Hunt to Harbor
A Maryland Cookbook

The Junior League of Baltimore

To: Jerry Duncan
5/94

If you are unable to obtain Hunt to Harbor through your local dealer, write to:
Perry Publishing, 5087 Columbia Road, Columbia, MD 21044

A portion of the proceeds from the sale of **Hunt to Harbor** go to community projects of The Junior League of Baltimore, Inc.

This cookbook represents a collection of recipes submitted by contributors who have vouched that they were not taken without adaptation from a copyrighted source.

All recipes in this book have been tested at least twice.

First printing, October 1985
Second printing, March 1988
Revised edition, November 1992
Fourth printing, October, 1996

Cover photograph copyright ©1996 David Hobby
Illustrations by Tom Tongue

ISBN 0-9643728-6-X
Library of Congress Catalog Card Number 96-70172

Published by: Perry Publishing
              5087 Columbia Road
              Columbia, Maryland 21044
              410-997-2731

Printed in Baltimore, Maryland by United Book Press, Inc.

CITY OF BALTIMORE

KURT L. SCHMOKE, Mayor

OFFICE OF THE MAYOR

250 City Hall
Baltimore, Maryland 21202

MESSAGE FROM MAYOR KURT L. SCHMOKE

It gives me great pleasure to introduce you to the Junior League's fourth edition of the popular *Hunt to Harbor* Cookbook.

Our City is known for the many cultural contributions made by our diverse ethnic groups. *Hunt to Harbor* exemplifies these contributions by providing a glimpse of the great variety of cuisine found in the Baltimore Metropolitan area.

Another Baltimore tradition is volunteerism and the Junior League is an excellent example of a volunteer group committed to making our City a better place to live. Help and hope are provided to many of our citizens through such programs as New Start Furnishings, Hampden Family Center, and the Johns Hopkins Children's House.

I commend and thank the Junior League of Baltimore for their commitment and caring.

Sincerely,

Kurt Schmoke

Mayor

The Junior League of Baltimore

The Junior League of Baltimore, Inc.

Since 1912, the Junior League has been a leader in volunteer service to Baltimore. Exclusively educational and charitable, the purposes of our organization are promoting volunteerism, developing the potential of our members for voluntary participation in community affairs and demonstrating the effectiveness of trained volunteers. Guided by this, thousands of women have volunteered their time, skills, knowledge and energy to initiate community programs and to work with cultural and civic institutions as with other not-for-profit organizations.

Over the years, the Junior League has played a key role in the development of many programs, including the Maryland School for the Blind, Santa Claus Anonymous, and Metropolitan Senior Citizens' Center, known as the Waxter Center. Currently, the Junior League of Baltimore is involved with the Hampden Family Center, providing prevention-oriented programs to adults, children and families. Through New Start Furnishings, the League collects and distributes furnishings and household items to individuals and families moving from homeless shelters to permanent housing. A new project of the League is the "Family Nights" program at the Johns Hopkins Hospital Children's House. Meals, special activities and other support are given to pediatric patients and their families. Other Junior League services include public advocacy, tutoring, and fundraising.

To those who purchase this cookbook, please accept our sincere thanks and gratitude on behalf of the many people, projects and programs relying on your support.

Table of Contents

Original Cookbook Committee

Marguerite Dixon Ayers
Chair

Polly E. Behrens
Vice Chair

Recipe Testing Committee

Charlotte S. Whitenight, *Chair*
Karen Ressler Jefferies, *Assistant Chair*

Production Committee

Elizabeth Church Mitchell, *Chair*
Jamie Hall Magovern, *Assistant Chair*
Anne Bear Powell, *Editor*
Ann Scarborough Dahne
Cecilia M. Ennis
Donnan C. Huddleston
Lorraine G. Merlis

Marketing Committee

Katherine Asam Rogers, *Chair*
Martha E. Shelhoss, *Assistant Chair*
Cynthia Shilliday Ebner

The Testers

Joanne Archibald, *Captain*
Frances Bergin, *Captain*
Claudia Bowe, *Captain*
Deborah Daugherty, *Captain*
Betsy Evans, *Captain*
Virginia Gilner, *Captain*
Donna O'Donnell, *Captain*

Barbara Beshel
Elaine Born
Linda Brenegan
Elizabeth Brooks
Linda Colombani
Pam Corckran
Lynn Cortezi

Dale Dingledine
Liz Edwards
Barbara Giudice
Judy Hilliard
Whitney Markley
Beverly Moore
Debbie Morton
Mary Alice Nolan
Carrine Reilly
Nancy Sherman
Susan Vohrer
Anna von Lunz
Terri Weller
Suzanne Whitney

Other League Members and Friends

Nancy Armstrong
Donna Bambrick
Meg Bank
Tina Baugher
Alice Bernstein
Ingrid Bortner
Bobbe Burke
Lisa Close
Chris Coale
Diane Daugherty
Doris and Ben Dixon
Frances Dixon
Toni Duke
Sandra English
Meg Fielding
Catherine C. Funk

Mary Patricia Ginter
Helen Graham
Mack Graham
Mrs. Edwin Gramkow
Janet Green
Violet Greenbank
Elizabeth Holland
Barbara Johnson
Townsend Kent
Fran Kleinfelter
Nancy Kromkowski
Karen Linaweaver
Ellen McGuire Lindew
Bobbie Lingard
Barrie McCleary

Vanna McDonald
Martha McIntire
Susan MacDonald
Maggie Madden
DeeDee Manuel
Annette Nagler
Denise Meyer Nail
Mrs. Fred Peterson
Mary Ann Quarngesser
Helen Rockwell
Louise Schadt
Elaine Smith
Sueanne F. Spivey
Sharon Walker
Nancy Webster
Karen Williams

Special Thanks

Alex. Brown & Sons, Inc.
Camp Manufacturing Company
Dolliver Church Design
Douglas-Innes & Co.
Douglas M. Ebner
Eddie's—Victor's Market
Giant Food
Cindy Goff

The Gourmet Shop
Graul's Market
Helene Hahn & Hahn Graphics
Mars Super Markets Inc.
Santoni's
Tom Tongue
The Typeworks
Wells Discount Liquors

The Contributors

Sally Abbott
Frances K. Albert
Judy D. Aldridge
Susan E. Alexander
Toni Lee Aluisi
Nancy E. Anderson
Joanne Archibald
Mrs. Bruce D. Ash
Genie Ayers
Marguerite Dixon Ayers
Cindy Bacon
Kathleen C. Badger

Susan M. Baker
Donna Marie Bambrick
Mrs. Stephen A. Bank
Debbie Bannister
Robin H. Bare
Joanna C. Barrell
Natalie B. Barringer
Pat Barry
Karin Batterton
Margaret W. Becker
Polly E. Behrens
Clara Close Benbow

Frances Bergin
Mrs. Robert C. Berson
Barbara Beshel
Peggy Bessent
Susan E. Bissell
Mrs. Wayne E. Bohannon
Sharyn T. Bolinger
Jane Bollman
Gretchen G. Bolton
Elizabeth O. Bond
Elaine Born
Ingrid L. Bortner

Harriett W. Bosiack
Claudia D. Bowe
Edie Boyce
Meredith Boyle
Elizabeth Bradley
Etta Brandt
Linda Funk Brenegan
Andy Brooks
Elizabeth Brooks
Leslie W. Brotman
Nancy Wilkins Brown
Mary Lea Bryant
Ouisie Bulkeley
Mrs. Frederick G. Burger
Vickie Burns
Bobbe Burke
Janice K. Bush
Sheila Butler
Lynn Byank
Kathryn Byrd
Gini Caldroney
Kitty Carter
Anne Cash
Patricia A. R. Chambers
Constance Carlson Chriss
Karin Chriss
Sherry Christhilf
Mary Clawsey
Mrs. Stevenson W. Close, Jr.
Mrs. Jeffrey D. Clute
J. L. Coale
Christine C. Coale
Beale Winfield Cockey
Lynda Weisheit Cogswell
Linda Colombani
Paul Colombani
Ana Maria Colwill
Martha A. Conlon
Dee Conners
Shirley O. Cook
Pam Corckran
Lynn Cortezi
Marian Costa
Mary Starz Cox
Emily Culley
Cheryl Cummerow
Alice Jackson Curtin
Mrs. Joseph M. Dahdah
Ann Scarborough Dahne
Sarah Pettit Daignault
Deborah K. Daugherty
Debbie Duke Davis
Yvonne Davis
Candy Davis
Stephanie Rice Davis

Gail Dawson
Joanne deBettencourt
Eva M. Devine
Sue Dillon
Dale Dingledine
Doris Lewis Dixon
Frances McKee Dixon
Marion Homes Dixon
Diane Donohue
Kathryn E. Douglass
Sally Douglass
Peggy Duer
Marty Durian
Gay A. Duty
Dolly Dyer
Maria Eagan
Kim Asam Eckert
Liz Edwards
Sylvia J. Eggleston
Genevieve P. Elliott
Betsy Evans
Barbara Anne Ewing
Elizabeth Fake
Betsy Ferguson
Marjorie C. Fink
Kathy S. Fleischman
Jeanne Floeckher
Donna Reid Foley
Kathlyn Ford
Nancy Ford
Jennie L. Fowlkes
Mary D. Franz
Carey Fravel
Liz Freshwater
Melissa M. Frey
Anna Funkhouser
Susan Galitzin
Maria Rixey Gamper
Alice Gary
Mrs. Daniel Gilner
Barbara Giudice
Leslie Goetsch
Mary Gorman
Dick Gower
Helen Graham
Kathleen Greenberg
Stephanie Danko Grill
Julia Peebles Grimes
Donna Guba
Mrs. Henry Hagan
Helene H. Hahn
Janet Hall
Nancy Poindexter Hall
Sandi Harper
Meredith S. Harrington

Sandra M. Harris
Jill L. Hauser
Nancy-Bets Hay
Elisabeth Albert Hayes
Roberta Gehman Heller
Marywill Dent Herrfeldt
Ann G. Hesselbacher
Judy Hilliard
Mrs. Thomas E. Holland, Jr.
Rosemary Hollick
C. Yvonne Holt-Stone
Coleman Hooper
Nancy Hopkins
Nancy W. Horst
Susan Hossfeld
Donnan Huddleston
Rebecca MacRae Huey
Mary Ann Hughes
L. Reed Huppman
Carol White Ingalls
Marguerite Ingalls
Karen Jefferies
Cathy Jenkins
Alice Pruitt Johnson
Barbara Johnson
Steve Johnson
Pansy B. Jones
Colleen Jordan
Debbie Belury Kastendike
Gigi Kegg
Mrs. Grafton S. Kennedy, Sr.
Leslie K. Kleban
Fran Kleinfelter
Virginia W. Kline
Leslie Klinefelter
Patricia Knight
Rosemary Knott
K. R. Kramer
Birdie B. Kraus
Nancy Kressin
Saundra Kahn Krieger
Mrs. John Kromkowski
Debbie Kurz
Frances Lamb
Janet Little Landay
Michele Levin
Jean Lewis
Beth Leyda
Bobbie Lingard
Karen Little
Janice Little
Kathleen Nash Lockhart
Randy Low
Cathy Lowe
Joyce K. Mace

Judy Mace
Susie Macfarlane
Sharon Macy
Jamie Hall Magovern
Julia Maier
Mrs. Allan J. Malester
Jean McDevitt Mallard
Debbie Mallon
Alexandra Mallus
Mary Anne Marsalek
Carol Dickenshied Martin
Cathy Martin
Whitney Markley
Betsy McDonald
Mary M. McFadden
Pattie McLane
Lucy B. Meade
Anne Mekalian
Lorrie Merlis
Lee Merrill
Margaret K. Merry
Mary Messmore
Mary M. Meyer
Janet Miller
Elizabeth Church Mitchell
Eleanor K. Moffat
Beverly Moore
Katherine Reeves Moore
Mrs. L. Franklin Moore, Jr.
Lanny Moore
Hannah Creighill Morehead
Deborah Morris
Kakki Morrison
Karen Pearce Morrow
Debbie Morton
Deborah E. Murphy
Carol Muskin
Annette Nagler
Denise Meyer Nail
Judith C. Naughton
Betsy Neale
Diane O. Newman
Edith Newton
Susan Kinley Niemeyer
Dulany H. Noble
Paula Davis Noell
Cathy Norton
Maureen E. Norton
Pat Nothstein
My Hanh Nguyen
Janette Nyce
Mary B. O'Connell
Sandy O'Connell
Susan L. O'Connell
Donna O'Donnell

Cordelia Ogrinz
Ann Mathias O'Neil
Ann Rogers Oster
Opie Owen
Kathy Paal
Nancy E. Palmer
Karen Elaine Pannell
Mrs. Edwin P. Parker
Helen M. Passano
Colleen L. Pearl
Anne Griswold Peirce
Sheila S. Peter
Diana J. Pillas
Anne Bear Powell
Jane B. Powell
Diana Prescott
Beth Purvis
Mary Ann Quarngesser
Lori Dennis Raneri
Mrs. Thomas C. Ray
Linda J. Rayburn
Laura C. Reed
Carrine Reilly
Stephanie Lassotovitz Rich
Cynthia Burker Rief
Mrs. George F. Ritchie
Lucy Ritter
Helen Rockwell
Mrs. John R. Rockwell
Kathryn Asam Rogers
Trish Rogers
W. Charles Rogers III
Debbie Rullman
Susanne McFarlane Runge
Judith B. Sanders
Hilary Sargeant
Mary Catherine Savage
Carol Bruce Sayre
Brenda Louise Schadt
Louise Jane Schadt
Susan Schindler
Mrs. John E. Schmick
Susan Parrish Schnering
Linda J. Schuerholz
Kathy W. Searcy
Robert M. Searcy, M.D.
Mary Sekerak
Sandra Semenuk
Leslie Seyffert
Jane Sharrocks
Martha E. Shelhoss
Nancy Collins Sherman
Carole Shewbridge-Dipple
Molly Shock
Barrie Sigler

Susie Silberstein
Barbara Sizoo
Dorothy Sizoo
Anna Leake Smith
Beetle Smith
Elaine Smith
Mary Ann Smith
Susan M. Smith
Sarah Follmer Snyder
Susan Ann Snyder
Betsy Y. Spath
Holly Spector
Cressy S. Spence
Andrea J. Steenburg
Katie Stevens
Maryellen F. Stier
Beverly Bell Straus
Garnett Strickland
Lucy Durham Strickland
Susan Styer
Lynn B. Summerlin
Anne Bennett Swingle
Rosemary Creighton Synkowski
Joanne Tew
Kathye P. Thomas
Nancy R. H. Tommaso
Mary Tracy
Peggy Traycoff
Susan Uhlig
Linda A. van Reuth
Karen Visser
Ilene Vogelstein
Susan Vohrer
Lucy M. Kirkman von Buttlar
Anna R. von Lunz
Millie Wachtl
Barbara Weeks
Gregory Weidman
Deborah D. Weidner
Terri Weller
Cathryn Wellner
Charlotte S. Whitenight
Suzanne Grell Whitney
Gayle Williams
Mrs. Alan C. Woods III
Charlene F. Woods
Susan Willand Worteck
Anne Worth
Kay Wriggelsworth
Hopie Wright
Judith M. Wright
Kathleen Kennelly Yuhanick
Kim Zaharris
Liza Zopp

Beverages

Blessing of the Hunt

Every Thanksgiving hundreds of friends and families gather inside and outside St. James Episcopal Church in the rolling hills of Monkton, Maryland, for the traditional blessing of the Elkridge-Harford Hunt. This is a colorful event that dates back to 1878 when the Elkridge Fox Hunting Club was formed. In 1934 it merged with the Harford Hunt Club, which had been in existence since 1912.

The chill of winter is in the air, and after the church service the minister dons a black wool cape with royal blue lining. He strolls through a side door of the 234-year old colonial church and walks by the tombstones in the church yard to a terrace overlooking the field of brightly dressed hunters, about 80 horses, and 30 fox hounds.

After all are assembled, the minister gives special thanks to God and His creation—the great outdoors and all His creatures great and small.

A prayer for those who go forth to hunt . . . . .

Heavenly Father, we return thanks to you with these your servants now gathered together in your name who this day go a-hunting with horse and hound.

Grant that they who delight in the freshness and beauty of the open fields may never your hand fail to see, and evermore be ready to lift up their hearts in thanksgiving to you.

Keep, O Lord, this day bright, the horses sure of foot, the fox swift and the hunters safe, that returning in vigor of health, they may evermore dedicate themselves to your Service in the setting forth of your Kingdom here on earth. Amen.

The Hunt is on!!

Orange Luscious

6 ounce can frozen orange juice
1 cup milk
1 cup water

¼–½ cup sugar
1 teaspoon vanilla extract
12–15 ice cubes, according to taste

Blend all the ingredients in a blender on high speed until smooth.

Serves 4

Fruit Slush

1⅓ cups water
1⅔ cups sugar
2 6-ounce cans frozen orange juice
5 6-ounce cans water
2 tablespoons lemon juice

32 ounce can crushed pineapple
3 or 4 bananas, diced
10 ounce jar maraschino cherries, drained

Boil water and sugar together for about 15 to 20 minutes, until it thickens and reaches the syrup stage. Add orange juice and 5 cans of water. Keep this mixture on the heat until well mixed. Remove from heat. Add lemon juice, crushed pineapple, bananas, and cherries. Freeze the mixture. Thaw slightly before serving.

Serves 20

Minute Fruit Tea

1 quart strong tea
14 sprigs fresh mint
6 ounce can frozen lemonade, thawed

6 ounce can frozen orange juice, thawed
24 ounces water
¼–½ cup sugar, to taste

Crush 3 to 4 sprigs of fresh mint into tea with your hands. Taste the tea to be sure there is a very strong mint flavor. Strain the tea to remove all mint leaves. Add remaining ingredients, and mix until the sugar is dissolved. Garnish each glass of tea with the remaining sprigs of mint.

Serves 10

Bloody Mary

⅓ cup 100 proof vodka
8 ice cubes
⅓ cup clamato juice
⅓ cup "V-8" Spicy-Hot Vegetable Juice

¼ teaspoon horseradish
Hot pepper sauce, to taste
Worcestershire sauce, to taste
⅛ teaspoon celery seed

In a 12-ounce glass, mix all ingredients in the order listed above.

Serves 1

Caribbean Cooler

¼ cup dry, sweetened lemonade mix
1 teaspoon sugar

¾ cup pineapple juice
¼ cup light rum
1 cup crushed ice

Mix all the ingredients, except ice, in a blender. Serve over crushed ice. Garnish with orange slices and maraschino cherries. Serve immediately.

Serves 2

Great Piña Coladas

¼ cup pineapple juice
¼ cup liquid piña colada mix
1½ ounces dark rum
3 ounces light rum

¼ cup canned crushed
   pineapple, drained
½ cup crushed ice
1–2 scoops pineapple sherbet

Put all of the ingredients in a blender, and blend until smooth. Pour mixture into glasses over additional crushed ice if desired.

Serves 2 to 4

Irish Cream

2 eggs, beaten
14 ounce can sweetened
   condensed milk
3 teaspoons chocolate syrup

7 ounces Irish whiskey
½ teaspoon coconut extract
3 ounces light rum
½ teaspoon instant coffee

Combine all ingredients in a blender and chill. Serve over crushed ice.

Serves 4

Mocha Punch

2 cups water
1¾ cups sugar
2 cups powdered instant coffee
4 quarts milk

½ gallon vanilla ice cream
1 teaspoon vanilla or rum
   flavoring

Bring water and sugar to a boil in a saucepan. Add the instant coffee and let the mixture cool. When you are ready to serve punch, add the milk, ice cream, and flavoring.

Serves 18 to 20

Mrs. Tottle's Fruit Punch

2 6-ounce cans frozen orange
juice, plus water required on
can
6 ounce can frozen lemonade,
plus water required on can
46 ounce can pineapple juice

1 pint of tea
Sugar to taste
1 bag frozen strawberries or
equal amount of fresh
strawberries

Combine all the liquids. Add sugar to taste. Float the strawberries on top of punch.

Serves 30

Sangria

½ cup lemon juice, preferably
fresh
1½ cups orange juice, preferably
fresh
½ cup sugar

1 one-fifth bottle dry red wine
7 ounce bottle club soda
1 cup sliced fruit (apples,
oranges, peaches, limes,
lemons)
1 tray ice cubes

Just before serving, mix the lemon juice, orange juice, and sugar together, stirring to dissolve the sugar. Add wine and club soda. Mix in fruit, add ice cubes, and serve.

Note: You may use white wine instead of red wine. Use sliced strawberries with white wine. You can mix all the ingredients except the club soda, ice, and fruit ahead of time, and chill it. Just before serving, add the club soda, ice, and fruit.

Serves 8

Whiskey Sour Punch

3 12-ounce cans frozen
  lemonade
3 envelopes whiskey sour mix
46 ounce can orange juice (not
  frozen)

46 ounce can apricot juice
1½ quarts whiskey (bourbon or
  blended)
Maraschino cherries
  (optional)

Thoroughly combine all the ingredients, and chill. Serve in a punch bowl. If you desire, mix ⅓ water and ⅔ parts punch to fill a ring mold. Freeze the filled mold, adding maraschino cherries for decoration. Unmold the ice ring into a punch bowl when you are ready to serve the punch.

Serves 30, 1½ gallons

Apricot Sours

12 ounce can frozen lemonade,
  thawed
12 ounce can water

12 ounces apricot brandy
6 ounce can frozen orange
  juice, thawed

Ice cubes

Mix all ingredients together in a large pitcher. Serve in glasses over ice. For best flavor, make this drink in advance.

Serves 6

Champagne Punch

1 one-fifth bottle cold duck
1 one-fifth bottle pink
  champagne

6 cups cranberry juice
28 ounce bottle ginger ale

Combine all ingredients, and chill in a large punch bowl.

Yield: 4 quarts

General's Punch

3 one-fifth bottles bourbon or
rye
1 quart maple syrup

1 quart fresh lemon juice
2–3 quarts ginger ale

Mix bourbon, maple syrup, and lemon juice together. Chill the mixture in the refrigerator. Add ginger ale just before serving.

Note: Freeze an ice ring decorated with fruit, and place it in the punch bowl immediately before serving.

Serves 35

Moselle Bowl

1 very ripe medium-sized
pineapple
½ cup sugar
12 ounces Grand Marnier

16 ounces brandy
4 one-fifth bottles Moselle
wine, chilled
1 quart large, ripe strawberries

Cut the ends off the pineapple, remove the shell and eyes, and cut the pineapple lengthwise into 4 pieces. Cut away the hard core from each piece; then cut the pieces crosswise into thin slices. Place the pineapple, sugar, Grand Marnier, and brandy in a mixing bowl and cover. Marinate the mixture in the refrigerator for at least 24 hours, and preferably 48 hours.

Pour the well-chilled wine into a punch bowl, adding a decorated ice ring. Add the pineapple mixture, and stir well. Let mixture ripen in the punch bowl 30 minutes before serving.

Remove the stems from the strawberries. Cut the strawberries lengthwise in half, and float them in the punch.

Yield: 5 quarts

Claret Wine Punch

⅓ cup sugar
   Juice of one lemon
4 4-inch cinnamon sticks
4 whole cloves

½ cup water
1 cup claret or light Bordeaux
   wine
   Lemon slices

Mix all the ingredients in a saucepan on very low heat. Warm mixture thoroughly, but do not boil. Serve in a punch cup garnished with a lemon slice.

Note: You may also heat the mixture in a microwave oven on high for about 1 minute. Do not boil.

Serves 2

Wassail

1 gallon apple cider
48 whole cloves
4 teaspoons whole allspice
12 4-inch cinnamon sticks

⅔ cup sugar
1 cup orange juice
6 tablespoons lemon juice
4 cups apple brandy (optional)

Combine all the ingredients in a large saucepan, and bring the mixture to a boil. Lower the heat, and simmer for 10 minutes. Just before serving the wassail, add the apple brandy.

Serves 24

McKee Eggnog

1 dozen eggs, separated
1 cup sugar
½ cup sugar
1 quart bourbon whiskey, no substitute

1 quart whole milk
1 quart whipping cream, stiffly whipped
2 cups Jamaican rum
Grated nutmeg

Beat the egg yolks with a mixer. Gradually add 1 cup sugar to the yolks while beating. In a separate bowl beat the egg whites, and add ½ cup sugar after the whites are very stiff. Very slowly add the bourbon to the yolks. The bourbon will cook the yolks if it is added too quickly. Now fold the egg whites into the yolk mixture. Gently stir the milk and whipped cream into the yolk mixture. Add Jamaican rum. Stir thoroughly, but gently. Serve eggnog very cold with a sprinkling of grated nutmeg on top of each cup.

Note: This is a very potent eggnog. It should be made ahead.

Yield: 5 quarts

Black-Eyed Susan

Shaved ice
1 ounce vodka
1 ounce rum
¾ ounce Triple Sec

Lime wedge
Pineapple juice
Orange juice

Fill a 12-ounce glass with shaved ice. Add vodka, rum, and Triple Sec. Squeeze in the lime wedge and drop into glass. Fill with equal parts pineapple and orange juice.

Serves 1

Appetizers

The Steeplechase Tradition

Steeplechasing, originally a chase on horseback to a church steeple, began in Ireland in 1752. Today, a typical steeplechase consists of six races on the flat and over fences. The Maryland Hunt Cup, America's foremost steeplechase over timber fences, came into being in 1894. Maryland boasts ten steeplechases which begin at the end of March and continue through the middle of June. One of the many rituals associated with the steeplechase is tailgating. The tailgate is a celebration of spring, sport, and a chance to share good food with good company.

Gagi's Stuff and Nonsense

1 teaspoon savory
1 teaspoon celery salt
1 tablespoon garlic powder
1 teaspoon chili powder
1 tablespoon hot pepper
  sauce
1 tablespoon or more
  Worcestershire sauce
¼–½ cup bacon or spicy
  sausage drippings
¼–½ tablespoon peanut butter

¼–½ tablespoon salted butter
½ box or 1 quart toasted oat
  cereal
½ box or 1 quart corn puff
  cereal
½ box or 1 quart Rice Chex®
½ box or 1 quart small
  shredded wheat cereal
2 pounds salted nuts
1 box pretzel sticks,
  broken in half

Mix spices, drippings, and butters together in frying pan over low heat until well blended. Put cereals, nuts, and pretzels in large baking pan. Pour spice mixture over cereal mixture in the baking pan. Bake in 200 degree oven for 1¼ hours, stirring every 20 minutes or so.

Note: Watch carefully as this burns easily. Can be made ahead and stored in airtight containers.

Yield: about 1 gallon

Pashka

1 envelope unflavored gelatin
¼ cup cold water
2 8-ounce packages cream
  cheese, softened
½ cup butter, softened
1 cup sour cream

½ cup sugar
1 cup chopped pecans
1½ cups seedless white raisins
  Chopped pecans or parsley
  (for garnish)

Dissolve the gelatin in water. Set aside. Mix the softened cream cheese with butter, sour cream, and sugar. Add nuts and raisins. Heat gelatin in top of double boiler until foamy. Add to other ingredients. Pour into a greased 4-cup mold. Refrigerate overnight. Unmold and garnish with additional chopped pecans or parsley. Serve with your favorite butter-type crackers.

Yield: 4 cups

Stuffed Edam Cheese

2 pound Edam cheese ball	½ teaspoon dry mustard
½ cup dry sherry or port wine	¼ teaspoon garlic powder
1 tablespoon grated onion	Paprika or parsley

Remove wax rind from cheese. Remove a 2- or 3-inch wide horizontal slice from top of cheese. Scoop out cheese using a sharp knife, leaving ¼ inch of cheese in the shell. Cut a sawtooth or zig-zag pattern around edge of the cheese shell. Chop or shred cheese in food processor or by hand. Using food processor or blender mix shredded cheese and other ingredients. Spoon mixture into cheese shell, and sprinkle with paprika or with finely chopped parsley for color. Cover and refrigerate for 2 hours before serving. Serve with your favorite wheat crackers.

Serves 16

Cheese Ball

½ pound cold-pack cheddar cheese	1 teaspoon grated onion
¼ pound bleu cheese	1 teaspoon chili sauce or ketchup
1 pound cream cheese	½ cup walnuts, chopped
1 teaspoon Worcestershire sauce	½ cup parsley, chopped

Let the ingredients reach room temperature. Combine all ingredients except walnuts and parsley. Shape into a ball. Roll in chopped nuts and then in chopped parsley until well covered. Chill. Serve with wheat crackers.

Note: Recipe can be divided for smaller parties. Will freeze well.

Herb Cheese Spread

8 ounces cream cheese,
   softened
⅓ cup sour cream
2 shallots, finely chopped
¼ cup fresh chives, chopped

1 small clove garlic, minced
¼ cup fresh parsley, finely
   chopped
½ teaspoon thyme
   Salt and pepper to taste
¼ cup heavy cream, whipped

Mix cream cheese and sour cream. Add herbs and spices, and mix. Fold in whipped cream. Refrigerate for at least 2 hours.

Note: Stuff cheese into blanched snowpeas that have been slit open along long side. Garnish with a sprig of mint just poking out the top. Omit heavy cream for a stiff filling, which can be piped with pastry tube into snow peas.

Yield: 1½ cups

Curry-Chutney Cheese Ball

½ cup slivered almonds
   Butter
2 8-ounce packages cream
   cheese, softened

½ cup chopped chutney
1 teaspoon dry mustard
1 teaspoon curry powder

Toast almonds in melted butter until crisp. Combine half the almonds with remaining ingredients. Shape into a ball. Roll in reserved almonds to coat. Serve with sesame seed crackers.

Yield: 2½ cups

Humos

16 ounce can chick peas	½ teaspoon salt
¼ cup lemon juice	Pepper to taste
½ cup olive oil	2 tablespoons chopped fresh
3 cloves garlic	mint and/or parsley
¼ cup tahini paste	Olive oil
Paprika	

Drain chick peas and reserve liquid. In a food processor, put ½ can chick peas with all ingredients, except mint and parsley. Blend. Add the remaining chick peas. Blend until smooth. If too thick, add olive oil or reserved liquid until desired consistency. The mixture should be thick. Sprinkle the mint and/or parsley on top of the humos in a serving bowl, and drizzle with olive oil and a little paprika. Serve with heated pita bread triangles.

Note: Purchase tahini paste in Middle Eastern or Italian grocery stores.

Serves 8

Avocado Crab Dip

1 large avocado	¼ cup sour cream
1 tablespoon lemon juice	¼ teaspoon salt or to taste
1 tablespoon grated onion	8 ounces crab meat, picked over
2 teaspoons Worcestershire	Mayonnaise (as needed)
sauce	Chopped tomatoes (optional)
8 ounces cream cheese,	Bacon, cooked and crumbled
softened	(optional)

Seed, peel, and cube avocado. In a blender or food processor, combine avocado, lemon juice, onion, and Worcestershire sauce. Blend until smooth. Add the cream cheese, sour cream, and salt. Blend well. Transfer mixture to a bowl and fold in crab meat gently. Cover with a thin layer of mayonnaise to prevent discoloration of avocado. Chill for 24 hours to let flavors blend. Serve with assorted crackers. Before serving, you may garnish with chopped tomato or crumbled, cooked bacon.

Note: Dip must be allowed to sit for 24 hours to bring out all flavors.

Yield: 2 cups

Bricklayer's Sauce with Cheese and Avocado

2 10-ounce cans tomatoes with green chilies	1 teaspoon sugar
½ small onion	2 tablespoons oil
1 clove garlic	1 pound cream cheese, chilled and very firm
2 sprigs fresh cilantro OR ½ teaspoon ground coriander	2 large ripe avocados, halved lengthwise, pitted, and peeled
¼ teaspoon salt	Tortilla chips

Combine tomatoes, onion, garlic, cilantro, salt, and sugar in food processor or blender until well blended. Heat oil in medium skillet. Add tomato mixture and bring to a boil; reduce heat and simmer 3 minutes. Remove from heat and cool. This can be prepared ahead of serving time.

Cut each block of cream cheese crosswise into ¼-inch thick slices. Place 3 cream cheese slices side by side on an oblong serving platter. Top with 3 avocado slices placed in the opposite direction and enough sauce to make a thin mortar-like layer. Repeat layers in a brick fashion 4 times to construct a brick wall. Make a second stack next to the first. Pour leftover sauce over top, and surround with tortilla chips. Serve at room temperature with a knife to slice through layers and spread on chips.

Serves 12

Guacamole

2 ripe avocados, peeled and mashed	½ teaspoon chili powder
1 teaspoon lemon juice	⅛ teaspoon garlic powder
2 tablespoons onion, chopped	⅛ teaspoon salt
	⅓ cup mayonnaise

Combine all ingredients except the mayonnaise. Mix well with fork. Cover with mayonnaise, and chill at least 45 minutes before serving. Thoroughly stir mayonnaise into mixture before serving. Serve with tortilla chips or crackers.

Serves 6 to 8

Jezebel Sauce

16-ounce jar apple jelly
2 16-ounce jars apricot preserves
1 2-ounce can dry mustard, sifted

1 5.6-ounce jar horseradish, drained
1 tablespoon white pepper

Melt jelly with preserves over low heat until well blended, about 5 minutes. Gradually stir in mustard and horseradish until blended. Add pepper. Remove from heat and cool. Serve well chilled over a block of cream cheese with your favorite crackers, or serve warm as an accompaniment to meats or poultry. Keeps three weeks in refrigerator. Freezes well.

Yield: 3½ pints

Fruit Dip

½ cup sugar
2 tablespoons all-purpose flour
¾ cup pineapple juice
¼ cup Liquore Galliano

1 egg, beaten
1 tablespoon butter or margarine
1 cup heavy cream, whipped

Combine sugar, flour, pineapple juice, Galliano, egg, and butter in a heavy saucepan. Cook over medium heat, stirring constantly, until smooth and thickened. Let cool completely. Fold in the whipped cream. Serve with fresh fruit.

Yield: 2½ cups

Marinated Carrots

2 pounds carrots, sliced
2 bell peppers, cut in 1-inch
   squares
1 onion, chopped
1 teaspoon mustard
¾ cup vinegar

1 cup sugar
1 can tomato soup
½ cup salad oil
1 tablespoon Worcestershire
   sauce

Cook carrots until tender. Drain and add remaining ingredients. Mix together well. To serve, drain and serve chilled or warm.

Serves 12

Spinach Pâté

3 packages frozen, chopped
   spinach, thawed
4 tablespoons butter
½ cup onion, finely chopped
⅓ cup celery, finely chopped
1 clove garlic, minced
½ teaspoon nutmeg

2 eggs
1 small package herbed cheese
   spread, garlic flavored
¾ cup Italian bread crumbs
½ cup grated Parmesan cheese
1 teaspoon salt

Squeeze spinach to extract all the liquid. Melt butter. Add onion, celery, garlic, and cook until tender. Beat eggs together with herbed cheese. Add bread crumbs, Parmesan, salt, nutmeg, onion mixture, and spinach. Grease a spring-form pan. Spread mixture evenly. Cover and bake for 45 to 50 minutes at 375 degrees. Cool in pan.

Serve at room temperature, thinly sliced, and garnished with julienned carrots and/or cherry tomatoes. Freezes well.

Serves 20 to 25

Liver Pâté

1 quart boiling water	1 cup soft butter
1 stalk celery	½ teaspoon nutmeg
2 sprigs parsley	2 teaspoons dried mustard
6 peppercorns	¼ teaspoon cloves
1 pound chicken livers	5 tablespoons minced onion
1 teaspoon salt	1 clove garlic, chopped
½ teaspoon hot pepper sauce	2 tablespoons cognac

2 hard-cooked eggs, chopped

Cook the celery, parsley and peppercorns in water for 5 minutes. Add chicken livers, and cook covered for 10 minutes. Drain. Combine in food processor with remaining ingredients, except eggs. Process until it forms a paste. Fold in the chopped eggs.

Pâté Mold

1 envelope unflavored gelatin	10-ounce can consommé
2 ounces bourbon whiskey	8 ounces cream cheese, softened

8 ounces Braunschweiger

Soften gelatin in bourbon. Boil consommé and add softened gelatin, stirring to dissolve. Divide into 2 parts. Chill first part in 4- to 6-cup mold or two smaller molds until firm. Mix cream cheese and Braunschweiger with remaining consommé mixture. Spread on first layer and chill until set. Unmold and serve with crackers.

Yield: 6 cups

Terrine Mâison

4 slices bacon	1 large onion
1 pound boneless pork	1 medium carrot
8 ounces boneless veal	4 cloves garlic
4 ounces prosciutto	1 tablespoon paprika
⅓ cup all-purpose flour	1 teaspoon salt
8 ounces chicken livers, halved	1 teaspoon dried rosemary,
¼ cup butter or margarine	crushed
2 eggs	½ teaspoon ground allspice
½ cup brandy	½ teaspoon pepper

2 bay leaves

In skillet, partially cook bacon; drain and set aside.

Using a food grinder or processor, grind pork, veal and prosciutto together. (If using processor, grind meat half at a time.) Stir in flour; set aside.

Cook chicken livers in butter until pink. In processor or blender, combine livers and remaining ingredients except bay leaves. Cover, process until smooth. Stir in meat mixture.

Line bottom and sides of a 9- by 5- by 3-inch loaf pan with partially cooked bacon. Spoon terrine mixture into pan. Top with bay leaves. Fold bacon slices over terrine. Cover pan tightly with foil. Place on a baking sheet. Bake in a 350 degree oven for 1½ hours.

Remove foil; drain off excess fat. Do not remove terrine from pan. Place pan on a rack.

To weight down terrine in pan, place several pieces of foil directly over terrine, then place a brick (or two 1-pound unopened food cans) on the foil. Cool to room temperature, then refrigerate overnight with weight atop.

To serve, remove bay leaves and reserve; unmold terrine. Slice thinly; serve with French bread or crackers. Garnish with reserved bay leaves. Makes a great first course.

Serves 20

Steak Tartare

3 pounds very lean ground beef
1 medium onion, minced
⅓ cup parsley, finely chopped
3 tablespoons Dijon mustard
3 egg yolks

2 teaspoons salt
¼–½ teaspoon freshly ground
  pepper
1 rounded teaspoon caraway
  seeds

Combine all ingredients thoroughly. Refrigerate.

Garnish:
1 head red leaf lettuce
12 ounce jar antipasto peppers
3 hard-cooked eggs, chopped
  fine
1 red onion, chopped fine

1 yellow onion, chopped fine
1 cup capers, drained
2 pints cherry tomatoes, sliced
100 thin slices party rye and
  black bread

Arrange lettuce on a large platter. Shape steak into a ring. Place antipasto peppers in a glass bowl in center. Arrange garnishes around steak on lettuce.

Serves 50

Shrimpy Dip

½ pound sharp cheddar cheese,
  grated
1 cup mayonnaise
1 small onion, grated
1 teaspoon Worcestershire
  sauce

1 cup shrimp, cooked and finely
  chopped
Dash of celery salt
Dash of garlic salt
1 teaspoon parsley flakes

Combine the cheese with mayonnaise in a medium bowl. Add the onion, Worcestershire sauce, and shrimp. Sprinkle with celery salt and garlic salt. Mix well. Garnish top with parsley flakes. Taste improves by refrigerating overnight.

Serves 40

Pickled Shrimp

3 pounds uncooked shrimp
2 medium Spanish or Bermuda
   onions, sliced very thin
8 bay leaves
1 cup olive oil

½ cup white vinegar
½ 4-ounce bottle capers and
   brine
2 tablespoons lemon juice
Dash of hot pepper sauce

Salt to taste

Cook shrimp until they rise to top of boiling water and turn pink. Drain in colander. Run cold water over shrimp to stop further cooking. Shell and devein the shrimp. Layer the shrimp, onion slices and bay leaves in lidded jars. Combine remaining ingredients to make marinade. Pour over the shrimp. Marinate for at least 24 hours in refrigerator. Stir occasionally. Serve with toothpicks.

Serves 12

Smoked Oyster Log

8 ounces cream cheese,
   softened
1½ tablespoons margarine
1 tablespoon Worcestershire
   sauce

Dash garlic salt
Dash hot pepper sauce
¼ teaspoon onion juice
1 3-ounce can smoked oysters,
   drained and coarsely chopped

Fresh parsley, snipped

Combine softened cream cheese and margarine. Stir in Worcestershire, garlic salt, hot pepper sauce and onion juice. Spread this mixture ¼-inch thick on foil or waxed paper, making a rectangle about 8 by 10 inches. Chill.

Spread oysters on cheese and roll jelly roll style to make a long, slender roll. Cover with snipped parsley. Chill overnight.

Serve with crackers.

Serves: 6 to 8

Hot Spinach Dip

1 10-ounce package frozen,
   chopped spinach
4 tablespoons butter
¾ cup heavy cream

⅜ cup grated Parmesan cheese
¼ teaspoon ground pepper
¼ teaspoon salt
⅛ teaspoon nutmeg

5½ tablespoons onion, chopped

Cook spinach just until thawed. Drain completely. Melt butter in a medium saucepan. Add drained spinach and heavy cream. Heat just to boiling. Remove from heat, and add Parmesan cheese, pepper, salt, nutmeg, and onion. Mix thoroughly. Serve in chafing dish accompanied with raw vegetables or crackers.

Serves 10

Hot Spinach and Cheese Dip

1 can cream of celery soup
8 ounces Monterey Jack cheese
   with jalapeña pepper, grated
OR 4 ounces Monterey Jack
   cheese with jalapeña pepper
   and 4 ounces plain Monterey
   Jack cheese, grated

2 10-ounce packages frozen,
   chopped spinach, thawed and
   well drained
Milk or cream
Pimiento, chopped for garnish
(optional)

Combine soup and grated cheese in a 2-quart saucepan. Cook over medium heat, stirring until the cheese is melted. Add thawed and well-drained spinach, and continue cooking the mixture until hot. Thin with milk or cream as needed. Garnish with chopped pimiento, if desired. Serve in chafing dish with tortilla chips. Freezes well.

Serves 6 to 8

South of the Border Dip

1 16-ounce can refried beans
1 1¼-ounce package taco
   seasoning mix
1 8-ounce carton sour cream
1 4½-ounce can ripe olives,
   chopped

2 tomatoes, diced
1 small onion, chopped
1 4-ounce can chopped green
   chilies
2 cups cheddar cheese, shredded

Preheat oven to 350 degrees. Combine beans and taco seasoning mix.
Spread the mixture in a 9- by 13- by 2-inch baking dish. Layer remaining
ingredients in order listed. Bake for 20 minutes or until cheese just melts.
Serve warm with corn or tortilla chips.

Serves 6 to 8

Hot Chipped Beef Dip

3 ounces chipped beef, finely
   chopped
8 ounces cream cheese,
   softened
2 tablespoons milk
¼ cup green pepper, chopped

2 tablespoons onion
½ teaspoon salt
¼ teaspoon pepper
½ cup sour cream
½ cup chopped pecans
2 tablespoons butter

Preheat oven to 350 degrees. Rinse chipped beef to remove salt. Combine
the cream cheese, milk, chipped beef, green pepper, onion, salt, pepper,
and sour cream. Mix thoroughly. Brown the pecans in butter. Place beef
mixture in small baking dish, and top with pecans. Bake 20 to 30 minutes.
Serve with crackers or biscuits.

Serves 10 to 12

Macadamia Crab Supreme

2 8-ounce packages cream cheese, softened	1 cup white wine
	1 cup mayonnaise
1 pound backfin crab meat	Salt and pepper to taste

2 cups macadamia nuts, chopped

Preheat oven to 320 degrees. Combine all the ingredients, and place in an ungreased casserole dish. Bake for approximately 25 minutes or until brown and bubbly. Serve with crackers.

Yield: about 6 cups

Hot Crab Dip

½ pint sour cream	Juice of one lemon
2 8-ounce packages cream cheese, softened	¼ teaspoon seafood seasoning
	3 tablespoons mayonnaise
1½ teaspoons dry mustard	Milk to thin (optional)
2–3 teaspoons Worcestershire sauce	½ cup grated cheddar cheese
	1 pound crab meat
2 teaspoons onion juice	Paprika

Preheat oven to 300 degrees. Combine all ingredients, reserving half the cheddar cheese. Add crab meat last. Place in a baking dish. Cover with the remaining ¼ cup cheese and sprinkle with paprika. Bake for 30 minutes or until thoroughly heated.

Serves 10

Oysters Beau Monde

¼ pound butter
1 quart oysters, preferably
   freshly shucked

Beau Monde seasoning
Crackers

Melt butter slowly in electric skillet or large frying pan. Drain oysters, and put in pan in a single layer. Sprinkle liberally with Beau Monde seasoning. Simmer 1 minute. Turn oysters over, and sprinkle again with Beau Monde seasoning. Simmer 1 minute. Serve on crackers.

Note: If Beau Monde seasoning is not available, you may substitute equal amounts of MSG and seasoned salt.

Hot Minced Clam Spread

2 cans minced clams
1 teaspoon lemon juice
8 tablespoons butter or
   margarine
½ green pepper, minced
   (optional)
¾ teaspoon parsley, chopped

1 clove garlic, minced
1 teaspoon oregano
⅛ teaspoon hot pepper sauce
⅛ teaspoon pepper
½ cup Italian bread crumbs
2 slices white American cheese
¼ cup Parmesan cheese

Preheat oven to 350 degrees. Combine undrained clams and lemon juice in a small saucepan. Simmer for 15 minutes over very low heat. In another saucepan, melt butter or margarine, and sauté green pepper, parsley, garlic, and spices. Add the bread crumbs and clam mixture. Pour into a greased casserole, and top with American and Parmesan cheeses. Bake for 20 to 25 minutes. Serve with crackers or miniature sliced rye bread.

Serves 12 to 16

Hot Shrimp Dip

2 pounds cream cheese
3 banana peppers, fresh or canned
3 chili peppers, fresh or canned
4 Italian plum tomatoes, canned

2 pounds shrimp, cooked, shelled, and chopped
1 large onion, chopped
1 teaspoon garlic juice
½ teaspoon salt

Mix all ingredients together in top of large double boiler. Cook covered over low heat for 1½ hours. Do not uncover or stir until finished. Pour off any excess liquid. Stir and serve in a fondue pot or chafing dish. Accompany with corn or potato chips.

Serves 25 to 30

Clams in Garlic and Herb Butter

6 dozen large cherrystone clams
Rock salt
1 pound butter
2 tablespoons fresh tarragon, chopped
9 cloves garlic, minced
9 shallots, minced
French bread

6 tablespoons parsley, chopped
Freshly ground pepper
2½ cups fine bread crumbs
2½ cups dry white wine
Lemon slices
Chopped parsley

Open fresh clams. Place opened clams in pan on bed of rock salt. Blend butter, tarragon, garlic, shallots, parsley, and pepper. Top each clam with one teaspoon of the herb butter. Sprinkle tops with bread crumbs, and drizzle with wine. Broil 3 to 5 minutes or until browned. Serve immediately. Garnish with lemon and parsley accompanied with crusty French bread to dip in remaining melted herb butter.

Serves 12

Sautéed Chicken Livers

6 tablespoons butter	¼ cup grated onion
½ cup flour	½ teaspoon celery salt
½ teaspoon salt	2 tablespoons sherry
1 pound fresh chicken livers, cleaned and cut if large	¼ teaspoon browning and seasoning sauce
1 can beef bouillon	

Melt butter in frying pan. Combine flour and salt in a bag. Add the chicken livers a few at a time to the bag. Shake to coat. Sauté in butter until brown, turning once. Repeat with remaining livers. Remove to plate when done. Add bouillon, onion, and celery salt to pan. Scrape bottom of pan for drippings. Simmer for 5 to 10 minutes. Add the sautéed chicken livers to the pan, and simmer for 30 minutes. Add the sherry and browning and seasoning sauce when cooking is complete. Serve in a chafing dish as an hors d'oeuvres or over toast for a light meal.

Serves 8

Chicken Nuggets

3 whole chicken breasts, skinned and boned	1 egg, slightly beaten
½ cup all-purpose flour	½ cup water
¾ teaspoon salt	Hot vegetable oil (375°)
2 teaspoons sesame seeds	Brown mustard
	Honey

Cut chicken into 1- by 1½-inch pieces, and set aside. Combine next 5 ingredients. Dip chicken into batter, and fry in hot oil until golden brown. Drain on paper towels.

To make sauce, mix equal parts brown mustard and honey. Use as a dip for nuggets.

Serves 6 to 8

Italian Chicken Bits

3 chicken breast halves, skinned
  and in bite-sized pieces
½ cup butter
2 tablespoons Dijon mustard
2 cloves garlic, pressed
2 tablespoons fresh parsley,
  chopped

Juice of 1 large lemon
⅛ teaspoon salt
½ cup white wine
1 cup fine dry Italian bread
  crumbs
¼ cup grated Parmesan cheese
¼ cup grated Romano cheese

Melt the butter in a large skillet. Sauté all ingredients except bread crumbs
and cheeses over medium heat for 10 minutes. Remove pan from heat.
Immediately sprinkle the chicken with bread crumbs and cheeses. Toss the
mixture lightly, but well. Serve in a chafing dish with toothpicks.

Serves 6

Sausage n'Sauce

1 pound Polish sausage
1 pound hot Italian sausage
1 pound smoked sausage
16 ounces canned tomato sauce
2 6-ounce cans tomato paste
1 teaspoon thyme

2 teaspoons parsley, chopped
2 teaspoons oregano
1 teaspoon basil
1 teaspoon garlic powder
2 teaspoons sugar
¼ cup dry red wine

Cook the sausages according to package instructions. Cut them into bite-
sized pieces and set aside. Combine all of the remaining ingredients in a
large pot (at least 2-quart size) and heat thoroughly. Add sausage pieces to
sauce and mix thoroughly. Cook over low heat until sausages are thoroughly heated. Serve in a chafing dish with toothpicks.

Flavors develop fully when prepared a day in advance.

Serves 20 to 30

Sauerkraut Balls

¼ pound ground pork sausage,
   crumbled
¼ pound ground cooked ham
¼ pound ground cooked corned
   beef
½ cup minced onions
2 teaspoons minced chives
1 cup flour
1 teaspoon salt
½ teaspoon pepper

1 cup milk
1 teaspoon Cayenne pepper
½ teaspoon caraway seeds
3 cups sauerkraut, drained,
   tightly packed
2 eggs, lightly beaten
¼ cup water
½ teaspoon salt
   Extra flour
3 cups dry bread crumbs

Lightly brown crumbled sausage in heavy skillet. Drain and add ground ham, corned beef, onion, and chives. Heat through. Stir in 1 cup flour, salt, pepper, milk, Cayenne, and caraway seeds. Bring to a simmer, and cook over low heat until mixture thickens. Remove from heat. Mince the sauerkraut. Combine with the sausage mixture. Chill thoroughly before frying. To fry: shape mixture into balls the size of a walnut. Heat at least 3 inches fat in a deep pan to 350 degrees. Mix together eggs, water, and salt. Roll balls in extra flour. Dip in egg mixture, and roll in bread crumbs. Fry the balls 1½ minutes or until golden. Drain on paper towels and serve hot.

Yield: 70 balls

Chili-Cheese Hors D'Oeuvres

½ pound Monterey Jack cheese,
   grated
½ pound sharp cheese, grated

2 4½-ounce cans whole chilies
   (mild), seeds removed and
   sliced

3 eggs, beaten

Preheat oven to 375 degrees. Grease a 9-inch square pan. Layer the Monterey Jack cheese, sharp cheese, and chilies twice. Pour beaten eggs over the layers. Bake for 30 minutes. Remove from oven, and cover with aluminum foil for 5 minutes. Serve warm with party pumpernickel.

Serves 6

Oven Meatballs

1 pound ground sirloin
¾ cup bread crumbs
¼ cup milk

2 tablespoons onion, chopped
1 egg
¾ teaspoon salt
½ teaspoon Worcestershire sauce

Preheat oven to 350 degrees. Combine all ingredients and mix thoroughly. Shape into 2-inch balls. Bake for 25 to 30 minutes.

Sauce:
¾ cup prepared mustard

8 ounce jar red currant jelly

Combine in saucepan and heat. Stir meatballs into sauce, and serve hot in chafing dish.

Yield: 2 dozen

Stromboli

1 loaf frozen bread dough
  (thawed overnight in
  refrigerator)
8–10 thin slices baked ham
  15 thin slices Genoa salami

8 ounces mozzarella cheese,
  shredded
½ jar Progresso Pepper Salad
  very well drained (comes in
  9½ oz. jar)
Melted butter

Preheat oven to 350 degrees. Roll dough to a 12-inch by 15-inch rectangle using a lightly floured rolling pin. Layer the ham to cover the dough. Then layer salami evenly. Sprinkle with shredded cheese. Chop the large pieces of pepper salad, and sprinkle the salad evenly over the loaf. Roll up lengthwise. Fold the ends, and turn the loaf over onto a greased cookie sheet. Bake for 30 minutes. Remove from oven and brush with butter. Let rest 5 to 10 minutes before slicing.

Alternate filling: sliced turkey, sliced ham, 8 ounces shredded cheddar cheese, ½ medium onion, finely chopped.

Serves 8 to 10 or 4 for lunch

Crab Rollups

½ pound pasteurized processed
   cheese spread
1 pound butter
1 tablespoon Worcestershire
   sauce (optional)

1 teaspoon dry mustard
   (optional)
1 pound crab meat, picked
   over
20–25 slices soft white bread
2 cups sesame seeds

Melt cheese and half of the butter in top of double boiler. Add the optional seasonings if desired. Cool slightly and add crab meat. Stir until mixture is spreadable.

Remove crusts from bread, and roll out flat with a rolling pin. Spread the bread with cheese-crab meat mixture, and roll up like a jellyroll. Melt remaining butter. Brush rolls with butter, and then roll in sesame seeds. Freeze on cookie sheets. Store in airtight containers. To serve, cut frozen rolls in thirds, and broil about 6 inches from the heat until golden on all sides.

Yield: 60 to 75 pieces

Crab Muffins

6 English muffins
½ cup butter or margarine
1 5-ounce jar sharp processed
   cheese
½ teaspoon garlic powder

¼ teaspoon salt
¼ teaspoon black pepper
1 tablespoon minced onion
1 7-ounce can crab meat
Paprika

Preheat oven to 350 degrees. Split the English muffins. Beat together butter or margarine and cheese. Add garlic powder, salt, pepper, and minced onion. Drain crab meat well and squeeze dry. Gently add crab meat to cheese mixture. Spread on muffins and sprinkle with paprika. Cut into sixths or eighths for appetizers, or leave as open halves for sandwiches. Bake on an ungreased cookie sheet for 12 minutes.

Yield: 72 appetizers or 3 to 4 sandwich servings

Petite Quiches

Pastry:

1 cup margarine, softened

2¼ cups flour

8 ounces cream cheese, softened

Cream margarine and cream cheese. Gradually add flour, mixing well. Form into a ball, and cover with plastic wrap. Refrigerate 6 hours or overnight.

Filling:

1½ cups half-and-half or evaporated milk

4 eggs, slightly beaten

½ teaspoon salt

Dash pepper

2 cups shredded Swiss cheese

2 tablespoons flour

8 slices crisp bacon, crumbled

Preheat oven to 325 degrees. Form 1-inch balls of pastry. Press against bottom and sides of miniature muffin pans. Combine half-and-half, eggs, salt, and pepper, and mix well. Toss cheese with flour, and add to egg mixture. Place some bacon in each pastry cup and fill two-thirds full with egg and cheese mixture. Bake 18 to 20 minutes. Cool in pan 5 minutes and remove. To freeze, cool completely on a rack. Place on a cookie sheet in single layer. When frozen, wrap well. To serve, thaw on cookie sheet for 1 hour. Heat in 350 degree oven for 6 to 8 minutes.

Yield: 60 to 70

Sesame Toast

½ cup margarine, softened   ¼ cup sesame seeds
½ cup Parmesan cheese   ½ teaspoon onion powder
                    Extra thin bread

Preheat oven to 350 degrees. Mix the first 4 ingredients in a small bowl. Remove the crusts from bread. Spread the butter/cheese mixture on bread and bake 8 to 10 minutes. Cut each toasted bread into 4 triangular pieces.

Yield: 50 pieces

Mushroom Canapés

½ pound mushrooms   1½ teaspoons minced onion
2 tablespoons butter   Salt
1 8-ounce package cream   Pepper
  cheese   Light cream
              Party rounds of rye bread

Slice mushrooms into tiny pieces, and cook in butter for 5 minutes. Remove from heat. Mix in cream cheese, onion, salt, pepper, and enough cream to soften mixture. Toast party rounds on one side. Spread untoasted side with mushroom mixture. Freeze on a cookie sheet until firm. Wrap carefully. Keep frozen until ready to use. When ready to serve, place under a broiler until bubbly and browned, approximately 5 to 7 minutes.

Serves 6

Cheese Pastries

1 cup flour	¼ pound butter, softened
4 ounces cream cheese, softened	Dash Cayenne pepper
¼ pound American cheese	

Preheat oven to 350 degrees. Blend together flour, cream cheese, butter, and Cayenne. Roll out the dough. Cut into circles approximately 3 inches in diameter. Place a small piece of cheese in center, and fold in half. Seal the semicircles together by pressing down with the tines of a fork. Bake for 15 to 20 minutes.

Note: Instead of American cheese, try cheddar, havarti with dill, or havarti with caraway. Substitute 2 teaspoons sesame seeds for Cayenne.

Yield: 4 to 5 dozen

Globetrotter's Sausage Appetizer

1 pound hot bulk sausage	3 cups biscuit mix
1 5-ounce jar processed cheddar cheese	½ cup milk

Preheat oven to 400 degrees. Combine all ingredients. Shape into 1-inch balls. Bake for 15 to 20 minutes on ungreased cookie sheet. These may be frozen if prepared ahead of time. Defrost and bake.

Yield: 50 balls

Spinach Cheese Triangles

3 10-ounce packages frozen,
   chopped spinach
½ pound cottage cheese
1 pound feta cheese
½ cup Parmesan cheese
4 eggs
1 small onion, grated

3 tablespoons oil
1½ teaspoons chopped fresh dill
1 teaspoon salt
¼ teaspoon pepper
1 package phyllo dough (not
   frozen)
1 cup butter, melted

Preheat oven to 350 degrees. Thaw spinach and squeeze dry. Combine with remaining ingredients except butter and dough. Open dough and carefully place on a damp towel. Cover with another damp towel. Remove 1 sheet of dough, replacing towel on rest of dough. Cut the dough into 3 long strips. At bottom of strip place 1 tablespoon of the spinach mixture. Start folding dough strip into triangle as you would fold a flag. Each time you fold, brush the dough with melted butter. When all folded, brush the top with butter. Place on lightly greased baking sheet, and bake for 20 minutes or until golden brown.

Serves 75

Olives in Pastry

¼ pound sharp cheese, grated
¼ cup butter, softened
¾ cup sifted flour
1 teaspoon salt
½ teaspoon paprika

¼ teaspoon hot pepper sauce
   (optional)
1 6-ounce jar stuffed olives,
   well drained

Preheat oven to 400 degrees. Blend cheese and butter. Add flour, salt, paprika, and hot pepper sauce (if desired). Wrap approximately 1 teaspoon of mixture around each olive, covering completely. Arrange on a baking sheet. These can be frozen or refrigerated at this point. Wrap well if freezing. Bake for about 10 minutes. If frozen, bake about 15 minutes. Serve hot.

Yield: 30 to 40

Pâte à Chou

¼ pound butter
1 cup water

1 cup unsifted flour
4 eggs, at room temperature

Cut butter up and place in saucepan with water. Bring to rolling boil. When the butter has melted, remove from heat. Add flour all at once. Return to the heat, and beat with a wooden spoon until the doughy mass leaves sides of the pan and forms a ball. Off the heat, stir in eggs one at a time, beating after each addition until paste is smooth and shiny. The eggs may be beaten in with a mixer.

Form dough into small balls, place 2 inches apart on greased cookie sheet, and bake at 400 degrees for 25 minutes. 60–70 puffs.

Cheese Beignets

1 recipe pâte à chou, uncooked
½ teaspoon dry mustard
1 teaspoon Dijon mustard
1 tablespoon cornstarch
1½ teaspoons salt

Dash hot pepper sauce
1½ cups imported Swiss cheese, coarsely grated
1 egg yolk
1 tablespoon milk or cream

Preheat oven to 425 degrees. Add the mustards, cornstarch, salt, and hot pepper sauce to pâte à chou. Stir in 1¼ cups grated cheese, reserving the rest. Taste and correct seasoning. Grease and flour a cookie sheet. Form the dough into small balls. Place 2 inches apart on cookie sheet. Paint beignets carefully with a mixture of egg yolk and milk or cream. Sprinkle with remaining cheese. Bake for 10 minutes. Serve immediately or reheat.

Yield: 60 to 70 1- to 1½-inch balls.

Chicken Puffs

1 recipe pâte à chou, prebaked
  in small puffs
4 chicken breasts, cooked and
  boned

¾ cup celery, thinly diced
½ cup mayonnaise
  Salt (optional)
  Garlic powder (optional)

Cut chicken into small cubes. Add celery and mayonnaise. More mayonnaise may be added until mixture reaches the desired consistency. Add salt and garlic powder to taste. Slit puffs and fill.

Note: Fill puffs with egg salad, ham salad, shrimp salad, or crab salad. Unfilled puffs may be frozen. Defrost at room temperature and recrisp in 250 degree oven for 5 minutes. Slit and fill puffs.

Yield: 12 dozen

Bleu Cheese Hors D'Oeuvres

¾ cup butter, softened
½ cup sharp cheddar cheese,
  grated
⅓ cup bleu cheese

½ clove garlic, minced
1 teaspoon parsley, chopped
1 teaspoon chives, chopped
2 cups flour

Preheat oven to 375 degrees. Cream the butter and cheeses. Add the remaining ingredients and shape into 1½-inch cylinders. Chill thoroughly. Cut into ¼-inch slices, and bake for 8 to 10 minutes.

Vietnamese Spring Rolls

1–2 tablespoons oil
1 clove garlic, minced
1 medium onion, diced
1 pound cooked pork,
  chicken, or shrimp, chopped
1½ cups bok choy, diced

1 cabbage, diced
1 cup carrots, shredded
2 cups bean sprouts, chopped
2 tablespoons soy sauce
1 package spring roll wrappers
  Oil

Heat oil on medium high heat. Sauté garlic and onion until clear. Add the meat, vegetables, except carrots, and soy sauce, and cook until crisp-tender. Drain the cooked meat and vegetables in a colander, and cool. Add carrots, and mix well. Separate the spring roll wrappers, and cover with a damp cloth. Place two tablespoons of the filling near one corner of a wrapper. Fold the corner tightly over filling and roll once. Fold the two side corners towards center. Dampen the remaining corner with a little water. Roll the spring roll towards the last corner that has been dampened with water. Lightly press the corner to spring roll. The water should make the corner stick to the spring roll.

Continue making spring rolls until all filling or wrappers are used. As you make the spring rolls, cover with a damp cloth. Heat oil in a wok or deep frying pan until very hot. Deep fry the spring rolls until golden. Use paper towels to drain fried spring rolls. Serve with duck sauce or soy sauce and sliced hot peppers.

Note: Be sure to wrap spring rolls very tightly, or they will come apart during frying. You can buy the wrappers, bok choy, and duck sauce in an Oriental grocery store. The wrappers are approximately 8-inch squares, and are larger than the regular egg roll wrappers. They may be labeled crispy egg roll wrappers.

Yield: approximately 18

Eggs, Pasta, & Cheese

White Fences and Silks

Horse raising and racing have been a way of life in Maryland since well before the Revolutionary War. Maryland gentlemen prided themselves on the nurseries and racing stables they built for their imported English thoroughbreds. In fact, races became so popular and numerous that the General Assembly legislated a special act to prohibit racing on Saturday afternoons, Sundays, and at Quaker Meetings.

The Preakness, second jewel in the Triple Crown, is a tradition from that era that has withstood the test of time and legislation. Sponsored by the Maryland Jockey Club, the oldest racing organization in the United States, the Preakness was first run on May 27, 1873. A crowd of 12,000 watched a field of 7 horses run 1 1/2 miles for a gross purse of $2,050 at Pimlico. Today the Preakness is still run at Pimlico where more than 80,000 watch their favorite thoroughbreds run 1 3/16 miles for a gross purse that has been known to exceed $346,000.

Egg and Sausage Casserole

6 slices white bread
2 pounds mild sausage
1 teaspoon prepared mustard
12 ounces sliced Swiss cheese
6 eggs

1¾ cups milk
1 cup half-and-half
¼ teaspoon salt
⅛ teaspoon pepper
⅛ teaspoon nutmeg

1 teaspoon Worcestershire sauce

Place bread in bottom of a greased 9- by 13-inch baking dish. Fry sausage, and drain excess grease. Mix sausage with mustard, and sprinkle over bread. Place Swiss cheese over sausage. Mix remaining ingredients thoroughly, and pour over cheese. Cover and refrigerate overnight.

The next day let casserole reach room temperature. Uncover, and bake in 350 degree oven for 30 to 45 minutes or until top is browned.

Note: Diced cooked ham may be substituted for sausage.

Serves 6 to 8

Scotch Eggs

4 hard-cooked eggs, shelled
¼ cup flour, seasoned with salt and pepper
11 ounces sausage meat

1 egg, beaten
Seasoned bread crumbs
1 teaspoon chopped parsley
Fat for deep frying

Worcestershire sauce

So that the sausage meat will stick, dust each egg with the seasoned flour. Flatten the sausage, and divide it into four portions which may be evenly molded around each egg. Mix parsley with bread crumbs. Brush molded eggs with the beaten egg, and roll them in bread crumbs. Place coated eggs in deep fat, and cook for 8 to 10 minutes. When the eggs are golden brown on the outside, remove from fat, and drain on paper towels. Slice the eggs lengthwise and serve with Worcestershire sauce.

Serves 4

Creamy Ham and Eggs

2 cups cooked ham, cubed
1 green pepper, coarsely
  chopped
1 tablespoon butter
1 can condensed cream of celery
  soup

½ cup sour cream
2 teaspoons horseradish
1 teaspoon Worcestershire
  sauce
3 hard-cooked eggs, sliced
¼ cup chopped pimiento
Paprika

In a 10-inch skillet, cook and stir ham and green pepper in butter over medium heat until green pepper is crisp-tender, 2 to 3 minutes. Mix soup, sour cream, horseradish, and Worcestershire sauce. Add to ham and green pepper. Heat to boiling. Simmer uncovered, stirring occasionally for 3 minutes. Stir in eggs and pimiento. Heat until eggs are hot. Serve over toast or English muffins. Sprinkle paprika on top.

Serves 4

Quiche Lorraine

9 inch deep-dish pie shell,
  unbaked
8 slices bacon or ham, diced
½ pound Swiss cheese, shredded
1 tablespoon flour

½ teaspoon salt
  Dash nutmeg
3 eggs, beaten
1¾ cups milk or 1 large can
  evaporated milk

Bake pie shell in 450 degree oven for 7 minutes. Remove and reduce heat to 325 degrees. Fry bacon until crisp. Drain and crumble. Reserve 2 tablespoons bacon for trim. Place remaining bacon in the shell. Add cheese. Combine remaining ingredients, and pour into pie shell. Sprinkle reserved bacon in a circle on top. Bake for 35 to 45 minutes until set in center. Let cool 25 minutes before serving.

Serves 6

Quiche Provencale

1 medium onion, sliced
½ cup green pepper, chopped
1 tablespoon vegetable oil
2 medium tomatoes, cut in wedges
1 cup zucchini, thinly sliced
1 tablespoon dried parsley
1–2 teaspoons garlic salt
½ teaspoon basil

¼ teaspoon pepper
9-inch deep-dish pie shell, unbaked
6 eggs, beaten
1¼ cups half-and-half or light cream
Grated Parmesan cheese (optional)

Preheat oven to 425 degrees. Cook onions and green pepper in oil in large skillet about 5 minutes. Add tomatoes, zucchini, and seasonings. Cook uncovered 10 minutes, stirring frequently. Drain well. Brush inside of pie shell with small amount of beaten egg. Prick bottom and sides of shell with fork. Bake shell for 5 minutes. Set aside. Reduce temperature of oven to 350 degrees. Combine beaten eggs, and half-and-half. Pour into pie shell, and spoon in vegetable mixture. Sprinkle lightly with grated Parmesan cheese. Bake for 45 to 50 minutes or until knife inserted near center comes out clean. Let stand 10 minutes before serving.

Serves 6

Crab Meat Quiche

6 ounce package frozen king crab meat
9 inch unbaked pie shell
4 ounces sliced mushrooms
¼ cup spring onion, chopped

1 cup Swiss cheese, shredded
3 eggs
1 cup half-and-half
¼ teaspoon salt
½ teaspoon Old Bay Seasoning

Preheat oven to 400 degrees. Drain and flake thawed crab meat. Layer mushrooms, onion, crab meat, and cheese in pie shell. Beat together eggs, half-and-half, and spices. Pour over ingredients in pie shell. Bake for 10 minutes; then reduce heat to 350 degrees, and bake an additional 30 minutes. Let stand 10 minutes before serving.

Serves 4

Ground Beef and Cheese Quiche

9 inch pastry shell, unbaked
½ pound ground beef
1 medium onion, chopped
1 can cream of mushroom soup
½ cup milk
2 eggs, beaten

¼ teaspoon salt
⅛ teaspoon pepper
2 tablespoons chives, chopped
4 ounce can mushroom pieces
1 green pepper, chopped
¾ cup Swiss cheese, grated

Preheat oven to 400 degrees. Prick bottom of pastry shell. Bake 10 minutes. Remove from oven, and reduce heat to 350 degrees.

Brown beef and onion. Set aside. Mix remaining ingredients, and add in beef and onions. Pour into partially baked pie shell. Cook approximately 30 minutes. Quiche is done when knife inserted in middle comes out clean.

Serves 6

Bacon, Spinach, and Mushroom Quiche

9 inch unbaked pie shell
¼ pound bacon or 4–5 slices
½ package frozen chopped
  spinach
1 can sliced mushrooms
1 onion, chopped
Dash pepper

1½ cups Swiss cheese, grated
3 eggs
1¼ cups half-and-half
¾ teaspoon salt
Dash nutmeg
Dash Cayenne pepper

Prepare pie shell. Fry bacon until crisp. Cook spinach, and drain very well. Sauté mushrooms and onion until tender. Crumble bacon and sprinkle on bottom of pie shell. Next add mushrooms and onion. Top with spinach and then cheese.

In medium bowl mix eggs with half-and-half and seasonings until well combined. Pour into pie shell. Bake at 350 degrees for 35 to 45 minutes or until top is golden, and the center seems firm. Let cool 10 minutes before serving.

Serves 6

Shrimp Strata

1 pound shrimp, shelled and deveined
12 slices white bread
½ pound cheddar cheese
¼ pound butter, melted
3 whole eggs, beaten
½ teaspoon dry mustard
1 tablespoon dried onion
OR ¼ cup chopped fresh onion
¼ cup parsley, chopped
1 pint milk
¼ teaspoon salt
½ teaspoon white pepper
Optional: ¼ cup sherry or white wine added to layers of bread.

Steam shrimp briefly, 3 to 4 minutes. Break or cut bread into pieces. (Coarsely textured bread is best for this.) Break or cut cheese into bite-sized pieces. Arrange shrimp, bread, and cheese in several layers in greased casserole dish. Pour melted butter over mixture. Beat eggs and add mustard, onion and parsley. Add milk and pour over ingredients in casserole. Cover and let stand in refrigerator overnight. Bake at 350 degrees for 1 to 1½ hours.

Serves 6 to 8

Ham and Cheese Strata

6 slices white bread
½ pound processed cheddar cheese
1 pound cooked ham, cubed
1 medium onion, chopped
¼ cup butter, melted
3 eggs, beaten
½ teaspoon dry mustard
1 pint milk

Break or cut bread in pieces about the size of a quarter. Break or cut cheese into bite-sized pieces. Arrange bread, ham, cheese, and onion in several layers in greased baking dish. Pour melted butter over this mixture. Add mustard, then milk, to the beaten eggs. Mix and pour over casserole. Refrigerate covered overnight. Bake uncovered at 350 degrees for 45 minutes.

Serves 6 to 8

Spaghetti Carbonara

½ pound country-style slab bacon
6 cloves garlic
2 tablespoons olive oil
2 tablespoons butter
⅓ cup white wine
2–3 tablespoons salt
1 pound spaghetti

3 eggs
2 tablespoons parsley, freshly chopped
¾ cup Parmesan cheese, freshly grated
¼ teaspoon freshly ground pepper

Cut bacon into thin strips. Peel and lightly crush garlic cloves. In saucepan heat oil and butter over medium heat. Sauté garlic until browned; then remove garlic from saucepan. Cook bacon in oil just until edges begin to brown. Add white wine, and boil for 2 minutes. Remove saucepan from heat, and set aside.

Boil salted water in 6-quart pot. Add spaghetti, and cook until al dente. Remove from heat and drain. In a large serving bowl, beat the eggs. Add the parsley, cheese, and pepper. Add the hot noodles to the egg mixture, and toss quickly. Carefully reheat the oil and bacon over high heat, pour over spaghetti, and mix thoroughly. Serve immediately.

Serves 4 to 6

Pasta Pesto

2 cups fresh basil leaves
3 cloves garlic, minced
Salt to taste (about ½ teaspoon)
½ cup olive oil

2 tablespoons butter, melted
½ cup grated Parmesan cheese
4 tablespoons pine nuts
Cooked and drained pasta

Combine basil, garlic, and salt in food processor until basil is finely chopped. Gradually pour in olive oil while processor is running. Add cheese and basil mixture to butter, and heat just until warm throughout. Do not cook. Toss cooked and drained pasta with pesto, and garnish each individual serving with a generous sprinkling of pine nuts.

Note: Fresh basil is available in summer. If desired, freeze pesto after puréeing. Before serving, thaw, add cheese, butter, and pine nuts.

Serves 4

Cheesy Clam Sauce for Spaghetti

2 10½-ounce cans clams,
minced with juice (reserve
¼ cup)
1-1½ cups half-and-half
2 tablespoons butter

½ pound Gruyère cheese
⅛ teaspoon oregano
2 tablespoons flour
¼ cup clam juice

Combine all ingredients except flour and reserved clam juice. Simmer over low heat until cheese has melted (about 30 minutes). If desired, mix flour and clam juice for thickening and add to sauce. Pour over 1 pound of cooked spaghetti.

Note: For a thicker sauce, increase the flour to ¼ cup.

Serves 4

Mr. Aluisi's Marinara

½ cup vegetable oil
6–12 cloves garlic, peeled and
sliced in half
2 large cans peeled Italian
tomatoes
7–10 fresh basil leaves
OR 3–4 teaspoons dry basil

Salt and freshly ground pepper
to taste
Freshly grated Romano, Parmesan or Assiago cheese
1 pound vermicelli or fettucine

Place oil in skillet, bring to medium heat and sauté garlic. Do not brown. Add drained tomatoes, reserving liquid. Sauté 10 minutes, then add basil, salt and pepper. Stirring, crush tomatoes in pan. Add reserved liquid from tomatoes, and simmer 20 to 30 minutes. Add freshly grated cheese to tomato sauce.

Toss cooked and drained pasta with sauce, being careful not to smother pasta with excess sauce.

Note: Add sautéed fresh vegetables to the sauce during the final simmering. Use broccoli, cauliflower or zucchini. Season with seasoned salt and cook until crisp, but tender.

Serves 4 to 6

Meaty Spaghetti Sauce

4 medium onions, chopped
2 green peppers, chopped
1 cup celery, chopped
3 cloves garlic, minced
2 tablespoons olive oil
1 pound hot Italian sausage, casings removed
1½ pounds lean ground beef
1 28-ounce can Italian tomatoes, drained and chopped

1 12-ounce can tomato paste
1 teaspoon sugar
1½ tablespoons fresh basil
OR 2 teaspoons dried basil
1½ tablespoons salt
¼ teaspoon freshly ground pepper
1–2 teaspoons Italian seasoning
1 cup Burgundy wine
1 20-ounce can tomato sauce (optional)

Sauté onions, green peppers, celery and garlic in olive oil until vegetables become transparent. Add meat, breaking it into pieces with a fork, and sauté until barely browned. Simmer mixture with all remaining ingredients, except for wine and optional tomato sauce, for 3 to 3½ hours, stirring occasionally. During last half hour of cooking, add wine and tomato sauce or extra seasoning if desired.

Note: This sauce freezes well.

Serves 16

Spaghetti Alberto

1 medium onion
35 ounce can Italian plum
   tomatoes
3 tablespoons olive oil
1 pound bacon

1 pound spaghetti
1 cup white wine
1 cup Parmesan cheese,
   freshly grated

Chop onion coarsely. Drain tomatoes, and cut in half; remove seeds. Slice bacon into thin pieces. Heat olive oil in a medium-sized skillet. When hot, sauté onion until translucent. Cook bacon in skillet, but do not allow to become crisp. Add tomatoes, reduce heat, and simmer 10 minutes, stirring often.

Heat water for spaghetti. When boiling, add pasta, and cook according to package directions. Three minutes before spaghetti is done, add wine to tomato sauce; turn up heat and boil, allowing alcohol to evaporate. When pasta is done, drain, and place in a serving bowl. Toss spaghetti with sauce, add cheese, and toss again. Serve immediately.

Serves 4

Pasta with Fresh Herbs

1 pound angel's hair pasta
1 cup heavy cream
3 tablespoons sweet butter
½ teaspoon salt
⅛ teaspoon ground nutmeg

1/16 teaspoon Cayenne pepper
¼ cup Parmesan cheese
1 cup finely chopped fresh herbs
   (basil, parsley, watercress,
   mint, and chives)

Cook pasta and drain. Combine cream, butter, salt, nutmeg, and Cayenne in a saucepan, and simmer for 15 minutes or until sauce is slightly thickened. Using a whisk, add Parmesan cheese and fresh herbs, and simmer an additional 5 minutes. Correct seasonings. Toss sauce with pasta in warm serving bowl, and serve immediately.

Serves 4

Linguine with Clam Sauce

1 pound linguine	1 tablespoon chopped parsley
2 quarts boiling water	2 teaspoons oregano
¾ cup olive oil	2 teaspoons basil
10 cloves garlic, minced	Hot pepper flakes
18 little neck clams (in shell, scrubbed in cold water)	1 small bottle clam juice
	½ teaspoon black pepper
1 cup white wine	1 teaspoon butter

Grated Parmesan cheese

Cook pasta until al dente in boiling water. Sauté garlic in olive oil. Add clams and white wine, and cover. Steam for 6 minutes. Add seasonings. Bring back to a boil until all clams open. Drain pasta. Rinse briefly to remove excess starch. Place in large heated bowl. Add butter and adjust seasonings of clam sauce to taste. Spoon clams over linguine, and pour remaining sauce over clams. Sprinkle Parmesan cheese over all if desired.

Serves 6

Pasta Primavera

½ pound snow peas, trimmed and stringed	1 cup small broccoli florets
	3 tablespoons sweet butter
¼ pound small white mushrooms, sliced	1 tablespoon vegetable oil
	1 cup cream
1 sweet red pepper, seeded and cut into thin strips	1 pound linguine, cooked al dente and drained
1 small yellow squash, thinly sliced	⅓ cup Parmesan cheese, freshly grated

Freshly ground pepper

Sauté vegetables in butter and oil until not quite tender. Do not overcook. While the vegetables are cooking, warm cream in small saucepan, and set aside. When vegetables are done, add the cream, and cook a few minutes over medium heat. Pour over linguine, toss with Parmesan cheese, and sprinkle with freshly ground pepper. Serve immediately.

Serves 4 to 6

Paglia e Fieno (Straw and Hay)

6 teaspoons butter
1 cup heavy cream
½ teaspoon nutmeg
½ teaspoon white pepper
½ pound fresh egg pasta fettucine
½ pound fresh spinach fettucine

3 tablespoons salt
12 large fresh mushrooms, sliced thin
¼ pound prosciutto, sliced thin and cut transversely into strips

Parmesan cheese, freshly grated

Melt 1 tablespoon butter in saucepan. Add remainder of butter, cream, nutmeg, and pepper. Stir over medium heat until it begins to thicken, about 15 minutes. Do not allow to boil, as boiling causes the cream to curdle.

Add pasta to vigorously boiling water in a 6-quart pot with salt added. When pasta rises to top of water and water resumes boiling, drain and place in large heated serving bowl. If using dry fettucine, cook until just al dente. Add the cream mixture to pasta, and toss thoroughly. Add more cream as desired. Toss in the mushrooms. Arrange prosciutto on top and serve. Provide grated Parmesan cheese at the table.

Serves 4

Penne with Asparagus and Artichoke Sauce

14 ounce can artichoke hearts
    packed in water, drained
¼ pound asparagus tops or thin
    tender asparagus cut to the
    length of the penne

1 pound penne (dry pasta)
5–6 tablespoons butter
1 cup cream
½ teaspoon nutmeg
½ teaspoon white pepper

Parmesan to taste

Quarter artichoke hearts (halve if small). Steam asparagus tips until fork tender. Cook penne in salted boiling water until al dente, and drain.

Place penne, artichoke hearts, and asparagus tips in casserole dish over low heat. Add butter, cream, nutmeg, pepper, and toss gently to allow cream to thicken. Add small amount of Parmesan cheese to hasten thickening. Serve immediately with Parmesan cheese.

Serves 4

Green Tortellini with Apple Walnut Cream Sauce

2–3 tablespoons salt
1 pound green tortellini (fresh
    frozen)
½ cup walnuts, crushed
6 tablespoons butter, melted

1 cup heavy cream
½ teaspoon nutmeg or to taste
½ teaspoon white pepper
1 cup apples, finely diced
    Parmesan cheese

Add tortellini to a 6-quart pot of salted boiling water. Cook until al dente and drain. Add the cream, nutmeg, and pepper to melted butter. Heat over medium heat, being careful not to boil sauce. Add apple and walnuts to cream sauce.

Place drained tortellini back in pan, and add cream sauce. Toss over low heat to thicken. You may top with freshly grated Parmesan cheese. Serve immediately.

Serves 4

Lasagne

1–1½ pounds ground beef or
   Italian sausage
1 large onion, chopped
1 clove garlic, minced
½ stalk celery, chopped
½ carrot, chopped
12 ounce can tomato paste
16 ounce can tomato sauce

2 teaspoons oregano
1 tablespoon basil, crushed
½ tablespoon parsley, chopped
6 ounces mozzarella cheese
6 ounces Swiss cheese
8 ounces Parmesan cheese,
   grated
8 ounces lasagne noodles

Brown beef in large skillet with onion, garlic, celery, and carrot. Drain excess fat. Place ground beef mixture in a 6-quart stock pot. Add tomato paste, tomato sauce, and spices. Simmer until thickened, about 30 minutes to an hour. Shred cheeses and set aside. Cook noodles until al dente, and drain.

White Sauce:
4 tablespoons butter
2 tablespoons flour

2 cups milk
Salt and white pepper to taste

Melt butter in saucepan, and gradually stir in flour. When smooth, stir in milk, salt, and white pepper with a wire whisk. Cook, stirring over low heat, until slightly thickened.

Preheat oven to 400 degrees. Spread a thin layer of ground beef sauce, then a layer of noodles in a 13- by 9- by 2-inch baking dish. Sprinkle noodles with each cheese. Over cheeses, pour some white sauce. Continue to layer beef sauce, noodles, cheeses, and white sauce, reserving enough meat sauce and Parmesan cheese for top. Bake 30 minutes. Let stand for 10 minutes before serving.

Serves 6 to 8

Spinach Lasagne

15 ounce can tomato sauce
2 6-ounce cans tomato paste
1 tablespoon basil
¼ teaspoon salt
¼ teaspoon pepper
½ teaspoon oregano
½ teaspoon garlic, minced
2 eggs, beaten
16 ounces cottage cheese

10 ounce package frozen
   chopped spinach, cooked and
   drained
½ cup grated Parmesan cheese
8 ounces uncooked lasagne
   noodles
8 ounce package sliced
   mozzarella cheese

Combine tomato sauce, tomato paste, basil, salt, pepper, oregano, and garlic. Cover and simmer for 30 minutes until thickened. Remove from heat. Combine eggs, cottage cheese, spinach, and ¼ cup Parmesan cheese, mixing well. Set aside.

Spread ¾ cup tomato sauce mixture in a greased 9- by 13- by 2-inch baking dish. Place half the uncooked lasagne noodles over sauce; spread with half the spinach mixture, half the mozzarella cheese, and half the tomato sauce. Repeat layers using remaining ingredients. Sprinkle with remaining Parmesan cheese. Cover dish securely with aluminum foil, and bake at 350 degrees for 1 hour and 15 minutes. Let stand 10 minutes before serving.

Serves 8 to 10

Three Cheese Manicotti

2 tablespoons vegetable oil	½ teaspoon oregano
½ cup onion, finely chopped	4 cups mozzarella cheese, shredded
1 clove garlic, diced	
2 8-ounce cans tomato sauce	15 ounces ricotta cheese
6 ounce can tomato paste	1 cup Parmesan cheese, shredded
1½ cups water	
1 teaspoon sugar	¼ cup fresh parsley, snipped
1 teaspoon salt	3 eggs, beaten
½ teaspoon pepper	½ teaspoon salt
14 cooked manicotti shells	

Sauté onions in oil. Add garlic. Sauté 1 minute longer. Add tomato sauce, paste, water, and seasonings. Cook over medium-high heat until bubbly. Reduce and simmer for 2 hours. Combine 3 cups mozzarella cheese, ricotta cheese, and Parmesan cheese. Add parsley, eggs, and salt. Mix all ingredients until blended.

Stuff cooked manicotti shells with approximately ⅓ cup cheese mixture. Pour 2 cups tomato sauce in bottom of 3-quart baking dish. Place shells in baking dish. Top with remaining sauce and sprinkle with remaining cup of mozzarella cheese. Bake at 350 degrees uncovered for 30 minutes. Freezes well.

Serves 6

Spinach Stuffed Manicotti

½ cup onion, finely chopped
2 tablespoons butter
2 cloves garlic, crushed
⅓ cup grated Parmesan cheese
½ teaspoon dried basil
½ teaspoon oregano
¼ teaspoon salt
¼ teaspoon pepper
16 ounces low-fat cottage cheese

¼ teaspoon nutmeg
2 10-ounce packages frozen spinach, cooked and drained well
10 manicotti shells, cooked and drained
2 6-ounce cans tomato paste
2 cups water
Chopped parsley

Sauté chopped onion in butter. Mix onion, garlic, Parmesan cheese, basil, oregano, salt and pepper, cottage cheese, and nutmeg with cooked spinach. Stuff mixture into cooked manicotti shells. Place in a greased 9- by 13- by 2-inch casserole dish. Mix tomato paste with water, and pour over shells. Bake at 350 degrees for 30 to 40 minutes. Garnish with parsley.

Serves 4 to 6

Noodle Pudding

¾ pound medium noodles
4 tablespoons butter
2 cups cottage cheese
2 cups sour cream
2–3 tablespoons onion, grated

1 teaspoon Worcestershire
  sauce
Salt to taste
6 tablespoons bread crumbs
Paprika

Cook noodles according to package directions, and drain. Stir butter into hot noodles. Fold in the next five ingredients. Pour into a greased baking dish. Top with bread crumbs and paprika. Bake at 375 degrees for 25 minutes. Serve with pork or poultry.

Serves 4

Kugel Soufflé

½ pound fine noodles
½ pound margarine, softened
¾ cup sugar
2 teaspoons vanilla

8 ounces cream cheese
1 pint sour cream
8 eggs, beaten
Cinnamon

Sugar

Cook and drain noodles, and set aside. Beat margarine until smooth. Add sugar, vanilla, and cream cheese. Blend together well. Add sour cream, then eggs.

Put noodles in buttered 9- by 13-inch pan. Pour custard mixture over noodles and cut through as if marbling. Bake 1 hour at 350 degrees. Sprinkle with cinnamon and sugar. Cut into squares.

Serves 12

Soups & Sandwiches

The Inner Harbor

On July 2, 1980, the memories of garbage floating in the harbor gave way to the opening of Harborplace. Offering restaurants, food markets, kiosks, and specialty shops, Harborplace soon became the gathering spot for Baltimoreans and non-Baltimoreans alike. It houses the Light Street Pavilion, a gourmand's delight and the Pratt Street Pavilion, a shopper's paradise.

The harbor also holds as part of its alluring bait the National Aquarium, home to approximately 5,000 fish, mammals, birds, and amphibians. It is crowned by a tropical rain forest lush with plants, exotic amazonian trees, lizards, snakes, and frogs.

I. M. Pei designed the 28-story World Trade Center where the "Top of the World" located on the 27th floor offers an excellent panorama of the city. Across the harbor, find the world of microscopes, ecology, and a planetarium in the Maryland Science Center. Here visitors are encouraged to participate in scientific exhibits. East of the Science Center is the Joseph H. Rash Memorial Field encompassing two sports playing fields and other recreational facilities.

Throughout the entire journey, if the winds are blowing in the right direction, your trip will be enhanced by the aromas of sweet-smelling spices emanating from the McCormick Spice & Tea Co., a Baltimore landmark for the past 64 years.

Vichyssoise

4 leeks (white parts only), sliced	1 quart chicken broth
1 medium onion, sliced	¼ teaspoon white pepper
¼ cup sweet butter	¼ teaspoon salt (optional)
5 potatoes, peeled and thinly sliced	3 cups milk
	2 cups heavy cream

Chopped chives

In a deep kettle, brown the leeks and onion very lightly in the butter. Add potatoes, broth, salt, and pepper, and boil 35 minutes.

Purée in a food processor or blender. Return mixture to the kettle. Add milk and 1 cup cream, and bring to a boil.

Return mixture to the food processor or blender and purée again. Chill. Add remaining cream. Chill thoroughly. Serve garnished with chives.

Serves 6 to 8

Curried Avocado Soup

2 large, ripe avocados	½–1 teaspoon curry powder
2 cups chicken broth	1 cup cream or sour cream
½ onion, chopped	Salt and pepper
Juice of 1 lemon	Chopped chives

Chop avocados, reserving seeds. Place in blender avocado, chicken broth, onion, lemon juice, and curry powder; blend until smooth. Stir in cream and season with salt and pepper.

Soup can be served hot or cold. If serving cold, place avocado seeds in soup to keep it from turning brown while refrigerating. Garnish with chopped chives.

Serves 4

Gazpacho

1¾ pounds tomatoes
1 large cucumber, pared
1 medium onion
1 medium green pepper
2 12-ounce cans tomato juice
   or vegetable juice
¼ cup vegetable or olive oil

⅓ cup wine vinegar
¼ teaspoon hot pepper sauce
1½ teaspoons salt
⅛ teaspoon black pepper,
   coarsely ground
2 garlic cloves, split
½ cup croutons

Combine half the tomatoes, ½ cucumber, ½ onion, ¼ green pepper, and ½ cup tomato juice in blender or food processor. Blend to purée vegetables. Mix puréed vegetables in a large bowl with the remaining tomato juice, oil, vinegar, hot pepper sauce, salt, and pepper. Refrigerate mixture about two hours.

To serve, cube remaining vegetables, and place in separate serving dishes. Place croutons in a serving dish. Rub individual soup bowls with garlic. Pour puréed soup into bowls, and garnish with cubed vegetables and croutons.

Serves 6 to 8

White Gazpacho

4 cucumbers or zucchini or a
   combination of the two,
   peeled
1 onion
½ green pepper
2 cups chicken broth
   Garlic salt

2 cups yogurt, sour cream, or
   cream
   Salt and pepper
   Optional garnishes: croutons,
   chopped tomato, crumbled
   bacon, chives, or fresh dill

Cook vegetables in a small amount of water. Do not drain. Purée vegetables and liquid in a blender or food processor. When cool, add remaining ingredients and season to taste. Refrigerate several hours and serve cold with garnishes listed.

Serves 6 to 8

Asian Lentil and Rice Soup

2 quarts water	3 large cloves garlic, minced
12 ounce package lentils	1 teaspoon ginger
3 cups cooked brown rice	⅔ cup soy sauce
3 cups water	1 teaspoon salt
¼ cup oil	3 tablespoons white wine
1 cup green onion, chopped	vinegar
½ cup parsley, minced	6 drops hot pepper sauce
1 cup celery, chopped	1 tablespoon oil

2 eggs, beaten

Bring water to a boil and add lentils. Cover and simmer until tender, about 1 hour. Add rice and water.

Meanwhile, heat oil and sauté onions, parsley, celery, garlic, and ginger until softened. Add to soup with soy sauce, salt and vinegar. Continue to simmer for another 45 to 50 minutes. Add hot pepper sauce.

Just before serving, heat oil in a 10- to 12-inch frying pan, and pour in eggs to cover bottom of pan. Cook until set and shred to use as garnish for soup.

Serves 8 to 10

Curried Chicken and Rice Soup

2 chicken breast halves (2 cups)	2 stalks celery, cut into chunks
3 cups water or chicken stock	⅓ cup uncooked rice
1 small onion, chopped	1 teaspoon curry powder
3 carrots, cut into chunks	Salt

Freshly ground pepper

Simmer chicken breasts in water for 30 minutes or until tender. Remove breasts from pot. Cool, remove skin and bones from chicken. Cube meat. Return meat to pot. Add onion, carrots, celery, rice, curry powder, salt, and pepper. Bring soup to a boil, lower heat, and simmer for 20 minutes.

Serves 2 to 4

French Onion Soup Gratinee

4 cups onions, thinly sliced	½ teaspoon Worcestershire
½ teaspoon sugar	sauce
¼ cup butter	½ cup dry vermouth or red or
1 tablespoon olive oil	white dry wine
1 clove garlic, finely minced	6 rusks or sour dough French
2 tablespoons flour	bread slices, toasted
¼ teaspoon dry mustard	6 tablespoons Gruyère, grated
¼ cup cognac, heated	6 tablespoons Parmesan, grated
2 cups beef stock	6 tablespoons Gorgonzola,
2 cups chicken stock	crumbled
10½ ounce can consommé	6 tablespoons Beaufort, grated
¼ teaspoon nutmeg	Parsley
⅛ teaspoon black pepper	Paprika

Slowly brown onions and sugar in butter and oil. Add garlic, cook 3 minutes, and sprinkle with flour and mustard. Cook 3 minutes, stirring; raise heat, and pour cognac over mixture. Ignite and let flame burn down. Add stocks, consommé, nutmeg, pepper, and Worcestershire sauce. Cover, bring to a boil, and simmer 20 minutes.

Cool and refrigerate overnight to mellow the flavor. Reheat and adjust seasonings to taste. Just before serving add vermouth.

Ladle soup into ovenproof bowls, top with rusks sprinkled with cheese, and broil to melt cheese. Sprinkle with parsley and paprika.

Serves 6

Oriental Chicken Noodle Soup

2 cups chicken, cooked and cubed
3 cups chicken broth
1 cup mushrooms, sliced
¼ cup sliced water chestnuts
¼ pound fresh low mein noodles

1 teaspoon minced fresh ginger
Freshly ground pepper
¼ cup scallions, thinly sliced (including some green tops)
½ cup bean sprouts
1 tablespoon soy sauce

Combine cooked chicken, chicken broth, mushrooms, water chestnuts, low mein noodles, ginger, and pepper in a large pot. Bring soup to a boil, lower heat, and simmer until noodles are done, about 10 to 15 minutes. Just before serving add scallions, bean sprouts, and soy sauce. Stir and serve.

Note: Fresh low mein noodles are available in Oriental food stores. Extra noodles can be frozen in plastic bags for future use.

Serves 2 to 4

Potato Soup

6 bacon slices
1 cup onion, chopped
2 cups potatoes, cubed
1 cup water
2 10½-ounce cans cream of chicken soup

2 13-ounce cans of evaporated milk
½ teaspoon salt
2 tablespoons parsley

Cook bacon in a large saucepan until crisp. Crumble and set aside. Pour off all except 3 tablespoons of fat. Add onions to saucepan and brown. Add potatoes and water, and cook 15 minutes until potatoes are tender. Blend in soup, milk, and salt. Heat, but do not boil. Serve garnished with bacon and parsley.

Serves 8

Pumpkin Soup

¼ cup butter
1 large onion, chopped
1 pound can pumpkin, puréed
4 cups chicken broth
1 teaspoon salt
½ teaspoon curry powder

¼ teaspoon grated nutmeg
¼ teaspoon pepper
¼ teaspoon ground ginger
1 bay leaf
1 cup half-and-half
4 teaspoons chopped chives

Melt butter in large saucepan. Sauté onion until tender. Stir in pumpkin, broth, and spices. Bring to a boil, stirring constantly. Reduce heat and simmer uncovered for 15 minutes. Remove bay leaf. Add half-and-half. Stir just until thoroughly heated. Adjust seasoning. Garnish with chopped chives.

Serves 8

Aunt Janet's Cream of Mushroom Soup

¾–1 pound of fresh mushrooms,
   thinly sliced
1 small onion, finely chopped
1 stalk celery, chopped
   ½ teaspoon black pepper

4 tablespoons butter
¼ cup flour
2 cups beef bouillon
1 cup light cream

Sauté mushrooms, onion, and celery in melted butter until tender, approximately 5 to 10 minutes. Gradually stir in flour. Add beef bouillon, and stir until slightly thickened. Cool for 10 minutes. Stir in cream and pepper. Heat thoroughly and serve.

Note: Can be made ahead. Freeze without cream. After thawing, add cream, pepper, and heat to serve.

Serves 4

Tomato Bisque

½ cup butter
1 cup chopped celery
1 cup chopped onion
¼ cup chopped carrots
⅓ cup all-purpose flour
4 cups chicken stock
6 large tomatoes, peeled and chopped
2 teaspoons granulated sugar

1 teaspoon dried marjoram
1 teaspoon dried basil
1 bay leaf
¼ teaspoon paprika
¼ teaspoon freshly ground pepper
½ teaspoon curry powder
Salt and pepper to taste
2 cups heavy cream

Sauté celery, onions, and carrots in butter for 3 to 5 minutes. Stir in flour. Pour in chicken stock and allow to thicken stirring constantly. Add tomatoes and spices, and simmer for 30 minutes. Add cream and heat just before serving.

Note: Can be made a day ahead. Add cream just before serving. Can be served hot or cold.

Serves 8 to 10

MacBain's Tomato Chowder

2 slices lean salt pork or bacon
1 medium onion, chopped
2 cloves garlic, minced
4 potatoes, peeled and cubed
4 ripe tomatoes, chopped (16-ounce can)

5 leaves fresh basil or ½ teaspoon dried basil
Salt and pepper to taste
Milk

In a large saucepan, fry pork and then sauté onion and garlic in drippings. Add potatoes, and cover with water. Boil gently until potatoes are soft. Add tomatoes and seasonings, and simmer 15 minutes. Add an amount of milk equal to tomato-potato mixture, and heat gently.

Serves 6

Broccoli Soup

2 tablespoons butter or margarine	14 ounce can chicken broth
1 medium onion, chopped	1 pound fresh broccoli, chopped
3 tablespoons flour	1 cup milk
½ teaspoon salt	1 cup half-and-half or light cream
½ teaspoon freshly ground pepper	

Melt butter in saucepan and sauté onion about 5 minutes. Add flour, salt, and pepper, stirring constantly about 1 or 2 minutes. Stir in chicken broth and broccoli. Bring to a boil, cover, and simmer 20 minutes or until broccoli is tender.

Purée in blender or food processor. Return to saucepan and stir in milk and half-and-half. Serve hot.

Note: Can be made ahead and refrigerated or frozen.

Serves 4 to 6

Cream of Zucchini Soup

6 small zucchini, cut into chunks	½ teaspoon dry mustard
1 cup onion, thinly sliced	3 cups chicken broth or bouillon
1 teaspoon curry powder	3 tablespoons uncooked rice
½ teaspoon ground ginger	1½ cups milk or cream

Minced chives

Combine the zucchini, onion, curry powder, ginger, and mustard in a saucepan. Add the chicken broth and rice. Bring to a boil. Cover and simmer 45 minutes.

Purée the mixture in a blender or food processor. Add the milk or cream. Salt and pepper to taste. Chill thoroughly or serve hot. Garnish with chives.

Serves 6

Spinach Soup

2 tablespoons butter
1 medium onion, chopped
3 tablespoons flour
½ teaspoon salt
½ teaspoon freshly ground
   pepper
14½ ounce can chicken broth

10 ounce package frozen,
   chopped spinach, defrosted
   and drained
1 cup milk
1 cup half-and-half or light
   cream
¼ teaspoon freshly grated
   nutmeg

Melt butter in a large saucepan over medium heat. Add onion and sauté until light golden, about 5 minutes. Blend in flour, salt, and pepper, stirring constantly, about 2 minutes. Gradually add broth, spinach, and bring to a boil. Cover and simmer until spinach is cooked, about 10 minutes.

Purée in a blender or food processor. Return to the saucepan, and add milk and cream. Bring to a simmer and add nutmeg to taste. Serve hot or cold.

Serves 4 to 6

Cheese Chowder

2 cups potatoes, diced
½ cup carrots, sliced
½ cup celery, sliced
¼ cup onion, chopped
1½ teaspoons salt
¼ teaspoon pepper
2 cups boiling water

4 tablespoons butter or
   margarine
¼ cup flour
2 cups milk
12 ounces cheddar cheese,
   shredded
1 pound can creamed corn

Combine potatoes, carrots, celery, onion, salt, and pepper. Add water. Cover and simmer 10 minutes. Do not drain.

In large saucepan make roux with butter and flour, and gradually add milk. Add cheese and stir until melted. Add corn and undrained vegetables. Heat; do not boil.

Serves 8 to 10

Crab and Shrimp Gumbo

¼ cup vegetable oil
8 ounces ham, chopped
2 large onions, chopped
2 cloves garlic, chopped
2 medium green bell peppers, chopped
1 pound okra, sliced
2 8-ounce cans tomato sauce
1 16-ounce can whole tomatoes
2 quarts water

1 teaspoon thyme
2 bay leaves
1 teaspoon chopped parsley
1 teaspoon salt
1 teaspoon crushed red pepper
1 teaspoon hot pepper sauce
1 pound claw crabmeat
1 pound raw shrimp, shelled and deveined
1 tablespoon gumbo filé powder

Cooked white rice

Heat oil in a 5-quart pot or Dutch oven. Add, one at a time, the ham, onions, garlic, green peppers, and okra; and cook over medium heat until they are light brown. Add the tomato sauce, tomatoes, water, thyme, bay leaves, parsley, salt, pepper, and hot pepper sauce; and bring the liquid to a boil over low heat, stirring constantly. Simmer, covered, for 2 hours. At this point, the gumbo can be cooled, refrigerated or frozen for later use.

Add the crabmeat and simmer for 30 minutes. About 30 minutes before serving time, add the shrimp, and simmer for 20 to 30 minutes or until shrimp are done. Remove gumbo from heat and stir in the filé powder. Remove bay leaves. Serve with one heaping tablespoon of hot, cooked rice in each bowl.

Serves 8

Crab Claw Soup

Steamed hard crabs, about 1 pound crabmeat
2 16-ounce cans tomato sauce
1 quart water

4 drops Worcestershire sauce
Old Bay seasoning, to taste
1 bag of frozen, mixed vegetables

Pick crabs, keeping claws whole. Meanwhile, heat tomato sauce, water, and seasonings. When boiling, add vegetables, crab meat, and claws. Heat thoroughly until vegetables are tender. Do not boil. Soup may be frozen.

Note: Excellent use for crabs leftover from a crab feast!

Serves 6

Crab Bisque

6 tablespoons butter	2 tablespoons flour
4 tablespoons green pepper, finely chopped	1 cup milk
	1 teaspoon salt
4 tablespoons onion, finely chopped	⅛ teaspoon white pepper
	⅛ teaspoon hot pepper sauce
1 scallion, chopped	1½ cups half-and-half
2 tablespoons parsley, chopped	1½ cups cooked crabmeat
1½ cups fresh mushrooms, sliced	3 tablespoons sherry

Heat 4 tablespoons butter in a skillet, add green pepper, onion, scallion, parsley, and mushrooms. Sauté until soft, about 5 minutes. In a saucepan, heat remaining butter and stir in flour. Add milk and cook, stirring until thickened and smooth. Stir in salt, pepper, and hot pepper sauce. Add sautéed vegetables and half-and-half. Bring to almost boiling, reduce heat, and add crabmeat. Simmer uncovered for 5 minutes. Add sherry just before serving.

Note: To make a shrimp bisque substitute 1½ cups cooked, deveined shrimp.

Serves 4

Maryland Crab Chowder

1 medium onion, chopped	1½ cups milk or half-and-half
2 tablespoons margarine or butter	2 tablespoons lemon juice
	⅛ teaspoon pepper
17 ounce can creamed corn	½ teaspoon Old Bay Seasoning
10¾ ounce can cream of mushroom soup	1 pound crab meat
	1 tablespoon sherry

Sauté onion in margarine. Add the corn, soup, milk, and lemon juice, stirring occasionally. Add the pepper, Old Bay Seasoning, and crab meat. When mixture is heated thoroughly, add the sherry, and simmer gently for 5 to 10 minutes.

Serves 4 to 6

Oyster Bisque

1 dozen large raw oysters,
  shucked, drained, and chopped
4 cups milk
1 slice onion
2 stalks celery

1 sprig parsley
1 small bay leaf
⅓ cup butter, melted
⅓ cup flour
1¾ teaspoon salt

⅛ teaspoon pepper

In a small saucepan, slowly bring oysters just to a boil. Enough oyster liquor will remain on oysters to cook without adding additional liquid. Cook until oysters curl around the edges. Remove oysters immediately.

Scald milk with onion, celery, parsley, and bay leaf. Remove seasonings from milk. In a large pan, blend butter, flour, salt, and pepper. Slowly stir in milk. Stir over low heat until thickened. Add oysters and serve.

Serves 3 to 4

Stack Ups

½ cup vinegar
½ cup sugar
16 ounce bag fresh sauerkraut
1 cup diced celery
1 cup diced green pepper
½ cup onion

Marble rye or dark rye bread
slices
Butter or mustard
Lebanon bologna or ham
Salami
Swiss cheese

To make relish, heat vinegar and sugar until sugar is dissolved. Cool. Combine undrained sauerkraut, celery, green pepper, and onion, and add to vinegar mixture. Drain.

To serve spread bread slices with butter or mustard. Stack slices of ham, salami, and cheese, and top with ¼ cup relish. Close sandwich with another piece of buttered rye bread.

Serves 12, 4 cups relish

Frosted Sandwich Loaf

1 loaf white bread, unsliced
3 tablespoons mayonnaise, divided
½ pound roast beef, thinly sliced
1½ cups egg salad

16 ounces cream cheese, softened
½ small onion
½ teaspoon paprika
Sliced Pimiento-stuffed green olives for garnish

Trim all crusts from bread, and slice the loaf horizontally into three layers. Spread the top of the bottom layer with 1½ tablespoons mayonnaise, and top with roast beef. Spread 1½ tablespoons mayonnaise on underside of the middle layer of bread, and place it on roast beef. Put egg salad on top of middle layer of bread. Place last layer of bread on top.

Mix softened cream cheese, minced onion, and paprika. Spread over sides and top of loaf. Arrange olive slices on top of loaf as a garnish. Chill before serving. Slice with sharp knife in ¾-inch sandwiches.

Note: Add minced red pepper to the egg salad for extra color inside. Garnish with radish slices, asparagus tips, parsley, watercress, pimiento strips, or sliced ripe olives. Additional softened cream cheese can be used for decoration with cake decorating bags and tips.

Serves 6 to 8

Pita Bread Sandwiches

Hard Genoa salami
Boiled ham
Swiss cheese
Italian cheese (mozzarella or
Provolone)

Cheddar cheese
Iceberg or romaine lettuce
Red or green peppers
Bermuda or green onions
Cucumber

Pita bread

Using a combination of approximately ¼ pound per person, choose any combination of meats and cheeses, and cut into strips. Tear lettuce into fine pieces. Dice vegetables. Toss meat, cheese, vegetables, and lettuce together in a serving bowl.

Dressing:
½ cup olive or vegetable oil
½ cup red wine vinegar
1 teaspoon oregano, dried
1 teaspoon MSG
1 teaspoon salt

1 teaspoon garlic salt or ¼
teaspoon garlic powder
1 teaspoon pepper
1 teaspoon minced parsley
¼ cup grated Parmesan cheese

1 teaspoon dried basil

Mix dressing ingredients and pour over sandwich fillers. Serve buffet style with pita bread.

Serves 8 to 10

Plum Alley Special

3 slices very thin wheat bread,
crusts trimmed
Soft cream cheese
Mayonnaise

Seasoned salt
Alfalfa sprouts
Sliced cucumber, peeled or
unpeeled (about 10 slices)

Take two slices of bread and spread one side of each with soft cream cheese. Spread both sides of the third piece of bread with mayonnaise. Take one piece of bread spread with cream cheese, sprinkle it with the seasoned salt; then add a layer of cucumbers, then alfalfa sprouts. Put the piece of bread which has been spread with mayonnaise on top. On that piece of bread, add a layer of cucumbers and alfalfa sprouts. Finally, add the other piece of bread spread with cream cheese.

Serves 1

Open Face Chicken Sandwich

4 leaves of head lettuce
4 boned chicken breast halves,
  sliced and cooked
8 slices tomato

12 slices bacon, cooked
4 slices rye bread
1 cup Thousand Island dressing

Place lettuce, chicken slices, tomato slices, and bacon on ryebread. Pour ¼ cup Thousand Island dressing over each sandwich.

Serves 4

Cannibal Sandwich

6 pieces of rye bread

¾ pound ground top round beef
Thin slices of Bermuda onion

Divide beef between 3 slices of bread, and top each with thin slice of onion and another slice of bread. Butter both sides of each sandwich, and place in frying pan on low heat. Turn when lightly browned, and brown the other side. Cut in quarters to serve.

Serves 3

Creamy Nutty Tuna Spread

8 ounces cream cheese, softened
2 tablespoons lemon juice
½ cup mayonnaise
4½ ounce can pitted black olives

1 cup tuna, drained (white
  albacore, water packed)
½ cup chopped pecans
Bread

Combine the cream cheese, lemon juice, and mayonnaise with a mixer until smooth. Chop the olives to yield ½ cup. Fold the olives, tuna, and chopped pecans into the cream cheese mixture. Spread thinly on bread of your choice.

Serves 12

Maryland Crab Melt

½ English muffin
  Butter
1 thin slice country ham
1 thin slice tomato

1 thin slice cheddar cheese
¼ cup backfin crab meat
1 teaspoon mayonnaise
  Dash paprika

Butter muffin and layer other ingredients in order given, ending with the mayonnaise. Sprinkle with paprika. Bake 15 minutes at 350 degrees until the mayonnaise is slightly browned.

Serves 1

Crab Soufflé Sandwiches

12 ounces backfin crab meat
½ teaspoon salt
¼ teaspoon pepper
1 tablespoon lemon juice
12 slices white bread, crusts
  removed

  Butter, softened
12 slices sharp cheddar cheese
4 eggs
2 cups half-and-half
6 tablespoons sherry

Pick over crab meat. Season with salt, pepper, and lemon juice. Mix and set aside. Butter bread slices on one side, and place 6 slices butter side down in glass baking dish. Place one slice of cheese on each slice of bread. Divide prepared crab meat, and spread it over the 6 slices. Cover with the remaining cheese slices and top with remaining bread, butter side up.

Beat eggs and mix with cream. Pour over sandwiches. Seal top with foil, and refrigerate 24 hours or overnight.

When ready to bake, let stand at room temperature for 1 hour. Pour 1 tablespoon sherry over each sandwich, then bake uncovered 1 hour at 325 degrees or until brown.

Serves 6

Chicken Soufflé Sandwiches

12 slices firm textured white
    bread, crusts trimmed
    Sliced cooked white chicken,
    enough for 6 sandwiches
 6 slices sharp cheddar cheese

3 eggs
1 cup milk
1 teaspoon dry mustard
1 teaspoon salt
½ cup cornflakes, crushed
½ cup butter, melted

Line greased 2-inch deep baking dish with 6 slices bread. Top with sliced chicken and then with sliced cheese. Cover with 6 bread slices. In a bowl beat eggs with the milk, mustard, and salt. Pour over casserole and refrigerate overnight.

The next day cover casserole with the crushed cornflakes, and pour melted butter over all. Bake 1 hour at 350 degrees.

Note: May be made with sliced turkey. Use approximately ¼ pound chicken per sandwich.

Serves 6

Hot Browns

½ cup butter or margarine
6 tablespoons flour
1 quart milk
1 teaspoon salt
½ teaspoon pepper
1 pound white American cheese

8 ounces Swiss cheese
1 pound turkey, sliced
1 pound ham, sliced
White bread
2 tomatoes, sliced
½ pound bacon, cooked crisp

In a medium saucepan melt butter, and whisk in flour. Add milk over medium heat, and stir until thickened. Add salt and pepper. Reduce heat and blend in cheeses.

Place two layers of turkey and ham on slices of bread. Pour sauce over, and top with a tomato slice. Brown sandwiches under broiler. When tomato and cheese sauce are beginning to brown, put bacon slices on top and brown for another minute. Watch carefully so they do not burn.

Serves 6 to 8

Egg Baskets

1 package brown and serve
  French rolls
2 tablespoons butter
¼ cup sweet red pepper,
  chopped
⅓ cup scallions, chopped,
  including some green tops

6 eggs
3 tablespoons milk
½ teaspoon seasoned salt
¼ teaspoon salt
¼ teaspoon pepper
  Paprika

Preheat oven to 425 degrees. With sharp knife, remove the top and center of each roll, leaving a shell about ½-inch thick. Place shells in the oven to brown, about 15 minutes.

Melt butter, and sauté scallions and red pepper. Beat eggs and milk together with salts and pepper. Pour into pan with scallions and scramble, cooking until eggs are done. Spoon into shells and serve, garnished with paprika.

Serves 4

Fish & shellfish

Bounty of the Bay

Maryland seafood—what a delight! Crabs, oysters, clams, and a variety of fish are found in abundance in the Chesapeake Bay. Lobsters, too, are another Maryland seafood delicacy which are harvested in the Atlantic Ocean 30 miles out from Ocean City.

The Chesapeake Bay is the world's largest producer of Blue Channel crabs, and they are recognized throughout the nation as an epicurean treat. Also more than 200 varieties of fish are found in the Bay, which is the world's greatest inland sea with 4,000 miles of shoreline. The Bay is home to white perch and striped bass (or rock fish as it is called by Marylanders). Some others, such as shad, herring, croaker, flounder, sea trout, and spot come in from the Atlantic Ocean to feed in the rich waters.

One hundred years ago, Maryland oysters were harvested by the famous fleet of Chesapeake Bay Skipjacks, driven only by sailpower. Today, oyster harvesting is done much the same way in addition to other more modern methods which are used to help Maryland maintain its position as the world's largest oyster producer. Each year Maryland watermen harvest more than 3 million bushels of oysters. In addition to oysters, Maryland waters are home to various sizes, shapes, and varieties of clams. Hard shell, little necks, cherrystone, chowder, soft shell, and surf clams are all harvested here in the Bay.

The famous seafoods of Maryland are harvested each year to be prepared in dozens of tantalizing ways by Baltimore's cooks, many of whom have a special touch with seafood. Come and enjoy!

Aunt Ruth's Imperial Crab

2 tablespoons butter	1 small jar pimiento, chopped
2½ tablespoons flour	1 teaspoon seafood seasoning
1 cup half-and-half	2 tablespoons white vinegar
1 medium green pepper, chopped	1 pound backfin crab meat, picked over
	Bread or cracker crumbs

Melt butter in skillet. Stir in flour and brown slightly. Add milk, green pepper, pimiento, and seafood seasoning. Cook on low heat until thickened, stirring constantly. Add vinegar and crab meat, and toss lightly. Place mixture in casserole dish or in baking shells. Sprinkle with bread or cracker crumbs, and bake at 350 degrees for 20 minutes or until lightly browned.

Serves 6

Baked Crab Meat in White Sauce

1 pound crab meat	4 hard-cooked eggs (optional)
¼ cup sherry	Salt and pepper
7 tablespoons butter	⅛ teaspoon Cayenne pepper
3 tablespoons flour	½ teaspoon dry mustard
2 cups light cream	1 cup toasted bread crumbs
1 tablespoon lemon juice	Parsley, for garnish

Place the crab meat in a mixing bowl, add sherry and let sit while making the white sauce. Melt butter in saucepan over moderate heat. Stir in flour. When smooth, gradually add cream. Cook stirring constantly until thickened. Stir in lemon juice. Put egg yolks through sieve and chop whites until fine. Add to sauce with salt and pepper. Mix dry mustard with 1 teaspoon cream or milk, and add to sauce. Fold in crab meat. Place in baking dish or serving shells. Top with bread crumbs and bake at 350 degrees for 25 minutes. Serve garnished with parsley.

Freezes well. Add bread crumbs just before baking.

Serves 6

Crab Cakes

2 eggs, beaten
¼ cup onion, chopped
½ cup cracker crumbs
3 tablespoons mayonnaise
1 tablespoon prepared mustard
¼ cup green pepper, chopped

1 teaspoon Worcestershire sauce
1 teaspoon seafood seasoning
1 tablespoon parsley, chopped
1 tablespoon baking powder
1 pound crab meat
1 egg, beaten (optional)
Dry bread crumbs (optional)

Combine eggs, onion, cracker crumbs, mayonnaise, seasonings, and baking powder in small bowl. Mix thoroughly. Gently blend in crab meat without breaking up any large chunks of crab. Mold into cakes. If desired, dip in egg, then bread crumbs. Brown in skillet with hot butter until heated through.

Serves 4

Crab Meat au Gratin

¼ cup butter
4 tablespoons flour
¼ cup milk
1 cup light cream
½ cup white wine
1 cup sharp cheddar cheese, grated

1 teaspoon salt
¼ teaspoon paprika
16 ounce can sliced mushrooms
2 tablespoons grated onion
1½ pounds crab meat, picked over
⅓ cup dry bread crumbs

To make white sauce, melt butter and stir in flour. When smooth, add milk, cream, and wine. Cook, stirring constantly, until smooth and thick. Add cheese, seasonings, mushrooms, and onion. Stir until cheese melts. Fold in crab meat; then pour into greased baking dish. Top with bread crumbs. Bake in 350 degree oven 15 to 20 minutes. Serve with rice or in patty shells.

Serves 6 to 8

Crab Meat with Ham en Casserole

1½ pounds crab meat, picked
over
½ cup diced country ham

¼ cup mayonnaise
6 tablespoons butter, melted
2 tablespoons lemon juice

Preheat oven to 400 degrees. Toss crab meat lightly with ham and put in buttered baking dish. Then mix lightly with mayonnaise, melted butter, and lemon juice. Bake for 10 minutes.

Serves 6

Creamed Crab with Artichokes

½ cup butter
½ cup flour
¼ cup onion, grated
½ cup green onion, chopped
2 tablespoons parsley, chopped
2 cups whipping cream
¾ cup dry white wine

2½ teaspoons salt
½ teaspoon white pepper
¼ teaspoon Cayenne pepper
2 tablespoons lemon juice
2 pounds crab meat
1 14-ounce can artichoke
hearts, drained and sliced

½ pound mushrooms, sliced

Melt butter, stir in flour, and cook for 5 minutes on medium heat. Add onions, parsley and cook 2 to 3 minutes. Gradually stir in cream and heat well. Add wine, salt, and peppers. Blend well and simmer stirring constantly. Remove from heat. When mixture is lukewarm, add lemon juice.

Place crab meat in bottom of 18- by 28-inch baking dish. Spoon a third of the sauce over top. Layer artichokes over sauce, then cover with a third of the sauce. Add mushrooms, and top with remaining sauce. Bake in 350 degree oven 30 to 45 minutes.

Serves 8

Seafood Jambalaya

5-6 large links mild sausage
⅓ cup onion, chopped
2 tablespoons butter
3 tablespoons parsley, chopped
2 cups water
16 ounce can tomatoes
1½ cups rice, uncooked

1 bay leaf
⅛ teaspoon freshly ground pepper
⅛ teaspoon Cayenne pepper (optional)
2 pounds shrimp, steamed, peeled, deveined
½-1 pound crab meat

Cook sausage in ½ inch of water, drain, and chop into bite-sized pieces. Sauté onion in butter until translucent. Add parsley and cook for 1 minute. Place sausage and onions in large baking dish. Mix with water, tomatoes, rice and seasonings. Cover and bake in 350 degree oven for 1 hour. When rice is cooked, and most of the liquid absorbed, mix in shrimp. Bake an additional 10 to 15 minutes to heat shrimp. Gently mix in crab. Cover for 5 minutes and serve.

Serves 6

Shrimp Antoine

1 pound shrimp, peeled and deveined
2 cups dry white wine
¼ cup margarine
¼ cup onion, finely chopped
½ pound mushrooms, sliced

2 tablespoons flour
2 tablespoons heavy cream
2 tablespoons fresh parsley, chopped
½ cup buttered bread crumbs
Long grain white rice

Place shrimp and wine in a skillet. Cover and simmer 5 minutes or until tender. Drain and reserve liquid. Melt margarine and sauté onions and mushrooms for 3 to 5 minutes. Stir in flour, and gradually stir in reserved liquid and cream. Bring to a boil, stirring constantly. Add shrimp and parsley. Place in greased ovenproof serving dish, cover with bread crumbs, and place under broiler briefly to brown. Watch closely. Serve over rice.

Serves 2

Artichoke and Shrimp Casserole

2 small jars artichoke hearts,
  packed in water
¾ pound shrimp, cooked briefly
1 tablespoon lemon juice
½ teaspoon thyme

½–¾ pound fresh mushrooms,
  sliced
2 tablespoons butter, melted
1½ cups Béchamel sauce
¼ cup Gruyère cheese

Paprika

Arrange artichoke hearts in buttered baking dish and sprinkle with half the lemon juice. If shrimp are large, halve them. Then place over artichokes, and sprinkle with remaining lemon juice and thyme. Sauté mushrooms in butter, and place over shrimp. Cover with Béchamel sauce and then Gruyère. Sprinkle paprika over all. Bake 30 minutes at 375 degrees.

Béchamel sauce:
2 tablespoons butter
2 tablespoons flour
2 cups half-and-half
½ teaspoon salt

½ teaspoon white pepper
Dash of nutmeg
1 tablespoon port wine or
  sherry

1 tablespoon soy sauce

Melt butter in saucepan. Add flour, stirring constantly until well blended. Gradually add half-and-half. Cook, stirring constantly, until sauce thickens. Add remaining ingredients, and stir until well mixed.

Serves 4

Shrimp Creole

¾ cup oil
1 large onion, chopped
1 large green pepper, chopped
3 ribs celery, chopped
2 cloves garlic, minced
½ cup fresh parsley, minced

1 bunch green onions, chopped
Salt
Black pepper
Red pepper
1 pound shrimp
1 28-ounce can tomatoes

1 cup rice, cooked

Sauté seasonings in oil until tender. Add shrimp and tomatoes. Simmer uncovered for at least 30 minutes. Serve over rice.

Serves 4

Prawn Curry

1 medium yellow onion, minced	4 cloves garlic, minced
2 tablespoons peanut oil	4½ cups unsweetened coconut milk
3 pounds peeled, canned tomatoes, drained	2 tablespoons tamarind sauce or plum jam
¾ teaspoon chili powder	2 pounds medium prawns or shrimp, peeled
¾ teaspoon turmeric	
¾ teaspoon powdered ginger	

In a heavy skillet, fry the onion in peanut oil until translucent. Add the remaining ingredients to pan except prawns. Simmer uncovered until thick. Add prawns and cook over low heat until done. Serve with rice, chutney, and condiments, such as Spanish peanuts, unsalted peanuts, grated coconut, pineapple chunks, raisins, chopped ripe tomatoes, or minced green onions. Mix tomatoes and onions with lemon juice, 1 tablespoon oil, salt, and pepper to taste.

Note: Purchase coconut milk and tamarind sauce from Oriental or Latin specialty stores. Substitute ½ cup tamarind juice for sauce if necessary.

Serves 6

Herbed Shrimp

1 cup butter	1 clove garlic, minced
¼ cup olive oil	¾ teaspoon salt
¾ tablespoon chopped parsley	1 tablespoon lemon juice
¾ teaspoon dried basil	2 pounds large fresh shrimp
½ teaspoon oregano	4 strawberries for garnish
1 lemon, sliced for garnish	

Melt butter over low heat. Add olive oil, spices, garlic, and lemon juice. Simmer for 10 minutes. Peel and devein raw shrimp, leaving tail section attached. Butterfly shrimp by slicing down length almost to vein and opening shrimp to flatten. Arrange in 9- by 12-inch baking dish and pour sauce over butterflied shrimp. Bake for 5 minutes at 450 degrees and then broil for 4 to 5 minutes until shrimp tails curl up. Serve with wild rice.

Serves 4

Shrimp Harpin

1½ pounds large shrimp	1 teaspoon salt
1 tablespoon lemon juice	⅛ teaspoon mace
3 tablespoons vegetable oil	1/16 teaspoon Cayenne pepper
¾ cup long grain white rice	1 can tomato soup, undiluted
2 tablespoons butter	1 cup heavy cream
¼ cup green pepper, diced	½ cup sherry
¼ cup onion, diced	½ cup slivered almonds
Paprika	

Boil shrimp briefly and peel. Place shrimp in 2-quart baking dish. Sprinkle with lemon juice and oil. Cook rice according to package instructions.

Melt butter in skillet. Sauté green pepper and onion for 5 minutes; then add to shrimp in baking dish. Combine rice with seasonings, soup, cream, sherry, and ¼ cup almonds. Add to shrimp. Sprinkle remaining almonds and paprika over top. Bake at 350 degrees about 55 minutes.

Note: Can be prepared in advance and refrigerated a few hours before baking.

Serves 6 to 8

Rosemary Shrimp

1 pound butter, no substitutes	1 teaspoon garlic salt
1 tablespoon seasoned salt	1 tablespoon rosemary
3 to 5 pounds fresh shrimp, unpeeled	

Melt butter and spices in 9- by 13-inch baking dish. Let cool a little. Add shrimp and marinate all day. Bake in a 400 degree oven for 20 to 30 minutes. Peel and serve with French bread to dip in herb butter.

Serves 6 to 8

Grilled Shrimp Kebabs

32 jumbo shrimp, shelled and deveined	1 teaspoon dried basil leaves
½ cup cognac	16 slices bacon, cut in half
½ teaspoon salt	Pineapple chunks, reserve juice
¼–½ teaspoon ground pepper	Apricot sauce

In large bowl, marinate shrimp in cognac, salt, pepper and basil in refrigerator several hours or overnight. Wrap each shrimp with ½ slice bacon and alternate with pineapple chunks on skewers. Broil 4 inches from heat for 5 minutes on each side or until bacon is crisp and shrimp are browned. Serve with apricot sauce.

Apricot sauce:

½ cup reserved pineapple juice	2 tablespoons soy sauce
2 tablespoons dry mustard	1 cup apricot preserves
1 lemon, juice and grated peel	

Whisk mustard into pineapple juice. Add soy sauce, preserves, lemon juice, and peel. Heat and serve with shrimp.

Serves 4

Spicy Shrimp

1 pound shrimp	2 tablespoons olive oil
3 green chilies	1 clove garlic (optional)
1 medium onion, chopped	1 tablespoon fresh thyme

Peel and devein shrimp. Remove seeds from chilies, and slice into small rings. Heat olive oil in large skillet. Sauté onion, chilies, and minced garlic until opaque, but not soft. Add shrimp and cook quickly until pink, about 5 minutes. Do not overcook. Add thyme and cook an additional 30 seconds. Serve with rice.

Serves 2

Shrimp and Scallop Casserole

1 pound shrimp, shelled
½ pound bay scallops
½ cup soy sauce
¼ pound butter
1 tablespoon fresh parsley, chopped
6 cloves garlic, minced

½ pound fresh mushrooms, sliced thin
8 ounce can water chestnuts, sliced
8 ounce can bean sprouts, rinsed and drained

Marinate seafood in soy sauce 15 minutes. Meanwhile, melt butter in saucepan. Add parsley and garlic. Remove seafood from soy sauce, and place in shallow baking dish. Top with mushrooms, water chestnuts, and bean sprouts. Pour seasoned butter over top, and bake at 350 degrees 25 minutes or until shrimp are done.

Note: Can prepare this ahead of time.

Serves 4

Broiled Scallops

1½ pounds fresh bay scallops
2 tablespoons lemon juice
3 tablespoons butter

1 clove garlic, finely chopped
¼ cup dry bread crumbs
⅛ teaspoon seafood seasoning

Pat scallops dry with paper towel and place evenly on broiler pan. Sprinkle with 1 tablespoon lemon juice. In small saucepan, melt butter. Add remaining lemon juice and garlic. Brush over scallops, sprinkle lightly with bread crumbs and seafood seasoning. Broil in oven 7 to 10 minutes, or until scallops start to brown slightly. Do not overcook, as scallops will become tough. Serve with parsleyed new potatoes.

Note: May prepare in advance.

Serves 4

Scallop Creole

1 large green pepper, chopped	½ teaspoon thyme
1 large onion, chopped	½ teaspoon oregano
2 tablespoons bacon drippings	1 teaspoon salt
16 ounce can stewed tomatoes	½ teaspoon pepper
4 tablespoons tomato paste	1½ pounds scallops

Sauté green pepper and onion in bacon fat until tender. Stir in tomatoes and tomato paste. Add thyme, oregano, salt, and pepper. Simmer for 10 minutes. Add scallops and cook for 7 minutes. Serve over rice.

Serves 6

Scallops in Sherry Cream

⅓ cup butter	1 pound sea scallops
2–3 shallots, finely chopped	2 tablespoons flour
1 clove garlic, finely chopped	½ teaspoon salt
¾ cup cooking sherry	1 cup heavy cream
½ pound fresh mushrooms, sliced	½ teaspoon paprika
	Parmesan cheese (optional)

Melt 1 tablespoon butter, and sauté shallots and garlic. Add sherry, mushrooms, scallops, and simmer until scallops are tender. Drain liquid and reserve. Place scallops in baking dish.

In saucepan melt remaining butter, whisk in flour and salt. When smooth, add cream and reserved liquid. Heat, stirring until very thick. Pour sauce over scallops, and sprinkle with paprika. If desired, sprinkle Parmesan cheese over top. Bake in 350 degree oven until bubbly.

Serves 2 to 4

Seviche

2 cups bay scallops
2 tablespoons onion, minced
1 tablespoon fresh parsley, chopped

⅓ cup fresh lime juice
Salt and pepper
Romaine lettuce
Tomato wedges

Place scallops in mixing bowl, and add onion, parsley, lime, and seasonings. Refrigerate overnight in tightly covered bowl. Serve on bed of lettuce leaves with tomato wedges.

Serves 6 to 8

Smoked Bluefish

1 cup non-iodized salt
½ cup brown sugar
¼ cup lemon juice

¼ tablespoon onion powder
2 quarts water
4 fresh bluefish fillets, with skin

To make brine, mix salt, sugar, lemon juice, and onion powder in water until dissolved. Soak fish in brine for 8 hours. Rinse, then pat dry. Leave at room temperature for 1 hour. Use hickory chips in smoker. Load fish into smoker skin down. Fish will not need turning. Check fish frequently as it cooks. Refer to your smoker's instructions for specific cooking time. It could range from 2 or 3 hours to 8 or 10 hours.

Note: To smoke more fish, increase brine proportionately.

Serves 2 to 4

Easy Cod Florentine

1 to 1¼ pounds fresh cod	10 ounce package frozen
¼ cup white wine	creamed spinach
Salt and pepper	2 1-ounce slices Swiss cheese

Place cod in broiler-proof pan. Pour in white wine and season with salt and pepper. Broil approximately 20 minutes until fish begins to flake slightly. While fish is broiling, prepare creamed spinach according to package directions. When fish and spinach are ready, pour spinach over fish. Cover with Swiss cheese and broil 2 minutes to melt cheese. Serve over rice.

Note: Season fish with a squeeze of fresh lemon juice or a dash of garlic salt before cooking.

Serves 2

Fish Poupon

3 cups soft whole wheat bread crumbs	1½ tablespoons Worcestershire sauce
1½ tablespoons Parmesan cheese, grated	½–1 teaspoon Dijon mustard
½ cup butter, melted	2 pounds haddock, sole or white fish fillets

Preheat oven to 325 degrees. Mix together bread crumbs, Parmesan cheese, ¼ cup butter, Worcestershire sauce, and mustard. Place fish fillets in single layer in a greased, shallow baking pan. Spoon sauce evenly over the fish. Pour remaining butter over top. Cover with foil greased on the inside. Bake about 15 minutes or until fish flakes. Remove foil, and broil 2 to 3 minutes until browned.

Serves 4 to 6

Flounder Fillets with Cheese Sauce

1½ pounds flounder fillets
   Salt and pepper to taste
½ cup mayonnaise
1/16 teaspoon Cayenne pepper
2 tablespoons chopped pickle

1 tablespoon parsley, chopped
⅓ cup sharp cheddar cheese, grated
1 egg white
   Pimiento, for garnish

Wipe fish with a damp cloth, and place on greased broiler rack. Broil under medium heat 8 to 12 minutes. Sprinkle with salt and pepper. Mix mayonnaise, Cayenne, pickle, parsley, and cheese. Beat egg white until stiff and fold into dressing. Spread over fillets and broil 5 minutes or until sauce has puffed. Garnish with pimiento strips.

Serves 4

Sole in Shrimp Sauce

1 pound sole fillets
½ teaspoon salt
½ teaspoon lemon pepper
¼ cup butter
1 teaspoon paprika

1 can cream of shrimp soup
¼ cup white wine
2 tablespoons lemon juice
⅔ cup Parmesan cheese, grated

Place fish fillets in a buttered 9- by 9-inch dish. Sprinkle with salt and lemon pepper. Dot with butter. Mix soup, wine, and lemon juice, and spread over fish. Sprinkle heavily with Parmesan cheese and paprika. Bake at 425 degrees for 25 minutes. Serve over rice.

Serves 3 to 4

Cold Poached Salmon with Dill Dressing

4 fresh salmon steaks (1½–2 pounds)	1 teaspoon salt
½ cup white wine	½ teaspoon Dijon mustard
1 cup boiling water	1 tablespoon lemon juice
2 lemon slices	1½ cups olive oil
2 eggs	2 tablespoons fresh dill, finely chopped

1 cup cucumber, thinly sliced

Place salmon in skillet with wine, water, and lemon. Simmer 10 minutes; then refrigerate in serving dish. To make dill dressing combine eggs, salt, mustard, and lemon juice in blender. Add oil very slowly. As mixture thickens, add more oil. When creamy, stir in dill and cucumber. Spoon over fish and garnish with additional sprig of dill.

Note: You may substitute vegetable oil for a portion of the olive oil.

Serves 4 to 6

Ginger Steamed Rockfish (Striped Bass)

1 tablespoon salad oil	¼ cup chicken stock
1 pound fresh rockfish fillets	¼ cup dry white wine
½ cup green onions, sliced	4 teaspoons soy sauce
1 cup fresh mushrooms, sliced	1 tablespoon cornstarch
1–2 tablespoons fresh ginger, peeled and minced	1 tablespoon water

Heat oil in large frying pan, add the fish and cook 1 minute. Turn pieces carefully with a wide spatula. Sprinkle the onions, mushrooms, and ginger evenly over the fish. Add the stock, wine, and soy sauce. Cover and let steam about 10 minutes, or just until the fish flakes when tested with a fork.

Remove fish to a warm platter and keep warm. Mix the cornstarch and water and gradually stir into the hot liquid. Cook, stirring, until sauce is slightly thickened. Pour over fish. Garnish with parsley. Serve with steamed white rice flavored with soy sauce.

Note: Slice any remaining ginger root into quarter-sized pieces and freeze in airtight container. Red snapper may be substituted for rockfish.

Serves 4

Eastern Shore Fried Oysters

2 tablespoons vegetable oil
1 quart oysters, freshly shucked
Pancake flour

1 teaspoon onion, minced
Salt, if oysters are from a river

Heat vegetable oil until very hot in a large skillet or electric frying pan. Place oysters, including liquid, in a bowl. Add onion, salt if needed, and pancake flour. Stir gently until oysters are coated. Remove from bowl with slotted spoon. Fry in a single layer no longer than 2 minutes on each side. Remove and drain on paper towel.

Note: Oysters will be soggy if oil is not hot enough.

Serves 4 to 6

Maryland Pan-Fried Oysters

24 ounces oysters
2 eggs, beaten
2 tablespoons milk
1 teaspoon salt
Dash pepper

1½ cups dry bread crumbs
1½ cups flour
Margarine or butter for frying

Drain oysters. Mix egg, milk, and seasonings in bowl. In another bowl, mix bread crumbs and flour. Roll oysters in crumb mixture, dip in egg mixture, and then roll again in crumb mixture. Fry in butter over medium heat 3 minutes each side.

Serves 6

Scalloped Oysters

2 cups saltine cracker crumbs
1 cup bread crumbs, made from
 toasted bread
½ cup butter, melted
2 pints oysters (or more),
 drained

Cayenne pepper
Salt and black pepper to taste
4 tablespoons butter
½ cup sherry

Combine the saltine crumbs and bread crumbs with melted butter, and mix together well. Butter a shallow, oblong baking dish, add one-third the cracker mixture to thinly cover the bottom of casserole. Arrange oysters on top of cracker mixture. Sprinkle with Cayenne pepper, salt, and black pepper. Layer half the remaining cracker mixture and oysters ending with cracker mixture on top. Dot with butter and sprinkle sherry over top. Bake at 375 degrees for 20 to 30 minutes.

Serves 8 to 10

Oysters Rockefeller Casserole

¾ cup butter
1 teaspoon thyme
1½ cups green onion, chopped
1 cup celery, chopped
1 large clove garlic, crushed
1 tablespoon Worcestershire
 sauce
1 teaspoon anchovy paste
1¼ cups seasoned bread crumbs
1 quart oysters, drained,
 reserve ½ cup liquid

½ cup parsley, chopped
½ cup Parmesan cheese, grated
1½ tablespoons Pernod liqueur
2 10-ounce packages frozen,
 chopped spinach, cooked
 and drained
½ teaspoon salt
¼ teaspoon pepper
¼ teaspoon Cayenne pepper

Melt butter in a large skillet over medium heat. Add the thyme, green onion, celery, and garlic; and sauté until tender. Add the Worcestershire sauce, anchovy paste, and bread crumbs; stir well for several minutes until crumbs are toasted. Gently stir in oysters, ½ cup of oyster liquid, parsley, Parmesan cheese, and Pernod. Cook several minutes until oysters curl. Add spinach; season with salt, pepper and Cayenne. Place in a 3-quart baking dish, and bake at 350 degrees for 30 minutes. Serve with rice.

Serves 8 to 10

Deviled Rock Lobster Tails

6 rock lobster tails
1¼ cups soft bread crumbs
¾ cup half-and-half
1 egg, beaten
1 teaspoon dry mustard

½ teaspoon salt
1/16 teaspoon Cayenne pepper
   Dash hot pepper sauce
½ cup cracker crumbs
¼ cup melted butter

Drop lobster tails into large pot filled with boiling salted water (6 quarts water, 2 tablespoons salt). Cover, bring back to boil and cook 2 minutes; then immediately put into ice water to stop the cooking. Cut away underside membrane completely, remove and dice meat into ½-inch pieces.

Mix lobster with next seven ingredients. Spoon mixture back into shells. Place in a shallow baking pan. Mix cracker crumbs and butter; sprinkle over top of shells. Bake at 375 degrees for 30 minutes.

Serves 6

Lobster with Marinara Sauce

3 cloves garlic, split
½ cup oil
1 cup onion, chopped
3 cups mushrooms, sliced
35 ounce can Italian plum
   tomatoes, undrained
2 teaspoons salt
½ teaspoon pepper

⅛ teaspoon ground cloves
½ teaspoon oregano
¼ teaspoon dried basil
1 tablespoon sugar
5 lobster tails
1 pound spaghetti
   Parmesan cheese
   Parsley

Brown garlic in hot oil in 4-quart saucepan. Remove and discard garlic. Add onion and mushrooms and sauté for 10 minutes. Add next 7 ingredients and bring to a boil. Reduce heat and simmer, uncovered, for 30 minutes. Cut undershell from lobster tails; then cut each tail into 3 pieces. Add lobster to sauce and simmer, uncovered, for 20 minutes. Cook spaghetti and drain. Place spaghetti around edge of large platter. Spoon lobster and sauce into center. Sprinkle with Parmesan cheese and parsley.

Serves 6

Lobster and Chicken Marengo

1 large onion, chopped	½ teaspoon thyme
1 clove garlic, crushed	⅓ cup dry sherry
½ cup olive oil	¼ teaspoon salt
2 cups chicken broth	¼ teaspoon pepper
2 16-ounce cans Italian tomatoes, chopped and drained	3 cups mushrooms, sliced
	2 pounds chicken breasts, cooked, boned, and cut into bite-sized pieces
½ cup celery, diced	
2 bay leaves	1 pound lobster meat, cooked
1 tablespoon chopped parsley	
1 teaspoon basil	

Brown onion and garlic in olive oil. Set aside. In a saucepan, combine stock, tomatoes, celery, and bay leaves. Bring to a boil; cover and simmer for 25 minutes. Add parsley, herbs, sherry, salt and pepper. Simmer 10 minutes more. Add mushrooms, onion mixture, chicken, and lobster. Simmer until thickened. If sauce seems too thin, it may be thickened with a little flour and water. Transfer to serving dish. Bake for 20 to 30 minutes at 350 degrees. Serve over rice.

Note: This is even better the next day. Freezes very successfully.

Serves 8

Paella

3 tablespoons olive oil
2 tablespoons onion, chopped (or more)
3 cloves garlic, minced
3 fresh tomatoes, chopped
1 green pepper, chopped in large pieces
3 cups rice, uncooked
6 cups hot chicken broth
1½ pounds raw shrimp, shelled and deveined
1½ pounds squid (optional), cleaned and cut in rings
½ teaspoon saffron or to taste

¼ teaspoon cumin
½ teaspoon oregano
2 packages frozen peas, cooked according to directions
1 3½-pound chicken, boiled, boned and cut into large pieces
2 chorizos (Spanish sausage), peeled and sliced
2 cans minced clams with liquid
Salt to taste
1 large jar pimiento, cut into thin strips
12 clams or mussels in shell

In large 12-inch skillet (or paella pan), sauté onion and garlic in olive oil. Add tomatoes and mash as they cook. Add green pepper and rice. Stir and brown a little, then add hot chicken broth, rinsed and dried raw shrimp, and squid. Add saffron, cumin, and oregano. Cook over very high heat about 25 minutes uncovered and without stirring until most of liquid is absorbed.

Add cooked peas, chicken pieces, sausage, canned clams, and liquid. Salt to taste. Mix or toss lightly. Transfer to baking dish or leave in paella pan. Place strips of pimiento on top. Bake covered in 350 degree oven until liquid is absorbed.

Meanwhile, wash mussels or clams well. Place in pan on top of stove, without additional water added to pan. Over medium heat, cook until clams or mussels open. Remove casserole from oven and arrange clams or mussels over paella. Pour any liquid from the clams or mussels over casserole and serve.

Serves 12 to 16

Poultry & Game

Eastern Shore Hunting

The Eastern Shore, or as we fondly know it, "The Sho'," provides a wealth of fowl and game for the hunter. It offers the largest variety of birds in the United States and Canada.

Until the construction of the Chesapeake Bay Bridge, the Eastern Shore was a world unto itself. Since then, hunters and sportsmen from throughout the country have come to Maryland's shore counties of Caroline, Cecil, Dorchester, Kent, Queen Annes, Somerset, Talbot, Wicomico, and Worcester. The red-haired Chesapeake Bay Retriever was bred on the Bay specifically to work the icy waters in fall and winter. This web-toed dog grows a double matting of hair and produces extra oil to act as insulation. It loves the water and is particularly adept at breaking through the ice.

A large variety of waterfowl has chosen the Eastern Shore as a winter home before making the spring journey North. Our farms, rivers, and marshes are populated by thousands upon thousands of ducks, geese, and swan.

Chicken Breasts with Wine Sauce

6 boneless chicken breast halves
4 tablespoons butter, melted
   Crushed cornflakes, seasoned
1 can cream of mushroom soup
¾ cup sherry, sauterne, or dry
   white wine

½ teaspoon Worcestershire
   sauce
¼ cup celery, chopped
1 small jar chopped pimiento
4 ounce can sliced mushrooms

Preheat oven to 400 degrees. Skin chicken breasts. Dip in melted butter or cream, and drain. Coat with cornflakes, and place in lightly greased baking dish. Bake 45 minutes.

While baking, combine remaining ingredients to make sauce. Remove chicken from oven; pour sauce over top. Return chicken to oven for additional 15 minutes.

Serves 6

Chicken Diane

2 tablespoons vegetable oil
4 tablespoons butter
4 boneless chicken breast
   halves
¼ cup shallots, minced
¼ cup parsley, minced
1 cup chicken bouillon

1 tablespoon cornstarch
1 tablespoon Dijon mustard
⅛ teaspoon Worcestershire
   sauce
   Juice of ½ lemon
½ teaspoon cognac
½ teaspoon port

In heavy 12-inch frying pan, heat oil and butter. Cut chicken breasts into 1-inch pieces. Sauté chicken until nicely browned. Add shallots and parsley. Mix bouillon, cornstarch, and Dijon mustard together. Then add to chicken. Add Worcestershire, lemon juice, cognac, and port, stirring and coating chicken pieces continually. Let cook slowly until the liquid becomes a thick gravy consistency. Serve with the sauce and noodles.

Serves 4

Chicken Parmigiana

1 small onion, chopped	¼ teaspoon sugar
2 cloves garlic, minced	¼ teaspoon pepper
4 tablespoons olive oil	4 chicken breasts
2 cups tomatoes, peeled and seeded	3 tablespoons butter
	Parmesan cheese
1 teaspoon dried oregano	Fettucine
1 teaspoon dried basil	Heavy cream
¼ teaspoon salt	

To make sauce, sauté onion and garlic in oil over medium heat for five minutes. Add next six ingredients. Simmer sauce partially covered for 25 minutes. If too thick, add a little water to thin. Sauce should be moderately thick and chunky.

Bone and skin chicken breasts. Sauté in melted butter in skillet for 4 to 5 minutes per side. Place in shallow baking dish. Put 2 to 4 tablespoons sauce over each breast. Sprinkle with Parmesan cheese. Place under broiler until cheese melts, browns a little, and casserole is hot. Serve with fettucine, tossed with heavy cream and freshly grated Parmesan cheese.

Serves 4

Chicken in Rum

6 boneless chicken breast halves	1 egg, beaten
6 tablespoons mango chutney	Seasoned bread crumbs
Cayenne pepper	2–3 tablespoons vegetable oil
1–2 cups rum	

Pound chicken breast halves briefly. Spread 1 tablespoon chutney on inside of each breast, and sprinkle lightly with Cayenne. Fold each breast in half, and seal closed with toothpicks. Dip filled breasts in beaten egg, then in bread crumbs. Brown in oil in skillet over medium heat. Pour rum over chicken to fill pan about ¼ inch. Cover and simmer 30 to 40 minutes. Serve with rice. Spoon sauce over rice and chicken.

Note: Freezes well. As an alternative, cube chicken and brown in oil. Add remaining ingredients, and simmer until done.

Serves 4 to 6

Crab-Stuffed Chicken Breasts

6 boneless chicken breast
   halves, skinned
   Salt and pepper
½ cup onion, chopped
½ cup celery, chopped
6 tablespoons butter or
   margarine, divided
7 tablespoons dry white wine,
   divided

12 ounces crab meat
½ cup herb-seasoned stuffing
   mix
3 tablespoons flour
½ teaspoon paprika
¾ cup milk
1 envelope Hollandaise sauce
   mix
½ cup Swiss cheese, shredded

Pound chicken to flatten. Sprinkle breasts with salt and pepper. Sauté onion and celery in 3 tablespoons butter until tender. Remove from heat. Add 4 tablespoons wine, crab meat, and stuffing mix, and toss. Divide mixture among the breasts. Roll up and secure with toothpicks.

Combine flour and paprika; coat the chicken. Place in 9- by 13-inch greased baking dish. Sprinkle with 3 tablespoons melted butter. Bake uncovered in 375 degree oven for 1 hour. Transfer to serving dish. Blend milk and Hollandaise mix. Cook, stirring constantly until thick. Add remaining wine and cheese, stirring until cheese melts. Pour over chicken and serve.

Serves 6

Glazed Chicken Breasts

8 ounce jar red currant jelly
½ cup water
1 tablespoon potato starch
1 tablespoon Robert's Escoffier
  Sauce

Juice of ½ lemon
Salt and pepper to taste
¼ cup ruby port
½ teaspoon allspice
6 chicken breasts

Preheat oven to 375 degrees. Place all ingredients except chicken in
1-quart saucepan, and bring to a boil. Stir slowly. Grease baking dish or
small roasting pan, and place chicken in it. Pour hot sauce over chicken,
and bake 45 to 60 minutes, basting frequently. Add more port if sauce
becomes too thick.

Serves 6

Mediterranean Chicken

4 chicken breast halves
1½ cups dry white wine
  White pepper
  Basil

Thyme
½ pint whipping cream
½ cup black olives, chopped
¼ cup capers, drained

Fresh parsley

Place chicken and wine in skillet on top of stove. Sprinkle with spices,
cover, and cook over moderate heat approximately 45 minutes. Stir occasionally to prevent sticking. Remove chicken from pan, and place in warm
oven. Reduce wine and pan juices to 1 cup. Add cream to thicken. Add
olives and capers. Pour sauce over warm chicken, garnish with parsley, and
serve.

Serves 2 to 4

Pecan-Stuffed Chicken Breasts

3 cups seasoned stuffing mix   ½ cup water
½ cup butter, melted   4 whole chicken breasts
½ cup pecans, chopped   2 teaspoons salt
                ½ teaspoon pepper

Preheat oven to 350 degrees. Combine stuffing mix, butter, pecans, and water. Make four mounds of mixture on a baking sheet. Spread chicken breasts open, and place skin side up over each mound of stuffing. Sprinkle each with salt and pepper. Cover with foil, and bake for 40 minutes. Fold back foil, and bake 20 minutes longer until breasts are browned and done.

Note: This can be made ahead of time. Refrigerate or freeze until ready to use.

Serves 4

Reed's Chicken Tarragon

4 boned and skinned chicken   2 tablespoons olive oil
  breast halves   ¼ cup brandy (optional)
½ cup flour   ½ cup onion, chopped
⅛ teaspoon pepper   2 tablespoons butter
⅛ teaspoon tarragon   2 cups white wine
2 tablespoons butter   1 teaspoon tarragon
                1 cup light cream

Dredge chicken in flour, pepper, and tarragon. Brown in butter and olive oil. Add optional brandy and carefully light it. Remove chicken from pan. Add chopped onions and butter, and sauté. Add white wine, and replace chicken in pan. Cook over medium heat until wine is reduced by half. Season with 1 teaspoon tarragon, and stir in cream. Serve over rice or toast.

Serves 2 to 4

Paprikas Csirke (Chicken Paprikas)

1 onion, chopped	4–5 pounds chicken, cut into
4 tablespoons shortening	pieces
1 tablespoon rose paprika	1½ cups water
1 teaspoon black pepper	½ pint sour cream
1 teaspoon salt	½ pint cream (optional)

Brown onion in shortening. Add paprika, pepper, salt, and chicken. Brown for 10 minutes. Add water, cover and let simmer slowly until tender. Remove chicken, add sour cream to drippings in pan, and mix well. Add dumplings; arrange chicken on top. Heat thoroughly and serve. For more gravy, add ½ pint cream to sour cream.

Dumplings:

3 eggs beaten	1 tablespoon salt
3 cups flour	½ cup water

Mix all ingredients together, and beat with a spoon. Drop batter by teaspoonfuls into boiling, salted water. Cook about 10 minutes. Drain and rinse with cold water. Drain again and add to paprikas.

Note: Authentic Hungarian dish. Purchase rose paprika, imported from Hungary, from gourmet grocer.

Serves 4 to 6

Neighborhood Chicken

½ cup vegetable oil	1½ teaspoons poultry seasoning
1 cup cider vinegar	¼ teaspoon pepper
2 tablespoons salt	1 egg, beaten
8–10 chicken pieces	

Mix first six ingredients to make marinade. Skin chicken pieces if preferred, and marinate several hours or overnight. Cook chicken on grill, basting every 15 minutes and turning. Chicken should be done in 45 minutes.

Serves 8 to 10

East Indies Barbecued Chicken

1 onion, finely chopped
3 stalks celery, finely chopped
¼ cup oil
2 cups chicken stock
3 medium tomatoes, skinned
and stewed

2 apples, pared and chopped
3 tablespoons curry powder
Salt and pepper
2½ pound broiler
Oil

Sauté the onions and celery in oil until soft and golden. Add the chicken stock, stewed tomatoes, apple, curry powder, salt, and pepper. Simmer for 30 minutes.

Cut the chicken into 8 pieces, brush with oil, and sprinkle with salt. Let the chicken pieces stand for 30 minutes. Grill over glowing coals basting frequently with sauce. Turn pieces from time to time until tender. Serve with sauce and rice accompanied by chopped fresh pineapple, fruit chutney, and chopped cashew nuts.

Serves 4

Chicken Kabobs

6 boneless chicken breast
halves, skinned and cut into
1-inch squares
5 cloves garlic, minced
2 tablespoons parsley
½ cup vegetable oil
¼ cup sherry

1½ tablespoons red wine
vinegar
1 tablespoon soy sauce
Salt and pepper to taste
8 strips bacon, cut into thirds
2 pints cherry tomatoes
2 large onions, cut into wedges

Place chicken in a bowl. Add all other ingredients except bacon, tomatoes, and onions. Mix well, and marinate overnight. When ready to cook, drain chicken, reserving marinade, and wrap each piece of chicken in a piece of bacon. Thread onto skewers with vegetables. Brush with remaining marinade. Place under preheated broiler 2 inches from heat. Cook 4 minutes or until bacon is done. Turn and cook 4 more minutes. Serve immediately.

Serves 6

Chicken and Artichoke Casserole

12 boneless chicken breast halves, in bite-sized pieces	8 ounces pimiento, chopped
Flour	15 ounce can artichoke hearts, drained and sliced in halves
6 eggs, beaten	½ cup parsley, chopped
Oil	6 ounces dry white wine
6 tablespoons butter	3 ounces dry sherry
½ pound mushrooms, sliced	Salt and pepper to taste
20 large pitted ripe olives	6 tablespoons butter
1 bunch green onions, sliced, including tops	½ cup flour
	15 ounces beef stock or broth

Roll chicken pieces in flour; then dip in beaten eggs. Heat oil in heavy skillet, and brown chicken. Remove chicken, and drain oil from skillet. Melt butter, add mushrooms, olives, green onion, and sauté 2 minutes. Add chicken, pimiento, artichoke hearts, ¼ cup parsley, wine, and sherry. Cook 7 minutes, add salt and pepper; then arrange in baking dish.

To make a brown sauce, make roux of butter and flour in saucepan. When smooth, gradually whisk in stock. Cook 5 minutes. Pour sauce over chicken, and sprinkle with remaining parsley. Bake 45 minutes at 325 degrees.

Note: Chicken mixture can be made a day ahead. Add brown sauce just before baking. Double or triple recipe for a crowd.

Serves 10

Chicken Casserole

8 ounces noodles	1 can cream of mushroom soup
4 tablespoons butter or margarine	1 can cream of chicken soup
½ cup green pepper, diced	8 ounces sour cream
½ cup onion, chopped	1 cup dry sherry
8 cups chicken, diced and uncooked (about 4 chicken breasts)	1 cup seedless green grapes
	1 cup slivered almonds

Cook noodles according to package directions. Set aside. Melt butter and sauté green pepper and onion in large skillet. Remove from skillet, and set aside. Add diced chicken to the same skillet, and cook 5 to 10 minutes. Set aside.

Combine soups, sour cream, and sherry in a large mixing bowl. Add onions, green peppers, chicken, and noodles. Mix well, and add grapes. Place in greased 9- by 13-inch baking dish, and sprinkle almonds on top. Bake at 350 degrees for about 30 minutes or until hot throughout.

Note: Freezes well. Thaw, and add nuts just before baking.

Serves 8

Sour Cream Chicken Enchiladas

1 small chicken	1 small onion
3 ounces cream cheese, softened	1 small can green chili pepper
1 package tortillas	Chili powder to taste
1 red tomato	½–1 cup water
2 green tomatoes	
	1 pint sour cream

Cook small chicken, debone meat, and mix with cream cheese. Put tortillas one at a time in hot oil about 7 to 8 seconds each side. Drain immediately, fill with chicken, and roll up while hot. In saucepan combine remaining ingredients, except sour cream. Cook until tomatoes and onion are soft. Put filled tortillas in baking dish, and top with sauce. Bake at 350 degrees for 20 minutes. Top with sour cream and serve.

Serves 10 to 12

Chicken Pot Pie

4–6 chicken breasts
 1 medium onion, chopped
 ½ teaspoon celery salt
 4 medium potatoes, peeled
    and diced
 5 tablespoons butter or
    margarine
 5 tablespoons flour

 1 can cream of chicken soup
 1 chicken bouillon cube
10 ounce package frozen peas or
    16-ounce can peas, drained
 1 pound package carrots,
    peeled or 16-ounce can
    carrots, drained
    Dough for 9-inch pie shell

Boil chicken with onion and celery salt for 1 hour. Parboil the diced potatoes until tender. If using fresh carrots, parboil these also. Remove chicken meat from bones. Strain stock and reserve.

Melt butter in saucepan. Blend in flour and 1½ cups stock. Add soup and bouillon cube. Place chicken and vegetables in deep 4-quart baking dish. Gently mix in sauce. Top with crust. Bake at 350 degrees until golden and bubbly, about 45 to 60 minutes.

Serves 6 to 8

Chicken and Crescent Almondine

3 cups chopped, cooked chicken
   or turkey
1 can cream of chicken soup
8 ounce can water chestnuts,
   sliced and drained
4 ounce can mushroom stems
   and pieces, drained
⅔ cup mayonnaise
½ cup celery, chopped

½ cup onions, chopped
½ cup sour cream
8 ounce can crescent dinner
   rolls
½ cup almonds, slivered
⅔ cup Swiss or American
   cheese, grated
2–4 tablespoons margarine,
   melted

Preheat oven to 375 degrees. Combine chicken, soup, water chestnuts, mushrooms, mayonnaise, celery, onions, and sour cream in large saucepan. Heat until hot and bubbly. Pour into ungreased 9- by 13-inch pan. Separate dough into two rectangles and place on top. Combine cheese, almonds, and butter, and pour over dough. Bake 20 to 25 minutes.

Serves 6 to 8

Chicken, Turkey, or Crab Curry

¾ cup butter
2 cups onions, finely diced
2 cups tart green apples, pared and finely diced
3 cloves garlic, minced
⅛–¼ cup curry powder
2 teaspoons celery salt
1 teaspoon dried thyme leaves, crumbled
1 cup chicken broth
½ cup dry vermouth
¼ cup pale, dry sherry
1½ cups heavy cream

1 cup half-and-half
¼ cup chutney, puréed
1 tablespoon cornstarch, dissolved in ⅛ cup cold water
1 pound chicken, cooked and shredded
OR 1 pound turkey, cooked and shredded
OR 1 pound crabmeat, picked over

Melt the butter in a heavy pot, and sauté the onions, apples, and garlic for 5 minutes, or until onion is transparent. Stir in the curry powder, celery salt, and thyme, and cook over medium-low heat 5 minutes to eliminate the raw taste of curry powder. Add chicken broth, vermouth, and sherry. Bring mixture to a boil, lower heat, and simmer for 15 minutes. Stir in cream, half-and-half, and chutney. Simmer. Taste and add salt if needed. To thicken sauce, slowly pour in cornstarch and water mixture, and stir until thickened, 1 or 2 minutes. Just before serving add chicken, turkey, or crabmeat. Simmer long enough to heat through. Serve hot with rice and condiments.

Note: For condiments use pineapple chunks, sliced cucumbers, diced onions, toasted coconut, unsalted peanuts, chopped eggs, pickled watermelon rind, raisins, sliced bananas, mandarin oranges, and your favorite chutney.

Serves 10 to 12

Wok Chicken and Cherries

4 large chicken breast halves, skinned
3 tablespoons peanut oil
1 large carrot, thinly sliced
1 clove garlic, minced
⅓ cup chicken broth
3 tablespoons honey
3 tablespoons red wine vinegar
2 tablespoons soy sauce
½ teaspoon grated fresh ginger root

1 tablespoon cornstarch
2 cups frozen pitted tart red cherries, thawed and well drained
OR canned pitted, tart red cherries, well drained
3 green onions and tops, sliced
Hot cooked rice
½ cup toasted sliced almonds

Cut chicken into 1-inch wide slivers, and set aside. Heat oil in wok or heavy skillet. Cook carrot and garlic in oil for 2 minutes. Remove, add chicken and cook 3 minutes. Stir in broth, honey, vinegar, soy sauce, and ginger root. Bring to a boil; reduce heat. Add carrots and cover. Simmer 10 minutes. Combine 1 tablespoon cold water and cornstarch, and stir into mixture. Cook, stirring, until boiling. Cook and stir 2 minutes more. Stir in cherries and onions; heat through. Serve over rice. Sprinkle with almonds.

Note: Do not substitute sweet cherries.

Serves 4

Cantonese Cashew Chicken

2 pounds boneless chicken, cubed	2 cups oil
3 eggs	½ cup cashews
¼ teaspoon garlic powder	½ cup pea pods
¾ cup sifted flour	¼ cup molasses or honey
3 tablespoons cornstarch	3 cloves garlic, chopped
	¼ teaspoon ground ginger

¼ cup soy sauce

Prepare chicken. Make batter by combining eggs, garlic powder, flour, and cornstarch. Coat chicken with batter, and fry in oil until browned and puffy. Remove and drain chicken. Drain oil from pan, reserving 2 tablespoons. Add cashews and pea pods. Stir fry for 2 minutes. Return chicken to pan. Make sauce using remaining ingredients. Pour over chicken, and toss.

Note: Add broccoli or water chestnuts with cashews and pea pods.

Serves 3 to 4

Marinated Chicken Livers with Rice

¾ pound chicken livers	1 cup rice, uncooked
¼ cup soy sauce	½ cup chopped water chestnuts
¾ teaspoon ground ginger	2 chicken bouillon cubes
1-2 cloves garlic, crushed	½ cup light brown sugar
6 slices bacon	½ cup chopped green onions

Marinate chicken livers in soy sauce, ginger, and garlic for at least one hour. Cook bacon until crisp. Drain bacon fat and reserve. Use 3 tablespoons of fat to sauté rice and water chestnuts until rice becomes opaque. Then cook rice in 2 cups boiling water to which bouillon cubes have been added.

Drain chicken livers, reserving marinade. Roll livers in brown sugar. Use remaining bacon fat to sauté livers and green onions in skillet for about 5 minutes. Stir in remaining marinade and sugar, and heat thoroughly. Serve chicken livers over rice mixture, topped with crumbled bacon.

Serves 4

Turkey Cutlet Linon

1 package turkey breast cutlets	1½ cups chicken broth
Unseasoned meat tenderizer	3 tablespoons parsley, minced
Flour	⅓ cup dry white wine
3 tablespoons butter	Freshly ground pepper to
3 tablespoons olive oil	taste
⅓ cup lemon juice	1 egg yolk

Pat the turkey breasts dry. Sprinkle with tenderizer, and pound lightly. Dredge in flour, shaking off the excess. Using a large skillet, melt butter. Add oil. Turn the heat up, and sear the turkey for about 2 minutes on each side. The turkey should remain pink inside. Cover and set aside.

Deglaze, and add the lemon juice, broth, parsley, wine, and pepper over medium-low heat. Quickly stir 4 tablespoons of warm sauce into egg yolk. Then whisk all sauce together to thicken. When ready to serve, place the turkey back with any accumulated juices and serve immediately.

Note: Optional additions are ½ cup thinly sliced ham, 2 tablespoons red caviar, or sliced mushrooms. This dish tastes like veal!

Serves 2 to 3

Roast Goose

1 young goose	½ tablespoon salt
1 apple, quartered	½ tablespoon pepper
1 onion, quartered	Onion salt
2 stalks celery	Garlic salt
3 tablespoons currant jelly	Oregano
1½ tablespoons butter	Thyme
½ tablespoon rosemary	Red wine (optional)

Draw goose immediately, saving heart and liver for pâté. Hang by feet as long as 3 weeks if temperature is below 45 degrees. Then pick and reserve feet, wings, head, and neck. Stuff cavity with apple, onion, and celery. In saucepan, combine remaining ingredients, except wine, and simmer for 10 minutes. Let cool while placing goose in roasting pan. Cover bottom of pan with red wine or water. Spoon sauce over breast of goose. Cook in 500 degree oven for 30 minutes for rare or 1 hour for well done.

Serves 4

Meats

The City Markets

City markets, scattered throughout Baltimore, are popular attractions. Each market has its unique personality and devoted clientele who often return to shop after moving from the neighborhood.

Lexington Market, founded in 1782, is the oldest continuously operated market in the United States. Here you can visit stalls selling fresh foods, lunch stands, sit-down restaurants, and even a grocery store. It is near the downtown business area and a favorite lunchtime spot as well as a popular attraction with our city's visitors.

Broadway Market, a popular ethnic market, was founded in 1785 and is located in the historic harborside neighborhood of Fells Point. Other city markets include Cross Street, Hollins, Belair, Northeast, and Lafayette Markets.

Baltimoreans may not agree on their favorite market, but they do agree that the wonderful freshness and diversity of food, and the nostalgia keeps them shopping in the footsteps of generations before them.

Honeymoon Roast (Prime Rib for Two)

1 rib of standing rib roast, about 2 pounds	1 clove garlic, mashed
	⅛ teaspoon thyme
1 tablespoon butter	½ teaspoon pepper
½ teaspoon salt	

Rub roast with a mixture of butter and seasonings, spreading completely over meat. Wrap well and freeze until solid. Take meat from freezer 1½ hours before serving time. Remove covering from meat, being careful not to disturb butter coating. Stand roast upright in a shallow pan using crumpled foil to support each side. Preheat oven to 400 degrees and cook 1¼ hours for rare, 1½ hours for medium rare, or 1¾ hours for well-done meat. Use a meat thermometer to check doneness. Let stand 5 minutes before cutting into 2 servings of meat.

Note: To serve 4, purchase 2 ribs and follow recipe as above, increasing cooking time proportionately. Ask the butcher not to cut through the chine bone when preparing this cut of meat.

Serves 2

Fabulous Fillet of Beef

2 pounds beef fillet (or more)	Dijon mustard
Salt	Fine bread crumbs

Cut 1-inch gash down length of fillet. Rub with salt. Coat the fillet with mustard, and roll in bread crumbs. Roast at 400 degrees until meat thermometer registers rare, about 50 minutes. Slice and reassemble the meat to serve on a warm platter. Serve with Béarnaise sauce.

Béarnaise sauce:

¼ cup tarragon vinegar	¼ teaspoon salt
6 green onions, minced	¼ teaspoon dry mustard
4 egg yolks	Dash hot pepper sauce
2 teaspoons dry tarragon	1 cup butter, melted

Combine vinegar and onions in skillet; simmer and reduce the liquid almost completely. Place in blender with egg yolks, tarragon, salt, mustard, and hot pepper sauce. Slowly add hot melted butter, and mix until smooth.

Serves 4 to 6

Fillet of Beef Roll

4½–5 pound fillet of beef	½ cup onion, chopped
Salt	¼ cup parsley, snipped
Pepper	6 ounces chicken livers, thinly
1 cup fresh mushrooms,	sliced (1 cup)
chopped	2 tablespoons butter

Cut thin end from fillet. Make a deep cut horizontally not quite through meat. Spread open meat and pound with mallet to an even thickness of about ¾ inch. Sprinkle well with salt and pepper. In covered saucepan cook mushrooms, onion, and parsley in butter until mushrooms and onion are tender, about 5 minutes. Add chicken livers. Cook uncovered 1 to 2 minutes more or until livers are lightly browned. Drain. Arrange mixture over meat. Roll up from the long side; tie with string at 3-inch intervals. Roast on rack in shallow roasting pan in 425 degree oven 40 to 50 minutes for rare. Check for doneness after 40 minutes by making small slit with paring knife in thickest part of the meat. Untie and slice. Serve with a wine sauce.

Note: Make filling the night before and refrigerate. Pound meat, and put on filling just before baking.

Serves 12

Rump Roast

4 pound rump roast	1 onion
2 cloves garlic	2 teaspoons oregano
¼–½ green pepper	2 teaspoons salt
1 tomato	1 teaspoon pepper
3–4 cups water	

Preheat oven to 350 degrees. Trim the fat from roast. Place in covered roasting pan. Cut up garlic, green pepper, tomato, and onion, and place in pan around roast. Sprinkle roast and vegetables with oregano, salt, and pepper. Brown, uncovered in oven for 45 to 60 minutes. Reduce heat to 325 degrees. Add water, cover, and cook 2 to 3 hours. Meat should be tender when fork is inserted. Cool meat. Slice thinly and warm in the gravy to serve.

Note: Can be made ahead. Freezes well.

Serves 8 to 10

Marinated Round Roast

4–5 pound top or bottom roast, or eye of round	3 cloves garlic, minced
Unseasoned meat tenderizer	½ cup oil
½ cup bourbon	2 tablespoons flour
1 tablespoon brown sugar	1 teaspoon pepper
2 tablespoons lemon juice	1 cup water
	1 beef bouillon cube

Pierce beef and sprinkle with meat tenderizer. In a large baking pan, make a mixture of bourbon, brown sugar, lemon juice, garlic, and oil. Add meat and marinate overnight, turning several times. Remove from marinade, and coat with flour and pepper. Cook in a 325 degree oven about 1½ hours or until meat thermometer registers 140 to 150 degrees. Remove beef; add water and bouillon to pan juices. Heat and stir until mixture is hot and has a smooth consistency. Slice meat very thin; serve immediately.

Note: This produces medium to well-done roast. Adjust time for rarer meat.

Serves 6 to 8

Marinated Flank Steak

2 pounds flank steak, scored	¼ cup Worcestershire sauce
1½ cups salad oil	2 tablespoons Dijon mustard
¾ cup soy sauce	1 tablespoon ground pepper
½ cup wine vinegar	1 large sprig parsley, chopped
⅓ cup fresh lemon juice	1 clove garlic, crushed

Mix all ingredients to make marinade, and pour over steak. Refrigerate for 12 to 24 hours. Drain off most of marinade. Grill steak over hot coals about 5 minutes each side for rare, or broil in oven. Carve diagonally across the grain in thin slices.

Serves 3 to 4

Barbecued Shish Kebab

1½-2 pounds sirloin, cubed
   1 package dry Italian
      dressing, prepared
   2 Spanish onions

   1 pound fresh mushrooms
  40 small tomatoes
      Zucchini (optional)
   1 pound bacon

Marinate beef in salad dressing for at least 3 hours. Wash vegetables, and cut into small pieces. Alternate bacon, meat, and vegetables on skewers. Cook about 15 to 20 minutes on grill, turning to cook all sides. Serve with mint sauce.

Mint sauce:
½ cup sour cream
½ cup yogurt

1 clove garlic, minced
½ teaspoon dried mint

1 small cucumber, pared and chopped

Place sour cream, yogurt, garlic, and mint in blender or food processor. Combine, then add cucumber. Serve over shish kebabs.

Note: Serve leftover shish kebabs stuffed in pita bread and topped with sauce. This would also be delicious using lamb meat.

Serves 4 to 6

Hawaiian Short Ribs

6 ounces pineapple juice
¼ cup soy sauce
¼ cup olive oil
¼ teaspoon ginger

2 cloves garlic, minced
¼ cup brown sugar
8 large, lean short ribs of beef
   Pineapple slices (optional)

To prepare marinade, combine pineapple, soy sauce, oil, ginger, and garlic in small saucepan over medium heat. Add brown sugar when mixture is hot; continue cooking until it dissolves. Place marinade in large bowl and add ribs. Turn ribs several times to coat. Marinate 3 to 4 hours at room temperature or overnight in refrigerator.

Preheat oven to 350 degrees. Place ribs in shallow pan, and bake 45 minutes for medium rare ribs. Baste occasionally during baking. If desired, place pineapple slices on ribs for the last few minutes of baking, and serve on top of ribs.

Serves 4

Green Pepper Steak

1 pound round steak	5 large mushrooms, sliced
¼ cup soy sauce	1 tablespoon cornstarch
1 tablespoon salad oil	¼ cup water
1 large green pepper, sliced	Rice or noodles

Slice steak into ¼-inch strips, and toss with soy sauce. Brown one side in oil. Add pepper and mushrooms, and stir until lightly browned. Dissolve cornstarch in cold water, and stir into pan over medium heat until ingredients are tender and sauce has thickened. Serve with rice or noodles.

Serves 4

Beef Stroganoff

1½ cups onion, sliced	2 tablespoons flour
½ cup shortening	2 cups canned tomatoes
1 4-ounce can sliced mushrooms	½ teaspoon Worcestershire sauce
1 pound round steak, cut into small strips	½ teaspoon salt
	¼ teaspoon pepper
½ cup sour cream	

Sauté onions in shortening until translucent. Add mushrooms with juice from can. Cover and cook slowly 5 minutes. Remove onions and mushrooms to bowl. Dredge meat with flour. Brown slowly in large frying pan. Break up tomatoes, and add them with the seasonings. Cover and cook slowly 1 hour or more, stirring occasionally. Add mushrooms, onions, and sour cream. Simmer 30 minutes. Serve with rice or noodles.

Serves 4 to 6

Marinated Chuck Steak

2 pounds boneless chuck steak, (1½ inches thick)
½ cup vegetable oil
¼ cup soy sauce
¼ cup vinegar
1 clove garlic
2 tablespoons lemon juice
1 tablespoon Worcestershire sauce
1 teaspoon Dijon mustard
¼ teaspoon pepper

To prepare marinade, combine all ingredients except beef. Pour over chuck steak. Marinate at least 4 hours in refrigerator turning over once. Cook on hot grill close to coals about 10 minutes on each side. Meat will be juicy and tender.

Serves 4 to 6

Lazy Day Beef Burgundy

2 pounds stew beef, cut into 1-inch cubes
1 large package onion soup mix
2 cans cream of mushroom soup
⅔–¾ cup Burgundy wine
⅛ teaspoon freshly ground pepper
1 8-ounce can mushrooms, sliced and drained
Long grain white or brown rice or noodles

Combine beef with soups, wine, and pepper in large, covered saucepan. Bake at 250 degrees for 6 hours, adding mushrooms during the last 30 minutes. Serve over rice or noodles. Freezes well.

Serves 6

Tangy Beef Brisket

4–6 pound beef brisket
1 teaspoon salt
1 teaspoon pepper
2 cloves garlic, minced

2 bay leaves
1 cup tomato sauce
1 package dry onion soup mix
½ cup red wine
½ cup grape jam

Coat a 5-quart baking dish with vegetable cooking spray, and line with foil. Season meat, and place in pan. Mix together tomato sauce, onion soup, red wine, and grape jam, and pour over meat. Cover and bake at 325 degrees for 3 hours.

Serves 6 to 8

Glazed Corned Beef

1 corned beef
2 tablespoons butter
1 tablespoon prepared mustard

3 tablespoons vinegar
5 tablespoons ketchup
½ cup brown sugar

Cook corned beef according to directions on package, and drain well. Combine remaining ingredients in a small saucepan, and bring to a boil. Pour sauce over cooked and drained meat, and roast at 350 degrees for about 30 minutes, basting occasionally. Slice and serve with remaining sauce.

Serves 6 to 8

Reuben Casserole

16 ounces sauerkraut, drained
12 ounce can corned beef,
   broken into small pieces
OR ½–¾ pound deli corned
   beef
2 cups Swiss cheese, shredded

½ cup mayonnaise
½ cup Thousand Island dressing
2 medium tomatoes, sliced
2 tablespoons butter or
   margarine, melted
¼ cup bread crumbs, rye or
   pumpernickel

Place sauerkraut in 1½-quart glass baking dish. Top with corned beef, then shredded cheese. Combine mayonnaise and dressing. Spread over cheese. Bake at 350 degrees 25 to 35 minutes. Place tomato slices on top of casserole. Stir bread crumbs into melted butter, and sprinkle over tomatoes. Return to oven an additional 10 minutes.

Note: To prepare in microwave, cover with waxed paper and cook 5 minutes. Add tomatoes and bread crumbs, and cook an additional 10 minutes on roast or 6 minutes on high.

Serves 6 to 8

B-B-Q Beef

4 cups shredded cooked beef
¼ cup vinegar
1 cup water
¼ cup sugar
4 teaspoons prepared mustard
¼ teaspoon pepper

1 tablespoon salt
¼ teaspoon Cayenne pepper
2 slices lemon
½ cup margarine
2 medium onions, sliced
1 cup chili sauce

3 tablespoons Worcestershire sauce

Combine all ingredients except beef and simmer over low heat for 20 minutes. Add meat and cook until sauce thickens.

Serves 8 to 10

Crock Pot Barbecue

3 pounds beef or pork
½ cup hickory smoked barbecue
  sauce
3 tablespoons Worcestershire
  sauce
3 tablespoons vinegar
2 cloves garlic
½ tablespoon pepper
1 tablespoon salt
1 tablespoon Dijon mustard

¼–½ tablespoon hot pepper
  sauce
2 large onions, chopped
3 tablespoons flour
2 tablespoons brown sugar
10 ounces frozen green
  peppers
1 large can tomatoes
  (optional)

Remove fat from meat, and cut meat into serving pieces. Put in crock pot. Add remaining ingredients. Cook on low about 12 hours, and stir several times. The longer it cooks, the better. Shred meat when tender, and cook another hour or so. Great for a hunt breakfast.

Serves 10

Meatballs Avgolemono

1½ pounds ground round or
  chuck
½ small onion, grated
  Salt and pepper
¼ cup parsley, minced

⅓ cup long grain rice
2 chicken bouillon cubes
2 tablespoons butter
4 eggs
  Juice of 2 lemons, strained

Mix together first five ingredients; moisten with a little water. Shape into 3- to 4-inch elongated meatballs. In Dutch oven bring 3 cups water to boil with bouillon and butter. Drop meatballs in broth, and reduce heat. Simmer covered for 20 minutes or until rice is tender.

Beat eggs until frothy. Gradually add lemon juice. Keep beating and add some warm broth a little at a time. When egg mixture is warmed, add to meatballs and cover pot. Shake pot, remove from heat, and let sit 20 minutes to thicken sauce. Serve sauce over meatballs.

Note: Reheat in top of double boiler. An authentic Greek recipe.

Serves 4 to 6, 14 large meatballs

Schnitzel Holstein

4 ½-inch thick veal or pork
   cutlets
½ cup milk
1 egg

⅔ cup flour
2 cups seasoned bread crumbs
½ cup vegetable oil
⅛ teaspoon paprika

1 lemon, quartered

Place cutlets between two large, plastic food storage bags and pound to a ⅛-inch thickness. Beat milk, egg, and flour in a small bowl. Dip cutlets into batter; then coat with bread crumbs. Warm oil in a large skillet over medium heat. Add cutlets and cook on both sides until golden brown. Sprinkle with paprika and a generous amount of lemon juice.

Serves 4

Scott's Veal Scallopini for Two

½ cup flour
1 teaspoon salt
¼ teaspoon pepper
½ pound veal scallops
¼ cup olive oil
6 tablespoons butter

2 cloves garlic, peeled and cut
   in half
½ pound mushrooms, sliced
2 tablespoons lemon juice
½ cup dry vermouth
½ cup chicken broth

2 tablespoons parsley, chopped

Mix flour with salt and pepper. Dip veal in flour, and shake off excess. Heat oil and butter together in skillet until hot. Add garlic. Sauté 3 to 4 pieces of veal at a time, cooking until veal is white, 2 to 3 minutes. Place in glass baking dish. Discard garlic. Sauté mushrooms in remaining oil in skillet for 3 to 4 minutes. Arrange mushrooms over veal in dish. Add lemon juice, vermouth, and broth to remaining particles in skillet, and cook over low heat for a few minutes. Pour over veal and mushrooms. Bake at 325 degrees for 30 minutes in covered dish. Sprinkle with parsley for last 5 minutes of cooking time.

Note: Can be made ahead, and kept in refrigerator before baking.

Serves 2

Veal with Lemon Wine Sauce

1 pound veal scallops or cutlets,
   pounded thin
   Flour
4 tablespoons butter
2 tablespoons olive oil

½ cup dry white wine
2 tablespoons lemon juice
   Salt and pepper
½ lemon, thinly sliced
   Parsley

Dredge veal in flour to coat lightly. Heat 2 tablespoons butter and oil. Add veal and cook over medium-high heat until lightly browned on each side (1 minute if very thin). Remove veal from pan, salt and pepper to taste. Place in warm oven.

When all cutlets are cooked, add white wine to skillet. Stir and scrape particles in pan over medium heat. Add remaining butter, lemon juice, and mix thoroughly. Place veal back in skillet, and toss in sauce. Then transfer to warm platter, and garnish with parsley and lemon slices before serving.

Serves 3 to 4

Veal or Lamb Patties

1⅓ pounds ground veal or lamb
½ cup soft bread crumbs
1 egg, slightly beaten
2 teaspoons lemon zest
1½ teaspoons salt
1½ teaspoons dried basil
   Pinch nutmeg

1 tablespoon parsley,
   chopped (optional)
½–1 teaspoon paprika
⅓ cup heavy cream or
   evaporated milk
OR ½ cup milk
   Lemon wedges

Combine all ingredients, except lemon wedges, and shape into 4 patties. Broil 10 minutes each side, and allow to brown nicely. Serve with lemon wedges and a dollop of coarse brown mustard.

Serves 2 to 4

Roast Crown of Lamb Florida Style

2 racks of lamb (16 ribs)	1 large grapefruit, sectioned
2 tablespoons onion, chopped	2 cups long grained rice, cooked
3 tablespoons celery, chopped	1 tablespoon salt
2 tablespoons butter	¼ teaspoon pepper
2 cups bread crumbs, toasted	1 teaspoon orange zest
4–6 oranges, sectioned	Mint jelly if desired

Preheat oven to 350 degrees. Place lamb on heavy duty aluminum foil in large roasting pan. Wrap foil around ends. Roast about 2 hours.

Meanwhile, sauté onion with celery in butter until vegetables are tender. Add bread crumbs. Remove from heat. Combine with fruit, rice, seasonings, and zest, reserving a few fruit sections.

Remove lamb from oven 30 minutes before done. Lift lamb and foil from roasting pan; stuff center with rice mixture, and baste meat. Return to oven and test for doneness using meat thermometer. Garnish with reserved fruit, and serve with mint jelly.

Serves 6 to 8

Lamb Grill

6–7 pound leg of lamb, boneless butterfly cut	½ teaspoon salt
	½ teaspoon cracked pepper
¾ cup olive oil	1 sprig fresh thyme
¼ cup tarragon wine vinegar	1 large onion, sliced thick

Combine oil, vinegar, seasonings, and onion for marinade. Marinate lamb at least 4 hours, turning several times. If necessary, before cooking slash thicker parts of meat to allow even cooking. Cook over hot coals 15 to 20 minutes each side on an open grill. Serve medium rare.

Serves 8 to 10

Polynesian Pork Roll

12 ounce jar bitter orange
    marmalade
1 heaping teaspoon brown
    sugar
2 tablespoons soy sauce
½ teaspoon garlic powder

1½ teaspoons powdered ginger
1½ pounds tenderloin pork roll
    Seasoned salt
    Pepper
½ apple, cut in wedges
½ medium onion, cut in slices

Prepare a sauce by mixing orange marmalade, brown sugar, soy sauce, garlic powder, and ginger. Cut pork roll ¾ of the way through into ¾-inch slices. Sprinkle with seasoned salt and pepper. Spread sauce between each slice; then insert a wedge of apple and slice of onion between each slice of meat. Coat entire roll with sauce saving some to baste with while cooking. Skewer roll lengthwise, or tie with string. Bake in oven at 375 degrees for 45 minutes to 1 hour. If grilling, wrap roast in heavy duty aluminum foil. Serve with saffron rice.

Serves 3 to 4

Tangy Pork Roast

4 pound boneless pork loin
½ teaspoon salt
½ teaspoon garlic salt
½ teaspoon chili powder

1 cup apple jelly
1 cup ketchup
2 tablespoons vinegar
1½ teaspoons chili powder

In small bowl combine salt, garlic salt, and chili powder. Rub into meat. Place roast, fat side up on rack in shallow pan, and cook at 325 degrees for about 2 hours. Meanwhile, make sauce by combining remaining ingredients in saucepan. Bring mixture to a boil, reduce heat, and simmer for 2 minutes. Baste roast periodically with sauce while baking.

Serves 8

Pork Chops with Apricots and Croutons

4 pork chops 1-inch thick	16 ounce can apricots, drain
1 box seasoned croutons	and reserve juice
¼ teaspoon thyme	1½ tablespoons bottled
Salt (optional)	steak sauce
Pepper (optional)	

Preheat oven to 350 degrees. Cut a pocket in each chop. Mix croutons with thyme, salt, and pepper. Spoon some of the stuffing into each chop. Do not overstuff. Place chops into 13- by 9-inch baking dish, cover tightly with foil, and bake for 30 minutes.

To make glaze, combine reserved apricot juice and steak sauce in saucepan. Simmer 30 to 45 minutes to thicken. Uncover chops, and spoon remaining croutons into dish around chops. Top with apricots. Brush glaze over entire casserole. Bake an additional 45 minutes.

Serves 4

Pork Chops and Pears

4–6 pork chops	¼ teaspoon cinnamon
Salt and pepper	⅓ cup dry sherry
3–4 fresh pears, peeled, halved,	1 tablespoon butter or
and cored	margarine
2 tablespoons orange juice	1 teaspoon cornstarch
¼ cup firmly packed brown	1 tablespoon water
sugar	

Preheat oven to 350 degrees. Grease bottom of skillet with small piece of pork fat. Brown chops over medium heat turning once. Place chops in shallow pan, sprinkle with salt and pepper. Arrange pears around and on chops. Drizzle orange juice over all; then sprinkle with brown sugar and cinnamon. Pour sherry over all. Divide butter, and place in hollows of pears. Cover and bake 40 minutes. Uncover during last 20 minutes. Place pears and chops on warm platter. Dissolve cornstarch in water, add to juices in pan, and cook until mixture thickens. Pour over chops and pears.

Note: Canned pears may be substituted for fresh. Add to pork chops 15 minutes before end of cooking time.

Serves 4 to 6

Plum Glazed Spare Ribs

¼ cup soy sauce
¼ cup honey
1 clove garlic, minced
2 pounds spare ribs, cut into
  1-inch strips

1 ounce jar plum jelly
2 tablespoons ketchup
2 tablespoons vinegar

Use a large baking dish to combine soy sauce, honey, and garlic. Add ribs and marinate for six hours. Drain. Cover and bake 1½ hours at 350 degrees. Meanwhile, make plum sauce by combining jelly, ketchup, and vinegar. Baste ribs, and continue to cook in uncovered dish for 30 minutes.

Serves 2

Oven Barbecued Ribs

4 pounds pork spareribs
1 tablespoon butter or
  margarine
1 clove garlic, minced
½ cup ketchup
½ cup chili sauce
2 tablespoons brown sugar
2 tablespoons onion, chopped

1 tablespoon prepared
  mustard
1 tablespoon Worcestershire
  sauce
1 teaspoon celery seed
¼ teaspoon salt
2–3 drops hot pepper sauce
3 thin lemon slices

Place ribs in salted water to cover. Simmer covered for one hour. In saucepan melt butter, add garlic and sauté 4 to 5 minutes. Add other ingredients and bring to a boil.

Drain ribs and arrange in shallow baking pan. Pour boiling sauce over ribs. Bake in 350 degree oven for 20 minutes. Baste occasionally with sauce during baking.

Serves 4

Western Shore Pork Barbecue

2 medium-sized pork
  shoulders (3–4 pounds
  each)
1 medium onion, minced
1–2 tablespoons cooking oil
1 cup vinegar (or less)

2–2½ cups ketchup
3 tablespoons Worcestershire
  sauce
2 tablespoons mustard
2 tablespoons sugar
  Dash of salt

3–6 drops hot pepper sauce

Bake pork shoulders in preheated 325 degree oven until tender and done,
approximately 40 minutes per pound. Heat oil and sauté onions in skillet.
Remove to a clean saucepan. Add vinegar, ketchup, Worcestershire sauce,
mustard, sugar, salt, and hot pepper sauce. Combine and simmer 10 minutes.

When pork is cooked, remove all fat and slice thin. Add to prepared sauce,
and simmer over low heat for at least 30 minutes. This tastes best if cooked
one day ahead and left in the sauce overnight.

Serves 8 to 10

Susan's Ham Loaf

1½ pounds ground ham
1 pound ground pork
2 cups wheat flakes cereal,
  crushed

2 eggs, well beaten
1–2 tablespoons cream
⅔ cup vinegar
2 tablespoons Dijon mustard

½ cup brown sugar

Mix together ham and pork. Add cereal, eggs, and cream, as needed to
moisten for shaping. Mold into loaf and place in 9- by 13-inch baking pan.
Make ahead of time and refrigerate if desired.

Bake at 400 degrees for 15 minutes. Reduce heat to 350 degrees, and bake
1 hour and 15 minutes. Baste often with glaze during last 30 minutes. To
make glaze, heat vinegar, mustard, and brown sugar in small saucepan until
mixture is well blended. Serve any remaining glaze as a sauce with the loaf.

Serves 6 to 8

Venison Bourguignonne

4 medium onions, sliced	¼ teaspoon thyme
8 ounces fresh mushrooms	⅛ teaspoon pepper
2 tablespoons oil	1½ tablespoons flour
2 pounds venison steak, cubed	1 cube beef bouillon
1 teaspoon salt	¾ cup water
¼ teaspoon marjoram	1½ cups Burgundy wine

Sauté onions and mushrooms in oil until tender. Drain, reserve drippings, and set vegetables aside. Brown meat in drippings, adding more oil if needed. Remove from heat. Sprinkle seasonings over meat. Combine flour, water, and bouillon, stirring well. Pour over meat. Stir and boil 1 minute. Stir in Burgundy. Cover and simmer 1½ to 2 hours until meat is tender. Add in mushrooms and onions. Simmer 15 minutes. Serve over hot rice.

Serves 6 to 8

Vegetables & Side Dishes

Maryland's Harvest

Farming in Maryland is diverse, producing everything from fruits and vegetables to chickens and cattle. Broiler chickens are the state's number one commodity while dairy products are Maryland's second most important cash value contributor. Agriculturally, tobacco is the largest cash-producing crop.

Farmers raise a wide variety of vegetables and fruits and are able to sell them without incurring high shipping costs because of the state's location in the nation's heaviest population center. Much produce is also sold at roadside stands which operate throughout the area during summer months. A sampling of the harvest may include sweet corn, vine-ripened tomatoes, succulent peaches, and the whitest of mushrooms. All are in abundant supply to keep Maryland's cooks creating wonderful dishes with the freshest of ingredients.

Artichokes à la Grecque

2 14-ounce cans artichoke
  hearts, packed in water
¾ teaspoon garlic powder
2 teaspoons oregano

¾ cup seasoned croutons,
  crushed
¼ cup olive oil
  Juice of 1½ lemons, strained

Drain artichokes, and place in a shallow baking dish. Sprinkle with garlic powder and oregano. Cover with crushed croutons, and pour olive oil over top. Bake covered for 15 minutes at 350 degrees. Add lemon juice and bake an additional 10 minutes. Serve with lamb or other red meat.

Serves 4 to 6

Stuffed Artichoke Hearts

2 14-ounce cans artichoke
  hearts, packed in water
8 ounces cream cheese, softened

1 tablespoon dehydrated
  onions
2-3 teaspoons curry powder
⅛ teaspoon pepper

Paprika

Preheat broiler to 475 degrees. Drain artichokes, open leaves, and press center flat for stuffing. Combine cream cheese, onion, curry, and pepper. Mix until smooth and well blended. Stuff each artichoke heart with a teaspoon of the cream cheese mixture. Sprinkle with paprika. Place under broiler for 3 to 5 minutes. Remove from oven when slightly browned.

Note: May be served as an hors d'oeuvre.

Serves 6

Marinated Asparagus

1 pound young asparagus	1 teaspoon salt
¼ cup vegetable oil	2 tablespoons chopped
1 tablespoon parsley flakes	pimiento
3 tablespoons vinegar	½ teaspoon pepper
½ teaspoon dry mustard	

Cook asparagus in simmering salted water in large skillet for 5 minutes. Drain and place asparagus in shallow serving dish. Combine remaining ingredients in a jar, and shake well. Pour over asparagus. Cover and chill at least 4 hours.

Serves 4

Green Bean Casserole

4 cups frozen French-style green beans	1 tablespoon grated onion
2 tablespoons butter	1 cup sour cream
2 tablespoons flour	6 ounces Swiss cheese, grated
½ teaspoon salt	2 cups corn flakes or butter crackers
1 teaspoon sugar	2 tablespoons butter, melted

Cook and drain green beans. Set aside. In a saucepan melt butter; add flour, seasonings, and onion. Stir in sour cream and cook until thickened, stirring often. Fold the green beans into sauce and heat thoroughly.

Pour into greased 1½-quart baking dish, and place Swiss cheese over all. Crush corn flakes or butter crackers into crumbs, and mix with melted butter. Sprinkle over casserole. Bake at 400 degrees for 20 minutes.

Serves 8

Stir-Fried Broccoli

1 bunch broccoli	2 tablespoons peanut oil
4 garlic cloves, minced	1 tablespoon soy sauce
2 teaspoons fresh ginger, minced	¼ teaspoon chili oil (optional)

Rinse broccoli. Cut top into florets and stems into julienne strips. Heat wok and add oil, coating surface of the wok well. Add garlic and ginger; stir-fry for a few seconds until you can just smell aroma of garlic and ginger. Add the broccoli and stir-fry for 1 minute. Add soy sauce and chili oil and stir; cover, lower heat and allow to steam for 30 seconds more until crisp-tender.

Note: Chili oil is available in Oriental food stores.

Serves 4 to 6

Mam's Creamed Cabbage

1 head cabbage	½ teaspoon salt
5 tablespoons butter	½ cup canned evaporated milk
White pepper to taste	

Chop cabbage into medium pieces. Place in a large pot of boiling salted water and cook 3 to 5 minutes. Remove from heat and drain cabbage thoroughly in a colander. In the same pot melt butter, then add the drained cabbage, salt, and milk. Simmer uncovered for about 20 minutes, or until milk has evaporated and cabbage has a creamy appearance. Add white pepper to taste and stir.

Serves 6

Carrot Soufflé

2 cups carrots, sliced	1 teaspoon salt
1¼ cups milk	3 tablespoons honey
3 tablespoons cornstarch	3 eggs, beaten

¼ cup butter, melted

Cook carrots until crisp tender. Dissolve cornstarch in milk, then place all ingredients in a blender or food processor. Combine, and pour into a buttered 1½-quart baking dish. Bake at 400 degrees uncovered for 45 to 60 minutes. Remove from oven when knife inserted in center comes out clean.

Note: May be prepared ahead of time and stored in refrigerator. Bring to room temperature before baking.

Serves 4 to 6

Eggplant Patties

1 medium eggplant, pared and cubed	2 tablespoons snipped parsley
1¼ cups rich round cracker crumbs	2 tablespoons green onion, sliced
1¼ cups shredded sharp processed American cheese	1 clove garlic, minced
2 eggs, slightly beaten	½ teaspoon salt
	⅛ teaspoon pepper
	2 tablespoons vegetable oil

In covered saucepan, cook eggplant in boiling water until tender, about 5 minutes. Drain very well and mash. Stir in crumbs, cheese, eggs, parsley, onion, garlic, salt, and pepper. Shape into 8 patties about 3 inches in diameter. Cook in hot oil for 3 minutes on each side until golden brown.

Serves 4 to 6

Heavenly Mushrooms

2 pounds fresh mushrooms	1 cup half-and-half
4 tablespoons butter	¼ teaspoon pepper
4 chicken bouillon cubes	2 teaspoons Parmesan cheese
½ cup water	2 cups stuffing mix
4 tablespoons flour	8 tablespoons butter, melted

Sauté the whole mushrooms in 4 tablespoons butter, and put in buttered 9- by 13-inch baking dish. Melt bouillon cubes in water, and stir in flour. Slowly add half-and-half, pepper, and Parmesan cheese. Cook over low heat, and stir until thick. Pour sauce over mushrooms. Combine stuffing mix and melted butter. Arrange on top of mushrooms. Bake at 350 degrees for 30 minutes covered and 15 minutes uncovered.

Serves 8 to 10

Stuffed Mushrooms

½ pound sweet Italian sausage	2 tablespoons butter, melted
1 tablespoon vegetable oil	1 clove garlic, chopped
1 pound large mushrooms	⅓ medium onion, finely
½ cup dry bread crumbs	chopped
3 tablespoons grated Parmesan	¼ teaspoon salt
cheese	¼ teaspoon pepper
1 tablespoon chopped parsley	6 tablespoons olive oil

Remove casing from sausage. Sauté in oil and crumble. Clean and remove stems from mushrooms. Mix bread crumbs, cheese, sausage, parsley, butter, garlic, onion, salt, and pepper. Fill mushroom caps with mixture. Pour 2 tablespoons olive oil in baking pan. Place mushrooms in pan, stuffed side up. Pour remaining oil equally over all mushrooms. Bake for about 20 minutes in 350 degree oven. When mushrooms are tender and tops are brown, remove from oven. Serve very hot.

Serves 4 to 6

Baked Onions

4 large Spanish onions, peeled   Salt
4 tablespoons butter   Pepper
4 tablespoons sour cream

Press one tablespoon butter into one end of each onion. Salt and pepper to taste. Wrap well in heavy aluminum foil. Place on rack in oven, and bake at 350 degrees for 1 hour. Unwrap, place onions in large bowl, and mash using potato masher. Combine with sour cream. Serve with beef.

Serves 4 to 6

Company Scalloped Potatoes

1	large clove garlic, halved	2 tablespoons butter
6–7	medium potatoes, pared and thinly sliced	¼ teaspoon nutmeg
2½	cups heavy cream	½ cup Swiss cheese, grated
		Salt and pepper to taste

Butter casserole dish and rub with one garlic clove half. Place cream, butter, garlic, nutmeg, and potatoes in saucepan. Simmer for 10 to 15 minutes. Remove garlic from the mixture. Layer one-third of the potatoes and one-third of the cheese, adding salt and pepper to taste. Repeat to form three layers. Pour remaining cream mixture over layered potatoes.

Cover casserole, and bake at 325 degrees for 45 minutes. Uncover casserole, and cook at 450 degrees for an additional 5 minutes.

Serves 6

Emmie's Cheese Potatoes

6 large potatoes
2 cups cheddar cheese, shredded
6 tablespoons butter
2 cups sour cream
¼–½ cup green onions, chopped
1 teaspoon salt
¼ teaspoon pepper

Bake potatoes in skins. Cool, peel, and grate coarsely. In pan over very low heat, combine cheese and 4 tablespoons butter. Stir until almost melted. Remove from heat and blend in sour cream, onion, salt, and pepper. Gently fold in potatoes. Grease 2-quart baking dish with remaining butter. Spoon potatoes into baking dish, and bake in a 350 degree oven for 25 minutes.

Serves 6 to 8

Greek Potatoes

4–6 medium-sized potatoes
2 tablespoons butter
2 tablespoons olive oil
1 tablespoon lemon juice
1 teaspoon oregano
1 teaspoon parsley
1 teaspoon salt
¼ teaspoon pepper

Wash, peel, and quarter potatoes into 1- to 1½-inch wedges. Heat butter and oil in a large skillet. Add potatoes and lemon juice. Sauté to an even brown, turning potatoes to brown all sides. Cover skillet, and continue to cook until potatoes are tender, approximately 20 minutes. Uncover skillet, sprinkle potatoes with seasonings, mix, and serve.

Serves 6

Holiday Sweet Potatoes

29 ounce can sweet potatoes,
drained
8¾ ounce can crushed pineapple
2 cooking apples, diced
1 small can water chestnuts
½ tablespoon ginger

Salt to taste
3 tablespoons butter
⅓ cup sugar
1½ ounces rum
½ tablespoon cinnamon

Mash potatoes and strain pineapple, reserving juice for syrup. To the potatoes, add pineapple, apples, water chestnuts, and salt. To make syrup, combine butter, sugar, pineapple juice, rum, and spices. Pour syrup over potato mixture, and blend well. Spoon into a buttered baking dish. Bake uncovered at 350 degrees for 45 minutes.

Serves 9 to 12

Sweet Potato Pecan Balls

4–5 medium sweet potatoes
¼ teaspoon salt
¼ teaspoon cinnamon
⅛ teaspoon nutmeg
2 tablespoons brown sugar
2 tablespoons butter
1–2 tablespoons sherry

1–2 tablespoons orange juice
concentrate
1 egg, beaten
1 cup pecans, finely chopped
¼ cup butter
½ cup dark brown sugar
3 tablespoons corn syrup

Cook sweet potatoes in skins until tender. Peel, and mash with a fork. Stir in salt, cinnamon, nutmeg, 2 tablespoons brown sugar, and 2 tablespoons butter. Add 1 tablespoon sherry and 1 tablespoon orange juice concentrate. Check consistency and if still dry, add another 1 tablespoon sherry and 1 tablespoon orange juice concentrate being careful that mixture can still be rolled into balls. If mixture becomes too soft, chill until firm.

Shape mixture into two-inch balls. Dip each ball into beaten egg and roll in chopped nuts. Place in baking dish.

Melt butter in separate dish. Stir in ½ cup brown sugar and corn syrup. Pour mixture over sweet potato balls and bake at 325 degrees until heated through.

Serves 6 to 8

Scott's Spinach with Artichokes

14 ounce can artichoke hearts
   packed in water, drained and
   halved
3 ounces cream cheese
1 teaspoon milk

1 teaspoon mayonnaise
1 medium onion, chopped
4 tablespoons butter
10 ounce package frozen
   spinach, cooked and drained

Bread crumbs

Place halved artichoke hearts in greased shallow casserole dish to cover bottom. Cream the softened cream cheese with the milk and mayonnaise. Sauté the onion in butter. Mix spinach, creamed cheese mixture, and onions. Pour over artichoke hearts, and top with bread crumbs. Bake at 350 degrees for 25 to 30 minutes.

Serves 4

Baked Acorn Squash

2 acorn squash
1 egg, beaten
1 chicken bouillon cube,
   dissolved in 1/3 cup water

1/4 cup chopped onion, sautéed
1/2 cup corn bread stuffing,
   crushed

Cut both squash in half. Bake cut side down in about 1/2 inch of water for 30 minutes at 400 degrees. Remove squash from oven, and scoop insides into mixing bowl. Mash squash with beaten egg and dissolved chicken bouillon cube. Add sautéed onion to mixture. Mix in half the crushed stuffing and fill squash shells. Sprinkle rest of stuffing on top. Bake at 400 degrees for 25 minutes.

Serves 4

Spinach-Stuffed Tomatoes

8 firm medium tomatoes
3 10-ounce packages frozen,
   chopped spinach
1 cup bread crumbs
1 cup grated Parmesan cheese
2 eggs, beaten
3 scallions, chopped

3 tablespoons butter, melted
1 clove garlic, minced
2 teaspoons salt
½ teaspoon thyme
½ teaspoon MSG
3 drops hot pepper sauce
¼ teaspoon pepper

Cook the chopped spinach, and drain very well. Hollow out the tomatoes, and turn upside down to drain. Combine the spinach with all the other ingredients, and spoon this mixture into the tomatoes. Bake at 325 degrees for 30 minutes. Can be prepared ahead and refrigerated.

Serves 8

Summer Squash Bake

1 pound yellow squash, sliced
1 onion, diced
1 can cream of mushroom soup

1 cup sour cream
½ cup grated carrot
1 package stuffing mix

½ cup margarine, melted

Boil squash and onion for 10 minutes. Remove from heat and drain well. Mix with soup, sour cream, and carrots, and put aside. Mix stuffing with melted butter. Line a 9- by 13-inch baking dish with stuffing mix, reserving ½ cup. Add squash mixture, and top with remaining stuffing. Cook for 45 minutes at 350 degrees. Freezes well.

Serves 10

Zucchini and Bacon Casserole

4 medium or 6 small zucchini
Salt and pepper
1 cup cheddar cheese, shredded
¾ cup bacon, cooked and
   crumbled
1 medium onion, chopped
2 tablespoons butter or
   margarine
2 tablespoons flour
1 cup milk
1–2 tablespoons sour cream

Slice squash, remove seeds, and cook until tender in small amount of salted water. Put in 1½-quart shallow baking dish and sprinkle with salt, pepper, and cheddar cheese. Fry bacon with onion. Place on top of casserole.

Make white sauce by melting butter in saucepan. Stir in flour. When smooth add milk and sour cream. Stir constantly over medium heat until thickened. Pour over casserole, and cover with foil. Bake at 325 degrees until bubbly. Remove cover and brown.

Serves 6

Zucchini in Dill Cream Sauce

2¼ pounds zucchini, sliced
¼ cup onion, chopped
½ cup water
½ teaspoon salt
1 teaspoon instant chicken
   broth
½ teaspoon dried dillweed
2 tablespoons margarine,
   melted
2 teaspoons sugar
1 teaspoon lemon juice
2 tablespoons flour
½ cup sour cream

In a saucepan combine zucchini, onion, water, salt, bouillon, and dillweed. Bring to a boil, and then reduce heat and simmer covered for 5 minutes. Do not drain. Add margarine, sugar, and lemon juice, and remove from heat. Blend flour into sour cream. Stir about half the hot cooking liquid into the sour cream. Return all to saucepan. Cook and stir until thickened.

Serves 6

Four Beans Baked

1 pound can pork and beans
1 pound can butter beans
1 pound can baby limas
1 pound can kidney beans
½ pound bacon

3 medium onions, chopped
½ cup vinegar
1 cup brown sugar
½ teaspoon garlic powder
¼ teaspoon dry mustard

Drain all beans and combine in a large baking dish. Fry bacon until crisp. Remove from pan to drain, and pour off half the bacon drippings. In the retained drippings, saute onions until translucent. Add the vinegar, brown sugar, garlic powder, and dry mustard to make sauce. Stir to dissolve sugar. Cook for 10 minutes, then pour sauce over beans. Crumble bacon over top, and bake 1 hour at 350 degrees.

Serves 8 to 10

Corn Pudding

1 cup frozen yellow corn, thawed
1 cup canned white corn
⅓ cup sugar

2 eggs, beaten
3 tablespoons butter, melted
½ teaspoon nutmeg
1 teaspoon salt

2 cups half-and-half

Mix all ingredients together. Pour into lightly greased 8-inch square baking dish, and bake in 350 degree oven for 40 to 45 minutes. Stir pudding occasionally while baking. Do not stir during the last 15 minutes. Remove from oven when knife inserted in center comes out clean.

Serves 6 to 8

Grits Soufflé

1 cup grits, uncooked	½ cup milk
½ cup butter	1 cup extra sharp cheddar
3 eggs, separated	cheese, grated

Salt and pepper to taste

Preheat oven to 350 degrees. Cook grits according to package directions, add butter, and set aside. Beat egg whites until stiff. In separate bowl beat yolks until light yellow in color. Beat milk into yolks.

Gradually add warm grits to the yolk mixture, being careful not to cook yolks with hot grits. Add cheese, salt, and pepper. Fold in egg whites, and pour into a buttered 2-quart baking dish. Bake 45 minutes. Do not open oven door during baking time.

Note: Cooked country ham may be placed on bottom of the dish before pouring in grits.

Serves 6 to 8

Tomato Pudding

2 tablespoons margarine	1 pound can whole tomatoes
¼ cup onions, chopped	⅓ cup sugar to taste
3 tablespoons chopped parsley	Salt and pepper

1–1½ cups fresh bread crumbs

Melt margarine in a skillet. Add onion and parsley and sauté. Squeeze or break up each tomato, chopping up lumps. Salt and pepper to taste, and simmer at low heat for ½ hour or until sauce is medium thick. Gradually stir in sugar. Add bread crumbs slowly while stirring constantly. Cook for another 5 minutes, stirring constantly over low heat.

Serves 4

Spanakopita

2 10-ounce packages chopped, frozen spinach	1 pound feta cheese
3 bunches spring onions, chopped fine	¼ cup butter, melted
	2 tablespoons dill, minced
6 eggs	1 cup butter, melted
	1 pound phyllo pastry

Cook spinach until thawed, and squeeze out all excess water. Chop onions. Beat eggs. Mix eggs with feta cheese, ¼ cup melted butter, and dill. Add onions and spinach.

Remove 1 or 2 sheets of phyllo pastry, unroll and brush with melted butter. Make a stack of about 6 sheets of phyllo, which have been brushed with butter. Keep all remaining phyllo covered with a dampened cloth. Spread about 1 cup spinach filling across the narrow end of phyllo pastry, and roll up. Makes about 2 rolls. Put in 9- by 13-inch baking dish, which has been coated with remaining butter. Bake in preheated 350 degree oven for 55 to 60 minutes, or until golden brown.

Note: Try making small portions, and serve as an appetizer.

Serves 6 to 8

Cheesy Broccoli and Rice

2 10-ounce packages frozen broccoli	1 cup half-and-half
1 cup onion, chopped	1 small jar jalapeño processed cheese spread
1 cup celery, chopped	2 cups cooked rice
2 tablespoons oil	Salt and pepper to taste
1 can cream of chicken soup	Parmesan cheese
Paprika	

Cook broccoli and drain well. Sauté onion and celery in oil. Add to broccoli, and then add the next 5 ingredients. Mix well and place in a greased shallow 2-quart baking dish. Top with Parmesan cheese, and sprinkle with paprika. Bake at 350 degrees for 30 minutes or until firm.

Serves 10

Baked Rice

6 tablespoons butter
1 medium onion, chopped

1 cup uncooked long grain white rice
2 cans beef consommé

Sauté onion in butter. Remove from heat and stir in rice to coat with butter. Pour into casserole. Bring consommé almost to a boil and pour over rice mixture in casserole. Cover and bake at 350 degrees for 45 to 60 minutes.

Variation I: Substitute 2 cans chicken broth for 2 cans beef consommé.

Variation II: Substitute ¼ cup wild rice and ¾ cup long grain white rice for the 1 cup white rice.

Serves 4 to 6

Baked Rice Casserole

2 cups Baked Rice
1 14-ounce jar artichoke quarters, drained

¾ pound mushrooms, sliced
2 tablespoons butter
1½ cups grated cheddar cheese

Prepare Baked Rice recipe. Cut artichoke quarters into eighths. Sauté mushrooms in butter. Layer one-third of rice, one-half of artichokes, one-half of mushrooms and one-half of cheese. Repeat layers. Cover all with final one-third of rice. Cover and bake at 350 degrees for 15 minutes or until heated through.

Serves 4 to 6

Pork Fried Rice

2 tablespoons bacon grease
2 tablespoons vegetable oil
1 teaspoon sesame oil
½ cup mushrooms, chopped
3 cups cold cooked rice,
prepared without salt
1 cup diced, cooked pork or
ham
OR 6 strips bacon, cooked and
crumbled

½ cup scallions, thinly sliced
including green tops
1 teaspoon fresh ginger,
minced
2 tablespoons fresh parsley,
minced
1½ tablespoons soy sauce
Freshly ground pepper
1 egg, lightly beaten

Heat the bacon grease and oils in a wok or a large skillet. When oil is hot, sauté mushrooms slightly. Add rice, meat, scallions, ginger, parsley, soy sauce, and freshly ground pepper to taste, stirring quickly for 3 to 5 minutes. Make a hollow in center of rice. Add lightly beaten egg, scramble until semi-cooked, then stir egg bits through rice mixture. Serve.

Serves 3 as main course or 6 as a side dish

Baked Curried Bananas

6 firm ripe bananas
Honey

1–2 teaspoons curry powder

Preheat broiler to 400 degrees. Peel bananas, and place in shallow baking dish. Sprinkle curry powder over the bananas. Generously drizzle honey over each banana. Broil until bananas are golden brown, and serve immediately.

Serves 6

Crunchy Pineapple

6 tablespoons flour
¾ cup sugar
8 ounces sharp cheese
2 15-ounce cans pineapple
  chunks, drained

4 tablespoons margarine,
  melted
2–3 cups RITZ® Cracker crumbs

Mix flour and sugar, and set aside. Grate cheese and mix it with drained pineapple chunks. Combine flour/sugar mixture with cheese/pineapple mixture. Spread in 9- by 13-inch casserole. Combine melted margarine and cracker crumbs. Pour over pineapple mixture. Bake at 350 degrees for 30 minutes.

Serves 8 to 10

Glazed Peaches

2 large cans peach halves,
  reserve ½ cup syrup
1 can whole cranberry sauce

½ cup sugar
Nutmeg
Cinnamon

Ground cloves

Place peach halves flat side down in a 9- by 13-inch baking dish or 12-inch pie pan. In saucepan heat cranberry sauce, sugar, and peach syrup until sugar dissolves and mixture is blended. Pour over peaches. Sprinkle with nutmeg, cinnamon, and cloves. Bake in moderate oven until it bubbles. Bake fruit at temperature you are using for other main dishes.

Serves 8 to 10

Luscious Fruit Compote

½ box of dried prunes
½ box dried apricots
16 ounce can pear halves
16 ounce can peach halves
16 ounce can bing cherries
16 ounce can pineapple chunks
½ cup raisins

11 ounce can mandarin orange slices
Zest and sections of 1 lemon
Zest and sections of 1 orange
1 cup brown sugar
1 cup macaroon crumbs
⅓ cup brandy

Preheat oven to 350 degrees. Drain the canned fruits, and combine all fruits in a large greased casserole. Mix the brown sugar and macaroon crumbs. Sprinkle over the fruits. Bake for 1½ hours. Remove from the oven, and sprinkle brandy over the top of the casserole. Return to oven and bake for an additional 15 minutes. May be served warm or cold.

Serves 16 to 20

Breads

The Renaissance Neighborhoods

Baltimore's citizens have successfully revitalized many neighborhoods. Many are of historical importance, and all have distinct personalities. Federal Hill is rowhouses, ranging from the stately to the dollhouse-size. Geraniums and impatiens adorn the marble stoops and harbor fragrances float by. The Otterbein is striking new townhomes clustered around the Old Otterbein Church, a block from Harborplace. Fells Point is a crazy quilt of artists' studios, posh waterfront restaurants, and covered markets where you can shop for fresh greens, ripe cheeses, and meats. Bolton Hill is the city's stately Victorian professional enclave. Union Square, proud to have H. L. Mencken as its most famous resident, is a cast-iron fountain, rose-tinted concrete walks, and reproduction gas lamps. Charles Village is rich in stained glass windows, big front porches, and golden oak woodwork. Little Italy is three-story houses packed into a neighborhood rich with family traditions.

And in each of these neighborhoods, there's the food—from oyster roasts in the backyards of Federal Hill to the Otterbein's deck-top barbeques to Fells Point's famous mussels to Little Italy's fresh pastas—that makes them all taste like home.

French Bread

Oil   2 tablespoons solid shortening
Cornmeal   1 tablespoon salt
2 packages active dry yeast   1⅓ cups water
⅓ cup hot water   5½ cups all-purpose flour
2 teaspoons sugar   1 egg, beaten

Oil French bread tin or baguette pan and sprinkle with corn meal. Proof yeast in hot water with sugar. Add shortening, salt, 1⅓ cups water, and flour. Knead 10 minutes; then let rise until doubled in bulk. Punch down and let rise again for 1½ hours. Shape into loaves, slash tops, and brush with egg wash made from beaten egg mixed with 1 tablespoon water. Let rise 1½ hours. Preheat oven to 425 degrees. Bake 10 minutes. Brush loaves again with egg wash. Reduce heat to 375 degrees and bake 30 minutes.

Yield: 2 loaves

Herb Bread

2 packages active dry yeast   ½ cup sugar
2¼ cups warm water, divided   ¼ cup oil
1 teaspoon sugar   2½ teaspoons Italian seasoning
1 tablespoon salt   1½ teaspoons oregano
                  7–7½ cups flour

In small bowl proof yeast in ¼ cup warm water and 1 teaspoon sugar. In large bowl mix salt, sugar, and oil. Add 2 cups water, Italian seasoning, and oregano. Mix. Add yeast mixture. Add flour and mix together. Wait about 10 minutes; then knead for 3 to 4 minutes. Cover and let rise until doubled in bulk. Form into 2 round loaves, or if desired braid dough. Cover and let rise 30 to 40 minutes. Preheat oven to 350 degrees. Bake for 40 minutes or until bread sounds hollow when tapped.

Note: To braid bread, divide dough into thirds, and roll each strand into a 10-inch length. Place strands 1 inch apart on greased baking sheet. Beginning in middle, braid loosely toward each end. Pinch ends together.

Yield: 1 braided loaf or 2 round loaves

Cilla's Three Wheat Bread

3 cups lukewarm water	1 tablespoon salt
½ cup honey	¼ cup oil
2 tablespoons molasses	5 cups whole wheat flour
3 tablespoons active dry yeast	3 cups white flour, divided

1 cup cracked wheat

In a large bowl, combine warm water, honey, molasses, and yeast. Let stand 5 minutes. Stir in salt, oil, whole wheat flour, two cups white flour, and cracked wheat. Mix well. Turn dough out onto floured board, and gradually incorporate enough of remaining white flour to make a dough that is not sticky. Knead until smooth and satiny, about 10 minutes. Place in large oiled bowl, and turn to oil top. Cover and let rise until doubled in bulk. Punch down, fold, and turn so that smooth side is up. Cover, and let rise again until almost doubled in bulk. Remove from bowl, divide in half, and shape into round loaves. Place on greased cookie sheets. Cover and let rise until doubled in bulk. Preheat oven to 350 degrees, and bake approximately 50 minutes.

Note: Purchase cracked wheat in health food store.

Yield: 2 large loaves

Fresh Apple Raisin Bread

2 packages active dry yeast
¾ cup sugar
1½ teaspoons salt
5½ cups flour, divided
½ cup water
¾ cup milk
6 tablespoons butter

2 large eggs
½ cup butter, melted
1 cup brown sugar
1½ cups raisins
2 cups apple, peeled and
   grated

In large mixing bowl, mix yeast with sugar, salt, and 2 cups of the flour. Heat water and milk with butter over low heat until very warm. Butter does not have to be completely melted. Add liquids to dry ingredients. Beat 2 minutes at medium speed. Add eggs and 2 cups flour; beat 3 minutes. Stir in 1 cup flour. Knead dough on floured board about 8 minutes, until smooth and elastic, using remaining ½ cup flour.

Place in buttered bowl. Cover and let rise 1½ hours in warm place until doubled in bulk. Punch down. Pinch off dough to form balls the size of golf balls. Roll balls first in melted butter, then in brown sugar. Arrange loosely in layers in buttered 10-inch tube pan distributing raisins, apples, and cinnamon between layers. Pour any remaining butter or brown sugar on top. Cover and let rise in warm place until dough almost reaches top of pan. Bake at 375 degrees for 50 to 60 minutes. Invert on rack. Serve warm and pull apart, or cool and slice.

Serves 12

Julekake (Norwegian Christmas Bread)

2 cakes compressed yeast	2 eggs
½ cup lukewarm water	½ cup currants
3 cups scalded milk	¾ cup raisins, chopped
½ cup shortening	½ cup citron, chopped
¾ cup sugar	½ cup candied cherries,
10 cups sifted all-purpose flour	chopped
2 teaspoons salt	1 egg white
½ teaspoon cardamom	3 tablespoons butter, melted

Dissolve yeast in ½ cup lukewarm water. Pour scalded milk over shortening. When milk mixture is lukewarm, add yeast and sugar. Sift flour, salt, and cardamom together. Add half the flour mixture to yeast mixture. Beat well for 10 minutes. One at a time add eggs, beating thoroughly after each addition. Mix fruit with remaining flour. Add fruit and flour mixture. Knead until dough acquires satiny texture. Place in greased bowl to rise. Grease top of dough, cover, place bowl in warm spot.

When doubled in bulk, punch down and knead again. Return to bowl, and let rise until doubled in bulk. Shape into loaves and place in greased 4- by 9-inch loaf pans. Brush tops of loaves with egg white. When doubled in bulk, bake 1 hour in preheated 350 degree oven. Remove from pans, and brush crusts with melted butter.

Note: Very nice made without pans in round loaves. Serve toasted with butter on Christmas morning.

Yield: 3 loaves

Baltimore Cheese Bread

2 loaves frozen plain bread
   dough, thawed together in bag
   in refrigerator overnight
1 pound muenster cheese,
   grated

2 eggs
¼ teaspoon salt
½ cup sour cream
1 tablespoon butter, no
   substitutes

Remove dough from bag and let rest on kitchen counter for ½ hour. Mix cheese, 1 egg, salt, and sour cream together to make filling. Set aside. Preheat oven to 375 degrees. Use butter to grease a 9-inch pie plate or shallow 2-quart round casserole.

Roll out dough to 18- to 20-inch circle. Place in pan. Put filling in center. Carefully fold dough to center as follows: With left hand pick up edge of dough between thumb and index finger, and hold over center of filling. With right hand, pick up edge of dough about 4 to 5 inches from left hand. Bring right hand to left and pinch portions together on ends. Use a little water to stick dough together. Continue around entire circle, folding umbrella style, always folding toward center. Do not get filling on dough, as it will not stick together. Brush with 1 beaten egg. Bake 35 minutes at 375 degrees. Let cool before slicing.

Note: Can also roll out as two loaves. Roll two rectangles. Put half of filling in center of each. Roll up jelly-roll fashion. Place each roll in a buttered loaf pan and bake as directed.

Yield: 10 to 12 slices

Swedish Tea Ring

1 package (¼ ounce) active dry
   yeast
¼ cup warm water
1 cup milk
½ cup honey
1 teaspoon salt
5½ cups flour, approximately
2 eggs

¾ cup butter, softened
¾ cup brown sugar, firmly
   packed
2 tablespoons cinnamon
1½ cups dark raisins
¼ cup butter, melted
½ cup confectioners' sugar
1 tablespoon milk
½ teaspoon vanilla extract

Dissolve yeast in warm water and set aside. Scald milk, and put in large bowl with honey and salt. When mixture is lukewarm, blend in 1 cup flour and beat until smooth. Add yeast and mix well. Add about 2 cups flour, and beat until smooth. Beat eggs into mixture. Vigorously beat in ½ cup softened butter 2 to 3 tablespoons at a time. Beat in enough of the remaining flour to make a soft dough. Turn dough onto a floured surface, and let it rest about 10 minutes; then knead until satiny in texture.

Form into a large ball and place in a deep greased bowl, and turn to grease all sides. Cover with waxed paper and a towel, and place in a warm area until dough is doubled, about 1 hour. Punch down dough with fist. Pull edges into center, and turn it over in bowl. Cover and let rise again until almost doubled, about 1 hour. Punch down, and place dough on floured surface. Divide in half, and roll or press each half into a rectangle approximately 9 by 18 inches.

Spread each rectangle with ⅛ cup softened butter. Combine brown sugar, cinnamon, and raisins. Sprinkle half of mixture on each piece of dough. Starting at the longer side, roll dough tightly, and pinch the edges to seal. Lightly grease two baking sheets. Place roll on baking sheet with sealed edge down. Pull ends together to make a ring, and seal ends by pinching. With scissors, snip dough at 1-inch intervals. Cut through ring almost to center. Turn each cut section on its side. Repeat to create the second ring. Brush rings with melted butter. Cover and let rise about 45 minutes or until doubled. Bake at 350 degrees for 20 to 25 minutes.

While rings are baking, mix confectioners' sugar, milk, and vanilla extract. When tea rings are done, place on cooling racks. Frost tea rings while warm.

Yield: 2 tea rings

Refrigerator Rolls

2 cups boiling water	2 packages active dry yeast
½ cup sugar	¼ cup lukewarm water
1 tablespoon salt	1 teaspoon sugar
2 tablespoons vegetable shortening	2 eggs
	8–10 cups flour

Combine boiling water, ½ cup sugar, salt, and shortening. Cool to luke-warm. Proof yeast in lukewarm water with 1 teaspoon sugar. After yeast dissolves add to first mixture. Add eggs, and blend in flour. Dough should not be sticky. Do not knead. Place in covered bowl in refrigerator for up to 3 weeks.

To bake, form 1½-inch balls. Place on greased cookie sheet in warm place, and allow to rise until doubled in bulk, about 3 hours. Bake in preheated 425 degree oven 15 to 20 minutes.

Note: Rolls taste best when freshly baked, although they may be frozen and reheated.

Yield: 20 to 24 rolls

Cinnamon Buns

16 ounce package hot roll mix	¾ cup raisins
1 cup brown sugar, divided	2 tablespoons butter
4 tablespoons cinnamon	½ cup pecans, chopped

Prepare hot roll mix according to package directions. Let rise; then on a floured surface roll out into 12- by 15-inch rectangle. Sprinkle ½ cup brown sugar, cinnamon, and raisins over top. Using long edge, roll up jellyroll fashion. Cut into ½-inch slices.

Melt butter in 9- by 13-inch shallow baking dish. Spread remaining brown sugar and pecans in bottom. Place rolls close together in pan, and let rise for 1 hour. Bake 15 minutes at 350 degrees. Remove from oven, and immediately turn pan over to remove cinnamon buns.

Serves 8

Homemade Pizza

Crust:

2 cups all-purpose flour
2 teaspoons baking powder
1 teaspoon salt

⅔ cup milk
⅛ cup vegetable oil
⅛ cup olive oil

Topping:

¼ cup Parmesan cheese,
    freshly grated
8 ounces spaghetti sauce
1 tablespoon onion, chopped
¼ teaspoon oregano, crushed
1¼ teaspoons basil, crushed
⅛ teaspoon freshly ground
    black pepper

Dash garlic powder
8 ounces sliced provolone or
    mozzarella cheese
4 ounces sliced mushrooms
1 green pepper, sliced thin
2 ounces sliced pepperoni
OR 8 ounces sausage, fried,
    drained, crumbled

Preheat oven to 425 degrees. Measure crust ingredients into bowl. Stir vigorously until mixture separates from sides of the bowl. Gather dough together, and press into a ball. Knead dough in bowl ten times to make smooth. On a lightly floured board, roll dough into circle slightly larger than pan. Turn up edge and pinch. Layer on pizza toppings in order listed. Bake 20 to 25 minutes.

Yield: 1 pizza

Herb Bread Sticks

1 package active dry yeast	3 teaspoons caraway seeds,
1¼ cups hot water	divided
3 tablespoons sugar	1 teaspoon ground sage
1½ teaspoons salt	1 teaspoon dillweed
1 tablespoon butter	3½ cups sifted all-purpose flour

Mix dry yeast in hot water in large bowl. Let stand a few minutes; then stir to dissolve. Add remaining ingredients using 2 teaspoons caraway seeds, and mix well. Turn out on lightly floured board, and knead 10 minutes or until smooth and elastic. Place in greased bowl, and turn to grease all sides. Cover and let rise 1 hour, or until doubled in bulk.

Punch down, turn out on floured board, and divide in half. Roll each half into 12-inch long rectangle. Cut into 12 pieces. Roll each piece on board to form rope ⅓ inch thick and 12 inches long. Place on greased cookie sheet. Sprinkle with remaining caraway seeds. Cover and let rise until doubled, about 1 hour. Bake in preheated 400 degree oven for 15 to 20 minutes.

Note: Children enjoy making these! Serve with soups or dips.

Yield: 24 sticks

Caraway Puffs

1 package active dry yeast
2⅓ cups sifted flour, divided
¼ teaspoon baking soda
1 cup cream style cottage
  cheese
¼ cup water

2 tablespoons sugar
1 tablespoon butter
1 teaspoon salt
1 egg
2 teaspoons caraway seed
2 teaspoons grated onion

In mixing bowl combine yeast, 1⅓ cups flour, and baking soda. Heat cottage cheese, water, sugar, butter, and salt until butter melts. Liquid should be 120 to 130 degrees. Add to dry ingredients. Then add egg, caraway seed, and onion. Using electric mixer, beat on low speed 30 seconds; beat 3 minutes on high speed. Stir in remaining flour.

Place in greased bowl, turning once. Cover; let rise about 1½ hours or until doubled in bulk. Generously grease muffin pan, and divide dough to fill muffin cups. Cover and let rise 40 minutes. Preheat oven to 400 degrees. Bake 12 to 15 minutes.

Yield: 12 puffs

Pineapple Zucchini Bread

2 eggs
1 cup oil
2 cups sugar
3 cups flour
1 teaspoon salt
½ teaspoon baking powder
1½ teaspoons baking soda

2 teaspoons cinnamon
1½ teaspoons nutmeg
2 teaspoons vanilla
1 cup crushed pineapple, with
  juice
2 cups zucchini, peeled and
  grated

Beat eggs, add oil and sugar, and beat again. Add dry ingredients, vanilla, and pineapple. Mix well. Add zucchini. Blend well. Pour batter into three greased 9- by 5-inch loaf pans, and bake in 325 degree oven for 1 hour.

Yield: 3 loaves

Lemon Bread

½ cup butter
1 cup sugar
2 eggs, slightly beaten
1⅔ cups flour
1 teaspoon baking powder

½ teaspoon salt
½ cup milk
½ cup nuts, chopped fine
1 lemon, juice and zest
¼ cup sugar

Cream butter and sugar; add slightly beaten eggs. Sift flour, measure and sift again with baking powder and salt. Alternately add flour mixture and milk to shortening mixture, stirring constantly. Mix in nuts and lemon peel. Bake in greased 9- by 5-inch pan in 350 degree oven for 55 to 60 minutes. Combine lemon juice and sugar, and pour over top of loaf when it comes from oven.

Yield: 1 loaf

Orange Bread

2 tablespoons butter
¾ cup sugar
  Zest of 1 orange
2 cups flour

2 teaspoons baking powder
½ cup milk
  Juice of 1 orange (about ¼ cup)

1 egg, beaten

Place butter and sugar in food processor bowl. Use steel knife blade, and mix for 30 seconds. Add orange zest. Mix until well blended. Through feed tube, add flour and baking powder; then add milk and juice until well blended. Add egg, mix 10 more seconds. Turn off machine. Pour batter into well-greased 9- by 5-inch loaf pan, and bake at 375 degrees for 45 minutes or until brown.

Yield: 1 loaf

Pear Nut Bread

2-3 fresh pears
½ cup vegetable oil
1 cup sugar
2 eggs
¼ cup sour cream
1 teaspoon vanilla extract

2 cups sifted flour
½ teaspoon salt
1 teaspoon baking soda
¼ teaspoon ground cinnamon
¼ teaspoon nutmeg
½ cup chopped walnuts

Preheat oven to 350 degrees. Pare, halve and core pears. Chop coarsely to yield 1½ cups of fruit. In large bowl beat together oil and sugar until well blended. Beat in eggs, one at a time, then sour cream and vanilla. Sift together flour, salt, baking soda, cinnamon, and nutmeg. Add to sugar mixture. Beat well. Add nuts and pears; mixing well with large spoon. Spoon into greased 5- by 9-inch loaf pan. Bake at 350 degrees for 1 hour and 10 minutes, or until knife inserted in center comes out clean. Let cool in pan 5 minutes. Remove from pan, and finish cooling on rack.

Note: You may substitute ½ cup honey for the sugar, and use 1 cup whole wheat flour with 1 cup of white flour.

Yield: 1 loaf

Strawberry Bread

2 10-ounce packages frozen strawberries in syrup, thawed
4 eggs
1¼ cups vegetable oil
1 cup nuts, chopped

3 cups flour
2 cups sugar
3 teaspoons cinnamon
1 teaspoon baking soda
1 teaspoon salt

Preheat oven to 350 degrees. Grease and flour two 5- by 9-inch loaf pans; set aside. In medium bowl stir thawed strawberries with their syrup, eggs, and oil. In large bowl combine flour, sugar, cinnamon, baking soda, salt, and nuts. Add strawberry mixture to dry ingredients, and stir until blended. Pour into pans. Bake 1 hour or until toothpick inserted in center comes out clean. Freezes beautifully.

Yield: 2 loaves

Gugelhopf (Austrian Coffee Cake)

1 cup butter or margarine
2 cups sugar
6 eggs, separated
1½ cups sifted all-purpose flour
½ teaspoon salt

2 teaspoons baking powder
6 tablespoons milk
1 teaspoon vanilla
OR ½ teaspoon almond extract
OR 2 teaspoons grated lemon
peel

Cream butter to consistency of mayonnaise. Add sugar slowly while continuing to cream. Beat until light. Beat in egg yolks one at a time. Mix and sift flour, salt, and baking powder. Combine milk and flavoring. Add flour mixture and milk alternately to butter mixture, stirring gently, but thoroughly. Beat egg whites until stiff, but not dry. Fold into batter. Spoon into well-greased 12-cup fluted tube pan. Bake at 350 degrees for 50 minutes or until cake tests done. Cool in pan 10 minutes. Loosen cake gently around rim and tube with sharp knife. Invert on cake rack 1 hour to finish cooling. Lift pan off of cake. Dust with confectioners' sugar. Best served the day it is made, but reheats well.

Serves 20

Mom's Blueberry Buckle

¾ cup sugar
¼ cup shortening, softened
1 egg
½ cup milk
2 cups flour, sifted
2 teaspoons baking soda

½ teaspoon salt
2 cups fresh blueberries
½ cup sugar
⅓ cup flour
½ teaspoon cinnamon
¼ cup margarine, melted

Mix together ¾ cup sugar, shortening, and egg. Stir in milk. Sift together and add 2 cups flour, baking soda, and salt. Blend in blueberries. Spoon into a greased and floured 9-inch square pan. For topping mix together ½ cup sugar, cinnamon, flour, and melted margarine. Pour evenly over batter. Bake at 375 degrees for 45 to 50 minutes. Serve warm as a coffee cake or dessert.

Serves 8

Plum Kuchen

2 cups flour	¾ cup milk (approximately)
2 teaspoons baking powder	20 fresh purple Italian plums
¾ teaspoon salt	¾ cup sugar
½ teaspoon cinnamon	1 teaspoon cinnamon
2 tablespoons sugar	2 tablespoons butter or
2 tablespoons shortening	margarine, melted
1 egg	

To make dough, mix first five ingredients; then cut in shortening. Beat egg slightly, and add milk to make a scant cup. Add milk mixture to flour, and mix all at once, stirring only to moisten. Pat dough into greased 9- by 13-inch pan, having edges higher than center.

To make topping, wash, halve, and pit plums. Arrange cut side up over dough. Combine ¾ cup sugar with 1 teaspoon cinnamon, and sprinkle over plums. Drizzle with melted butter. Bake at 425 degrees for 30 minutes. Serve warm or cool as coffee cake or dessert. Substitute other fresh fruits for plums, such as peaches, apples, or apricots if desired.

Serves 12

Bermuda Johnny Bread

¼ cup sugar	2 teaspoons baking powder
1½ cups flour	1 egg
¼ teaspoon salt	½ cup milk
	2 tablespoons butter

Mix dry ingredients. Add egg, milk, and mix. Melt butter in frying pan. Spoon a third of the batter into pan. Fry on low heat until brown. Turn and brown second side. Repeat twice with remaining batter . Split bread in half, and serve with plenty of butter and jam.

Note: Serve with fresh berries at breakfast.

Yield: Serves 3

Maryland Beaten Biscuits

5 cups flour
½ cup lard
1 teaspoon baking powder

1 teaspoon salt
1 teaspoon sugar
1⅓ cups water

Combine flour, lard, baking powder, salt, and sugar. Add water to form dry dough. Beat with hammer, wooden pounder, or mallet to remove air from dough. Turn dough periodically while pounding. Beat 20 to 30 minutes until dough pops, is smooth and elastic. Form dough into balls. Bake in 450 degree oven 15 to 20 minutes.

Note: These biscuits are prepared and served at Colonial Christmas at Mount Clare Mansion.

Yield: 2 to 3 dozen

Miniature Southern Biscuits

2 cups self-rising flour
1⅓ cups sour cream

1 cup butter, melted, no
    substitutes

Combine all ingredients in large bowl. Spray tiny muffin tins with cooking oil. Spoon batter into prepared tins. Bake at 450 degrees for 10 to 12 minutes.

Note: To make large biscuits, use larger muffin tins, and bake 15 to 17 minutes.

Yield: 3 dozen biscuits

Skillet Cornbread

2 tablespoons bacon drippings
1 cup self-rising corn meal
1 cup sour cream

½ cup corn oil
8 ounce can creamed white
    corn

2 eggs

Place bacon drippings in 9-inch iron skillet, and place in 400 degree oven. Combine remaining ingredients. When skillet is hot and grease has melted, pour batter into skillet. Bake for 25 minutes or until golden brown.

Serves 6

Martha's Muffins

1 egg
1 cup buttermilk
1 cup all-purpose flour
¾ cup whole wheat flour

½ cup honey or brown sugar
1 teaspoon baking powder
1 teaspoon salt
½ teaspoon baking soda

½ cup butter, melted, no substitutes

Preheat oven to 375 degrees. Combine egg and buttermilk. In large bowl, combine remaining ingredients, and then add egg mixture. Spoon into greased muffin tins, and bake for 20 minutes.

Yield: 1 dozen muffins

Whole Grain Muffins

2 cups stone-ground whole wheat flour	2 teaspoons baking powder
	¼ cup honey
3 eggs	½ cup raw bran
1½ cups milk	½ cup wheat germ
4 tablespoons butter, melted	1 cup raisins
2 ripe bananas, finely chopped	

Preheat oven to 425 degrees. Mix all ingredients together. Pour into greased muffin tins, about two-thirds full. Reduce heat to 400 degrees and bake 20 to 25 minutes. Freeze well.

Yield: 30 muffins

New England Blueberry Muffins

½ cup butter or margarine, softened	2 teaspoons baking powder
	½ teaspoon salt
1¼ cups sugar	½ cup milk
2 eggs	2½ cups fresh blueberries
2¼ cups flour	2 tablespoons sugar

Cream butter and sugar. Add eggs one at a time, stirring well after each addition. Sift flour, baking powder, and salt together. Add to butter mixture alternately with milk. Mash ½ cup blueberries. Add to batter with remaining blueberries. Grease top of muffin tin, and line cups with foil liners. Fill each cup with batter. Sprinkle top of each muffin with sugar, and bake 25 to 30 minutes at 375 degrees.

Note: To make apple raisin muffins, use cake ingredients for blueberry muffins. Delete blueberries and add: ½ cup raisins, 1 teaspoon cinnamon, and 3 medium apples, peeled, cored, and chopped. Bake as directed for blueberry muffins.

Yield: 12 large or 18 medium muffins

Orange Glazed Muffins

1 cup butter
1 cup sugar
2 eggs
1 teaspoon baking soda
1 cup buttermilk

2 cups sifted flour
Orange zest
½ cup raisins
Juice of 1 orange
1 cup brown sugar

Preheat oven to 400 degrees. Cream butter and sugar. Add eggs and beat well. Dissolve soda in the buttermilk, and add alternately with the flour to butter mixture. Add orange zest and raisins. Stir. Butter muffin tins and fill two-thirds full. Bake for 20 to 25 minutes. Mix orange juice with brown sugar. Pour over cooked muffins, and remove from pans immediately.

Yield: 3 dozen small muffins

Pumpkin Muffins

1 egg
½ cup milk
½ cup canned pumpkin
¼ cup butter or margarine,
   melted
1½ cups flour

2 teaspoons baking powder
½ cup sugar
½ teaspoon cinnamon
½ teaspoon nutmeg
½ teaspoon salt
½–¾ cup raisins

Sugar for topping

Preheat oven to 400 degrees. Beat egg slightly. Stir in milk, pumpkin, and melted butter. Sift dry ingredients, and stir into pumpkin mixture just until moistened. Batter should be lumpy. Fold in the raisins. Pour into greased muffin cups two-thirds full. Sprinkle batter with sugar, and bake 18 to 20 minutes.

Yield: 1 dozen

Salads

Mount Vernon Place

Visiting Mount Vernon Place is a wonderful way to acquaint yourself with old Baltimore. It is a distinctive neighborhood of four square blocks surrounding the site of the first Washington Monument. The Washington Monument is a 160-foot shaft of native marble and holds one of the most rewarding views of the city for those who wish to climb the 228 steps inside. This "rural" site was chosen after considerable debate, as the City Fathers felt this tall column was "exceedingly dangerous" and could topple over and injure someone. Surrounding the monument are rows of brownstones in various architectural styles popular in the Nineteenth Century. The newest building was completed in 1926, and none has been replaced since 1929. Among the more famous of these buildings are the Walters Art Gallery and the Peabody Institute.

At the beginning of May each year, when the azaleas are just coming alive with color, Mount Vernon rejuvenates itself to host the Flower Mart. The Flower Mart is a fund-raising project of the Women's Civic League. Encircling the monument are booths filled with springtime's bounty—lilies of the valley, impatiens, geraniums, and all sorts of beautiful plants. Also for sale are crafts, flowered hats, open-pit beef sandwiches and Maryland's famous crab cakes served on saltine crackers. Finally, no Flower Mart would be complete without the traditional lemon stick. Spring in Baltimore is synonymous with this porous peppermint stick served in the center of a lemon!

Beef and Avocado Salad

4 cups cold, rare roast beef strips	4 cups lettuce in bite-sized pieces
2 cups fresh mushrooms, sliced	1 large avocado, sliced
2 cups cherry tomatoes	Lemon juice

Combine roast beef, mushrooms, cherry tomatoes, and lettuce. Sprinkle avocado slices with lemon juice, and add to roast beef mixture.

Dressing:

¾ cup olive oil	2 teaspoons Dijon mustard
¼ cup red wine vinegar	2 teaspoons horseradish
½ teaspoon salt	

Combine dressing ingredients, and toss salad lightly. Refrigerate several hours before serving.

Serves 4

Antipasto Salad

1 pound small pasta shells or rotini	1 small onion, chopped
½ pound provolone, cut in ½-inch cubes	3 tomatoes, chopped
½ pound hard salami, cut in ½-inch cubes	1½ ounces green olives, drained
½ pound pepperoni, cut in ½-inch cubes	6 ounce can black olives, drained
2 green peppers, chopped	1 teaspoon oregano
2 stalks celery, chopped	1½ teaspoons salt
	1 teaspoon pepper
	¾ cup oil
	½ cup vinegar

Cook pasta according to package instructions, drain and cool. Several hours before serving, combine pasta, provolone, salami, pepperoni, peppers, celery, onion, tomatoes, olives, salt, and pepper. Two hours before serving, mix the oil and vinegar, and toss with the salad.

Serves 10 to 12

Immortal Reuben Salad

1 large head leaf lettuce, torn
  into bite-sized pieces
1 pound sauerkraut, drained
½ cup cooked corned beef, cut
  into strips

¼ cup sliced dill pickles
2 tomatoes, cut in wedges
1 cup grated Swiss cheese
1 cup Thousand Island dressing

In a salad bowl, combine lettuce, sauerkraut, corned beef, pickles, and
tomatoes. Toss lightly. Sprinkle with cheese. Heat the salad dressing, and
pour over salad mixture. Toss lightly. Sprinkle freshly ground pepper to
taste.

Serve immediately with Campari and soda, plenty of dark bread, and sweet
butter.

Serves 4 to 6

Taco Salad

1 pound lean ground beef
1¼ ounce package taco
  seasoning mix
8 ounces sharp cheese
15 ounce can ranch-style or
  barbecue-flavored baked
  beans

1 head lettuce, chopped
2–3 tomatoes, chopped
1 cup guacamole
1 cup sour cream
  Hot sauce (optional)
  Tortillas or corn chips

Brown beef and drain. Stir in taco seasoning mix, adding water and cooking
according to package directions. Cool.

Mix seasoned meat with cheese and beans in a large salad bowl. Add
lettuce and tomatoes. Top with guacamole, sour cream, and hot sauce.
Serve with tortillas or corn chips.

Serves 4 to 6

Chicken Chutney Salad

2 cups chicken, cooked and diced	⅔ cup mayonnaise
13½ ounce can pineapple chunks, very well drained	¼ teaspoon lime zest
	2 tablespoons chopped chutney
1 cup celery, diced	2 tablespoons lime juice
¼ cup salted peanuts or almonds	½ teaspoon curry powder
	¼ teaspoon salt

Mix together the chicken, pineapple, celery, and peanuts. Make a dressing of the remaining ingredients, and toss with the chicken mixture. Chill at least 2 hours, and serve on a bed of lettuce.

Serves 4

Vietnamese Chicken Salad

1 medium head cabbage	6 chicken breast halves, boiled, boned, and skinned
1 tablespoon salt	
1 cup salted, roasted peanuts	Chopped parsley
1 large onion, sliced very thinly	Salt and pepper to taste
1 or 2 carrots, shredded	Italian dressing to taste

Shred the cabbage into long, thin pieces. Place the cabbage in a large colander. Sprinkle the salt over the cabbage, and under cold water wash and squeeze the cabbage until it is soft. Chop the peanuts in a blender or food processor. Shred chicken. Combine the shredded chicken, carrots, onion, peanuts, and parsley with the cabbage. Add Italian dressing, salt, and pepper to taste.

Serves 8

Cold Seafood Pasta Salad

1 pound small rotini or shell
  pasta
12 ounce can artichoke hearts,
  rinsed, drained, and
  quartered
10 ounce jar roasted red
  peppers, thinly sliced

1 pound large shrimp, barely
  cooked and diced into ¾-inch
  pieces
½ pound small scallops, barely
  cooked
6 ounce can pitted ripe olives,
  drained

Cook pasta al dente. Drain. Stir in a small amount of oil. Toss and cool.
Combine with remaining ingredients.

Dressing:
1 large clove garlic, crushed
⅔ cup olive oil
⅓ cup wine vinegar
½ cup Parmesan cheese, freshly
  grated

2 ounce tin anchovies with oil
¾ teaspoon dried basil
  Salt and freshly ground
  pepper to taste

Combine dressing ingredients in blender or food processor. Pour over
salad ingredients, and toss well. Serve while still warm, or chill and serve
one or two days later. Seafood must be just done, not overcooked.

Serves 6

Shrimp Salad Oriental

2½–3 pounds shrimp, cooked
    and peeled
1 can sliced water chestnuts
1 whole onion, sliced and
    chopped

1 bunch celery, sliced thin on
    diagonal
2 cups bean sprouts
1 large can Chinese noodles

Mix together all salad ingredients, except noodles. Crisp Chinese noodles
in 350 degree oven for 5 minutes, and add to salad.

Dressing:
2 cups mayonnaise

3 tablespoons soy sauce
½ teaspoon ground ginger

Mix dressing ingredients together, and toss with salad.

Serves 12

Caesar-Lime Salad

⅓ tube anchovy paste
⅛ teaspoon pepper
¼ teaspoon dry mustard
¼ teaspoon Worcestershire
    sauce
1 large clove garlic, minced

½ cup olive oil
   Juice of 1½–2 limes
1 egg
⅓ cup Parmesan cheese
1 large head romaine lettuce
½–¾ cup seasoned croutons

In a large bowl, mix anchovy paste, pepper, mustard, Worcestershire
sauce, and garlic. Add olive oil, lime juice, and raw egg. Mix thoroughly
until dressing is smooth. Add the Parmesan cheese and mix.

Rinse and dry the romaine. Tear and add to the salad dressing. Add seasoned croutons, and toss to mix. If a saltier flavor is desired, increase
anchovy paste.

Serves 6

Nancy Maloley's Wonderful Salad and Dressing

5 ounce jar marinated
  artichoke hearts

11 ounce can mandarin oranges
  Red leaf or romaine lettuce

1 cup walnut pieces

Drain artichoke hearts, reserving marinade. Cut in quarters. Drain mandarin oranges, discarding juice. Tear lettuce into pieces. Toss lettuce, orange segments, and walnuts. Pour dressing over and toss to blend.

Dressing:

Vegetable oil
½ teaspoon paprika
¼ cup tarragon vinegar (or red wine vinegar)
½ teaspoon oregano

2 tablespoons sugar
1 clove garlic, crushed
1 teaspoon salt
1 bay leaf
Black pepper to taste

Measure reserved artichoke marinade, and add vegetable oil to measure ¾ cup. Combine oil mixture, and remaining dressing ingredients in jar. Shake well, and refrigerate overnight. Remove bay leaf before serving. Makes 1 cup.

Serves 4

Delmonico Salad

½ cup olive oil
2 tablespoons wine vinegar
2 tablespoons light cream
3 tablespoons Roquefort cheese, crumbled
Freshly ground black pepper
Dash of hot pepper sauce

1 head lettuce (red leaf, bibb, or Boston)
1 hard-cooked egg, peeled and chopped
2 slices bacon, cooked and crumbled
5 ounce jar marinated artichoke hearts, drained and quartered

Combine olive oil, wine vinegar, cream, and crumbled Roquefort in a small bowl. Whisk until smooth. Season to taste with pepper and hot pepper sauce.

Tear lettuce into bite-sized pieces, and place in salad bowl. Add egg, bacon, and artichokes. Pour dressing over all and toss.

Serves 6

Tomato Onion Salad

4 large, ripe tomatoes
1 large green pepper
Vinaigrette or Italian dressing

1 medium onion
⅓ cup bleu cheese, crumbled

Slice tomatoes and green pepper thinly. Chop onions. Combine all with bleu cheese. Add dressing of your choice, and chill until serving.

Serves 4

Curried Spinach Salad

3 tablespoons butter
2 teaspoons curry powder
1 teaspoon garlic salt
2 teaspoons Worcestershire
   sauce
⅛ teaspoon hot pepper sauce

5 ounce can Chinese noodles
1 package fresh spinach
½ head lettuce
1 avocado
6 ounce can pitted black olives
   Italian salad dressing to taste

Melt butter; then add curry powder, garlic salt, Worcestershire sauce, hot pepper sauce, and blend together. Preheat oven to 250 degrees. Scatter the noodles on cookie sheet, and pour butter mixture over noodles. Cook the Chinese noodles for 20 minutes.

Meanwhile, wash and break up spinach and lettuce. Slice avocado and olives, and mix with spinach. Toss with the Italian dressing. Add curried noodles, and mix well. Serve immediately.

Serves 12

Broccoli Salad

6 cups broccoli florets and
   stalks, cut just below florets
1 red onion
3 slices bacon
4½ ounces cream cheese,
   softened

⅛ teaspoon salt
⅛ teaspoon pepper
3 tablespoons vinegar
3 tablespoons sugar
3 tablespoons oil
1 large egg

Scrape or peel the broccoli, and steam briefly. Thinly slice red onion. Cook, drain, and crumble the bacon. Meanwhile, mix cream cheese with remaining ingredients in a blender or food processor. Pour over hot broccoli. Serve immediately, or refrigerate and serve chilled.

Serves 6

Mushroom Salad

¾ pound fresh mushrooms,
cleaned and sliced
⅓–½ cup parsley sprigs,
chopped
1 small clove garlic, minced
⅓ cup salad oil

2 tablespoons red wine
vinegar
1½ tablespoons mayonnaise
¼ teaspoon salt
⅛ teaspoon pepper
1 teaspoon Dijon mustard

Combine mushrooms with parsley and refrigerate. Mix the remaining ingredients in a lidded jar. Shake well, and chill for at least 30 minutes. Before serving toss mushrooms and dressing in a bowl. Place on a bed of Boston or bibb lettuce to serve.

Serves 4

Herbed Four-Bean Salad

1 pound can green beans
1 pound can yellow beans
1 pound can kidney beans
1 pound can garbanzo beans

½ pound snow peas, blanched
1 Bermuda (red) onion, thinly
sliced
2 hard-cooked eggs, sliced

Drain all beans. Mix with snow peas and onions in a large bowl. Combine dressing ingredients and pour over vegetables. Cover and marinate overnight, stirring several times. Before serving, toss vegetables with dressing again. Garnish with egg slices.

Dressing:
½ cup sugar
½ cup wine vinegar
½ cup salad oil
1 teaspoon salt

1 teaspoon dry mustard
½ teaspoon dried tarragon
½ teaspoon basil
2 tablespoons parsley

Mix all ingredients and add to salad.

Serves 8 to 10

Oriental Salad with Honey Dressing

½ pound fresh snow peas
11 ounce can mandarin oranges
1 cup fresh mushrooms, sliced
½ cup red onion, chopped
1 cup red apple, cored and sliced

Steam snow peas for 3 minutes and divide them equally on 4 salad plates. Cool to room temperature. Arrange mandarin oranges and mushrooms on snow peas. Sprinkle with red onion. Refrigerate at least one hour. Just before serving, slice red apple and place on salad.

Serves 4

Dressing:
⅔ cup sugar
1 teaspoon dry mustard
1 teaspoon celery seed
¼ teaspoon salt
½ teaspoon paprika
⅓ cup honey
5 tablespoons vinegar
1 tablespoon lemon juice
1 cup salad oil

Mix dry ingredients. Add honey slowly, mixing with a whisk. Gradually blend in vinegar and lemon juice. With an egg beater or electric mixer, beat in salad oil very slowly. Use with any fruit salad.

Yield: 2 cups

Luncheon Fruit Salad

1 head Boston or bibb lettuce	11 ounce can mandarin oranges
1 head red leaf lettuce	1 bunch seedless green grapes
1 head romaine lettuce	8 ounces slivered almonds,
½ pint fresh strawberries	toasted
2–3 kiwi fruits	

Wash lettuce, spin it dry, and tear it into pieces. Mix fruit in a large salad bowl with at least 2 tablespoons of salad dressing. Add lettuce and toss. Garnish with toasted almonds.

Dressing:

½ cup red wine vinegar	1 cup vegetable oil
¼ cup sugar	1 tablespoon minced onion
½ cup ketchup	½ teaspoon salt
1 teaspoon Worcestershire sauce	

Mix dressing ingredients in food processor or blender, and chill overnight.

Serves 10

Winter Potato Salad

½ cup olive oil
¼ cup grated Romano cheese
2 tablespoons white wine
   vinegar
2 tablespoons lemon juice
2 teaspoons Worcestershire
   sauce
5 cups potatoes, cooked, peeled,
   and cubed, still warm

1 cup carrots, slightly cooked
   and sliced
½ medium onion, finely
   chopped
3½ ounce can pitted ripe olives,
   drained
3–4 hard-cooked eggs, peeled
   and chopped
2 tablespoons parsley, minced

Salt and pepper to taste

Combine oil, cheese, vinegar, lemon juice, and Worcestershire sauce. Toss with warm potatoes, carrots, onion, olives, eggs, and parsley. Add salt and pepper to taste. Serve immediately. If the potatoes have absorbed the dressing by serving time, sprinkle with a little more vinegar and lemon juice.

Serves 4 to 6

Potato Salad

5 pounds potatoes, pared and
   cooked
¼ pound bacon, cooked until
   crisp and crumbled
4 large stalks celery, chopped
1 large onion, chopped

½ cup sugar
1 tablespoon flour
2 eggs
½ teaspoon salt
¾ cup water
½ cup vinegar

1 pint mayonnaise

Dice potatoes while still warm. Add the bacon, celery, and onion to the potatoes. In a separate bowl, mix together the sugar and flour. Beat the eggs slightly in a saucepan, and place over medium-low heat. Stir the eggs constantly, and add the sugar, flour, salt, and water. When this is warm, add the vinegar, still stirring constantly until the mixture thickens. Remove from heat, add mayonnaise, and mix well. Pour the dressing to taste over potatoes, and chill to serve.

Serves 12

Summer Salad

1½ pounds medium potatoes	1 small red onion, sliced and
Salt	separated into rings
1 medium green pepper	1 medium tomato
1 cucumber, peeled and sliced	2 tablespoons fresh parsley,
	chopped

Boil potatoes in salted water until tender, about 20 to 30 minutes. Do not overcook. Cool, peel, and slice thinly. Layer slices in a glass bowl and sprinkle with salt. Cut green pepper in half-rings and arrange on top of potatoes. Next add the sliced cucumber, and then the onion rings. Slice the tomato, and add to bowl. Sprinkle with parsley.

Dressing:

¼ cup white wine vinegar	2 tablespoons sugar
1 teaspoon salt	1 teaspoon dry mustard
¼ teaspoon freshly ground	½ clove garlic, minced
pepper	⅔ cup olive or salad oil

Shake dressing ingredients in a jar. Pour over the salad. Refrigerate for several hours or overnight, tilting bowl and basting salad with a bulb baster occasionally.

Serves 6

Rice Salad

2 6-ounce packages of chicken-	3 green onions, sliced
flavored rice	16 stuffed green olives
2 6-ounce jars marinated	¾ cup green pepper, chopped
artichoke hearts	⅔ cup mayonnaise
1 teaspoon curry powder	

Cook rice according to package directions, omitting the butter. Cool. Drain artichokes, saving liquid. Slice artichokes; add onions, olives, and green pepper, and add to rice. Mix artichoke liquid, mayonnaise, and curry powder. Toss well with rice mixture. Serve chilled.

Serves 6 to 10

Barcelona Rice Salad

1 pound shrimp, cooked,
  peeled, and deveined
½ cup oil
¼ cup wine vinegar
1 teaspoon salt
½ teaspoon pepper
1 tablespoon chopped onion

1 teaspoon minced garlic
1 tablespoon parsley, chopped
2 cups cooked rice, chilled
⅓ cup green pepper, chopped
½ cup mushrooms, sliced
1 cup tomatoes, peeled and
  cubed

Cut shrimp into bite-sized pieces. Combine oil, vinegar, salt, pepper, garlic, onion, and parsley. Marinate shrimp all day in half the marinade. At serving time, combine rice, green pepper, and mushrooms. Pour remaining marinade onto rice mixture. Drain shrimp. Combine with rice mixture, and add tomatoes. Toss and serve.

Serves 4 to 6

Confetti Rice Salad

2 cups cooked rice, cooled
4 celery stalks, chopped
½ cup onion, chopped
½ cup green pepper, chopped
½ cup stuffed green olives,
  chopped

2 ripe tomatoes, chopped
½ cup mayonnaise
¼ cup Italian or Caesar salad
  dressing
½ teaspoon each tarragon, basil,
  parsley, oregano

Place cooled rice with celery, onion, green pepper, olives, and tomatoes in serving bowl. Combine mayonnaise, salad dressing, and herbs. Toss with rice mixture. As substitutions try ranch-style dressing or yellow rice.

Serves 8

Asparagus Aspic

8 ounces cream cheese
1 cup mayonnaise
10 pimiento-stuffed green olives,
  halved
1 small onion, finely chopped

14 ounce can asparagus tips,
  drained
1 envelope unflavored gelatin
¼ cup cold water
  Hot water
  Salt and pepper to taste

Blend cream cheese and mayonnaise until smooth. Add olives, onion, and asparagus. Dissolve gelatin in cold water; add hot water to measure 1 cup. Mix gelatin with other ingredients. Pour into mold, and chill until firm.

Serves 6

Aunt Binny's Tomato Salad

46 ounce can tomato juice,
  divided
1 envelope unflavored gelatin
3 3-ounce packages lemon-
  flavored gelatin
3–5 drops hot pepper sauce
2 teaspoons Worcestershire
  sauce

6 carrots, grated
5–8 scallions, chopped
4 celery stalks, chopped
1 avocado, chopped
½ teaspoon salt
  Juice of 1 lemon

Combine 1 cup tomato juice and the unflavored gelatin, stirring until dissolved. Boil 3 cups tomato juice with above mixture. Pour into lemon gelatin, and stir to dissolve. Add remaining tomato juice. Chill until partially set. Add remaining ingredients. Pour into 8-cup mold and chill until firm. If desired, blend 1 cup mayonnaise and 1 cup sour cream to serve as a sauce.

Serves 20 to 30

Mandarin Orange Salad

6 ounces orange gelatin
2 cups boiling water
6 ounce can frozen orange juice
  concentrate
2 11-ounce cans mandarin
  oranges, drained

20 ounce can crushed pineapple,
   undrained
1 pint sour cream
1 teaspoon dried dillweed or
  more to taste

Dissolve gelatin in boiling water. Add orange juice, and cool slightly. Mix in oranges and pineapple. Pour into a large salad mold, and chill at least 8 hours. Unmold onto a plate with lettuce leaves. Fill center of mold with a dressing of sour cream mixed with dillweed.

Serves 10 to 12

Grandma Bridget's Cranberry Salad

2 cups ground cranberries
  (1 pound)
2 cups sugar
2 packages lemon gelatin
3½ cups boiling water

1 cup celery, chopped
1 cup pecans, chopped
1 whole orange, ground
  (the entire orange)

Combine cranberries and sugar. Let stand. Dissolve gelatin in boiling water, and chill until partially set. Add remaining ingredients, and pour into a ring mold, individual molds, or a 9- by 13-inch pan. Refrigerate until firm.

Serves 12

Frozen Fruit Custard

2 eggs, beaten
2 tablespoons white vinegar
2 heaping teaspoons sugar
1 heaping cup miniature
   marshmallows

17 ounce can fruit cocktail,
   chilled and drained
¾ cup heavy cream

Combine the egg, vinegar, and sugar in the top of a double boiler. Cook over medium heat, stirring until thickened. Add marshmallows, and stir constantly until they have melted. Remove from heat, and allow mixture to cool. Add fruit cocktail and cream, mixing well. Pour into an 8-inch square baking dish, and store in freezer at least 4 hours before serving. Cut in squares, and serve on leaf lettuce.

Serves 8

Poppy Seed Dressing

½ cup sugar
⅓ cup honey
1 teaspoon grated onion
6 tablespoons tarragon vinegar
3 tablespoons lemon juice

1 cup salad oil
1 teaspoon dry mustard
1 teaspoon paprika
¼ teaspoon salt
2 teaspoons poppy seeds

Mix all ingredients well, and store covered in refrigerator for up to two weeks. Serve over fruit. If less sweetness is desired, reduce sugar to ¼ cup.

Yield: 2 cups

Creamy Bacon Salad Dressing

½ pound bacon
2 cloves garlic, finely chopped
1 medium onion, finely chopped
1 tablespoon prepared brown mustard
1 teaspoon Worcestershire sauce

2 drops hot pepper sauce
1½ tablespoons parsley, finely chopped
2 tablespoons honey
¼ cup cider vinegar
1½ cups mayonnaise
½ cup heavy cream
½ cup milk

½ teaspoon ground black pepper

Cut bacon into julienne strips, and fry until crisp. Remove bacon from pan, and place on paper towels to drain. Saute the garlic and onion in hot bacon drippings until soft. Remove from the pan.

In a large mixing bowl combine bacon, garlic, and onions with prepared mustard, Worcestershire sauce, hot pepper sauce, parsley, and honey. Whisk all the ingredients together. Add vinegar, mayonnaise, cream, and milk; whisk vigorously until blended. Add black pepper. Serve on spinach salad or other greens.

Yield: 3 cups

Clear Lemon French Dressing

1 clove garlic, minced	¼ teaspoon sugar
½–1 teaspoon salt	½ teaspoon lemon zest
1 teaspoon coarsely ground	½ cup fresh lemon juice
pepper	1¼ cup salad oil

Combine all ingredients, and mix thoroughly in blender. Store covered in refrigerator.

Yield: about 2 cups

Cheese Salad Dressing

2 cups olive oil	1 teaspoon salt
1 cup white vinegar	1 teaspoon pepper
Juice of 1 lemon	1 cup grated Romano cheese
1 cup grated Parmesan cheese	

Combine all ingredients in a blender or food processor. Vary the thickness by adjusting oil or vinegar to your taste. Refrigerate and serve over a garden salad.

Yield: 2 cups

Sauces & Spreads

White Marble Steps

Rowhouses are one of the major ingredients in Baltimore's architectural flavor. Built since before the Civil War, the evolving rowhouse is a symbol of the city's historic era. Baltimore's first rowhouses were built to house the rapidly growing artisan and working class populations attracted to the city by the booming port.

Traditionally, rowhouses in Baltimore have always been brick. Surmounting the brick front is another standard rowhouse component, the cornice. Another Baltimore trademark invented in 1937 for use on rowhouses is Formstone—cement formed to look like stonework. It is still manufactured today by several companies as a permanent solution to the problems of scaling brick and crumbling mortar. Many neighborhoods of rowhouses have white marble steps in front built from marble quarried in northern Baltimore County. These have become a symbol of Baltimore's rowhouses. Various periods of building brought other characteristics—porches, bay windows, and stained glass. In east and south Baltimore many houses exhibit two other local art forms, the painted screen and the decorated window. The painted screens allow those indoors to have privacy with open windows, while those outdoors see lovely scenery. The decorated windows consist of a lacy curtain as a backdrop to a collection of ceramics, candles, flowers, and other seasonal displays. For the passersby, it is one of the many gifts of the Baltimore rowhouse.

Easy Hollandaise

1 egg yolk   4 tablespoons butter
                    Juice of ½ a lemon

Place all ingredients in heat-resistant glass cup. Place the cup in a saucepan of water. Bring water to a low boil, stirring the sauce constantly. When the sauce begins to thicken, remove cup from boiling water. Let stand for several minutes. Stir and serve.

Serves 4

Mustard Cheese Sauce

½ cup mayonnaise   ¼ cup Dijon mustard
                    2 ounces cheddar cheese, grated

Mix the mayonnaise and mustard. Place the vegetable of your choice in an ovenproof casserole. Pour sauce over the vegetable. Top with grated cheese and bake at 400 degrees for 20 minutes. Use with parboiled cauliflower florets, broccoli florets, or Brussels sprouts.

Yield: 1 cup

Blender Béarnaise

1½ cups margarine   1 tablespoon tarragon leaves
  9 eggs   3 tablespoons red wine
    Salt   vinegar
    Pepper   1 tablespoon green onion,
  1 tablespoon parsley   chopped
                    1½ cups boiling water

Place all ingredients except water in blender or food processor. Combine ingredients well, then very slowly add boiling water. Blend until smooth. Put in top of double boiler, and cook until thick. If sauce curdles, return to blender, and blend again. Can be made several days in advance and refrigerated.

Yield: about 5 cups, serves 12

Tomato Sauce

1 medium onion, minced	1½–2 teaspoons oregano
1 carrot, grated	1½–2 teaspoons basil
2–3 tablespoons olive oil	½ teaspoon garlic, minced
28 ounce can imported tomato	Red pepper flakes to taste
puree	Salt and pepper to taste
6 ounce can tomato paste	¼ cup dry red wine
35 ounce can imported plum	(optional)
tomatoes	

Sauté onion and carrot in oil until wilted and golden. Add puree and paste, and blend well. To eliminate pulp and seeds, force tomatoes through sieve held over large saucepan. Combine with carrot mixture. Add seasonings to taste, and stir in wine if desired. Bring to slow boil, and reduce heat immediately. Simmer slowly for about 45 minutes. Do not let sauce boil. Serve over pasta, chicken, or meat loaf.

Note: If too salty, add ½ teaspoon sugar. Sauce is light and sweet if you use imported tomatoes. Flavor improves the next day. Store in airtight container in refrigerator. Keeps several weeks.

Yield: 6 cups

Barbecue Sauce

½ onion, chopped	1 tablespoon Worcestershire
2 cloves garlic, minced	sauce
2 tablespoons oil	1 tablespoon chili powder
8 ounce can tomato sauce	½ teaspoon freshly ground
1 teaspoon prepared mustard	pepper
2 tablespoons vinegar	1 teaspoon salt
1 tablespoon brown sugar	¾ cup water

Sauté the onion and garlic in oil until onion is transparent. Add remaining ingredients, and stir to mix. Bring the mixture to a boil, lower heat, and simmer 20 to 30 minutes. Add more water if necessary. Delicious served on chicken or spare ribs.

Yield: 2 cups

Papa's Hot Sauce

5 ounces cider vinegar	1 teaspoon black pepper
3 ounces ketchup	½ teaspoon red pepper
1 ounce Worcestershire sauce	1 tablespoon butter
1 teaspoon salt	Juice of ½ lemon

Place all ingredients in a small pan and heat thoroughly. Serve over sliced lamb or pork. It is very spicy, and is not intended for use as a barbecue sauce.

Yield: about 1½ cups

Old Style Cocktail Sauce

½ cup mayonnaise	⅛ teaspoon hot pepper sauce
½ cup heavy cream, whipped	1 tablespoon crushed
½ cup ketchup	pineapple, drained and juice
1 teaspoon chutney, chopped	reserved
	1 teaspoon of brandy

Combine all ingredients, and blend well. Thin mixture with pineapple juice if desired. Chill for 1 hour, and serve over crab meat, lobster, or shrimp. Try this recipe as a dressing on chicken salad to which a few peeled, slivered apples have been added.

Yield: 1 cup

Dill Mustard Sauce

3½ tablespoons oil
2 tablespoons vinegar
2 tablespoons Dijon mustard

1 egg yolk
1 tablespoon sugar
¼ teaspoon salt

½ teaspoon dillweed

Combine all ingredients in covered jar, and shake vigorously. Store in refrigerator. Serve over salmon or other fish.

Yield: about ¾ cup

Hot Cooked Mustard

4 ounce can dry mustard
1 cup tarragon vinegar

3 eggs, beaten
1 cup sugar

Mix the mustard and vinegar in a glass bowl, and refrigerate overnight. The next day, add sugar and eggs. Transfer mixture to a saucepan, and cook until thick, stirring constantly with a wooden spoon.

Note: Very hot and spicy. Use with cheese, pretzels, or meats. Will keep in refrigerator for several months.

Yield: 1 pint

Frances' Ham Sandwich Spread

½ cup margarine, softened
3 tablespoons prepared mustard
1 teaspoon Worcestershire sauce
3 tablespoons poppy seeds
1 small onion, grated

Mix margarine with mustard. Add remaining ingredients and blend well. Store in covered jar in refrigerator. Will keep several weeks.

Note: Spread on party rye or croissants. Fill sandwich with shredded ham and Swiss cheese. Heat in 400 degree oven for 5 minutes, and serve hot.

Yield: 1½ cups

Pimento Cheese

1 10-ounce package mild
   cheddar cheese
1 10-ounce package sharp
   cheddar cheese
1 10-ounce package extra sharp
   cheddar cheese
1 medium onion, finely chopped
1 2-ounce jar pimiento, chopped
2 cups mayonnaise (see below)

Shred the cheese with a hand grater or food processor. Add onion, mayonnaise, and pimiento, and mix well. Use as a sandwich spread, a dip for vegetables, or serve with crackers.

Mayonnaise:

4 eggs
1 heaping cup sugar
1 teaspoon salt
1 teaspoon dry mustard
4 tablespoons butter
1 cup milk
1 tablespoon flour
½–⅔ cup vinegar (fill rest of
   measuring cup with water
   to make 1 cup)

Place all ingredients in a saucepan. Cook over medium heat until creamy, stirring constantly.

Note: This mayonnaise is very sweet, and is delicious mixed with ground country ham, curry chicken, or tuna for sandwich spreads.

Cranberry Chutney

½–1 teaspoon cinnamon
½–1 teaspoon ground ginger
1 cup orange sections, cut up
¼ cup orange juice
4 cups cranberries
   (12 ounces)

2 cups sugar
1 cup apples, unpeeled, cored,
   chopped
½ cup raisins
¼ cup walnuts, chopped
1 tablespoon white vinegar

Zest of orange (optional)

Place all ingredients in saucepan, and bring to a boil. Reduce heat, and cook until all cranberries have burst. Chill overnight to thicken and allow flavors to blend. Serve with turkey dinner and on holidays.

Serves 15 to 20

Grandmother's Lemon Curd

¼ pound butter
4 eggs, well beaten
Grated rind of 2 lemons

⅔ cup fresh lemon juice (4
   lemons)
5 grains of salt

3 cups granulated sugar

Melt butter in the top of a double boiler over simmering water. Do not boil water. Add remaining ingredients in the order given. Cook uncovered, stirring occasionally, until it is thick enough to spread. This takes about 45 minutes. Lower heat when thickening starts, so that the water in bottom of double boiler is no more than a simmer. Transfer to an airtight container, and store in the refrigerator. Serve with toast, biscuits, on pancakes, or as a tart filling.

Note: Small jars of this make delicious gifts. It keeps indefinitely in the refrigerator.

Yield: 3 to 4 jelly jars

Desserts

Our Maritime History

Merchant ships first set sail from what is now the Port of Baltimore in 1706, 23 years before Baltimore Town existed. Eighteenth century settlers were attracted to the Patapsco River Basin because of its natural harbor and streams to power mills. Shipbuilding was a natural industry, and it flourished. The U.S.F. CONSTELLATION, the first U. S. Navy ship put to sea, was launched in Baltimore in 1797. She was decommissioned after World War II and returned to Baltimore for restoration and public tours. The PRIDE OF BAL-TIMORE is an authentic recreation of a Baltimore Clipper schooner which was used to carry goods around the world and is now used as an ambassador of goodwill touring worldwide to promote Baltimore. Many skipjacks, like the MINNIE V, were built in Baltimore to harvest oysters and seasonal produce. The tugboat, S.S. BALTIMORE, built in 1906, is one of the last steam-powered tugs in the nation and is being restored at its dock at the Museum of Industry. The Baltimore Maritime Museum is the home for both the Lightship CHESA-PEAKE, which served as a floating lighthouse off the mouth of the Chesapeake Bay for merchant vessels and the U.S.S. TORSK, the submarine which fired the final torpedos of World War II. Baltimore's maritime history is unique in the number and variety of historic ships it offers.

Coffee Pecan Fantasy

1 cup light brown sugar, packed	½ teaspoon vanilla
½ cup light corn syrup	1 cup pecans
½ cup heavy cream	2 tablespoons butter
¼ cup butter	1 quart coffee ice cream

To prepare sauce, combine brown sugar, corn syrup, heavy cream, and ¼ cup butter in a saucepan. Cook over low heat for 5 minutes, stirring constantly. Remove from heat, and add vanilla. Set aside to cool.

To assemble, sauté pecans in 2 tablespoons butter until lightly browned. Cool, then place a few in the bottom of individual dessert dishes. Add a spoonful of sauce, a scoop of ice cream, and another spoonful of sauce. Top with pecans. Cover with foil, and freeze until ready to serve.

Serves 6 to 8

Betty McKimmon's Chocolate Icebox Dessert

12 ounce package semisweet chocolate chips	6 eggs, separated
6 tablespoons water	½ pint whipping cream
6 tablespoons sugar	2–3 tablespoons sugar
2–3 packages plain ladyfingers	Unsweetened bar of chocolate

Melt chocolate chips, water, and sugar in top of double boiler. Stir constantly. Remove top of double boiler from heat. Arrange ladyfingers on bottom of deep oval bowl and vertically around the sides. Add egg yolks to chocolate one at a time, and beat immediately after each addition. Beat whites until stiff, and fold into chocolate mixture.

Put half of the chocolate mixture into bowl, then add more ladyfingers and then rest of chocolate mixture. Can be prepared to this point 2 to 3 days in advance. Before serving, whip the cream until stiff with 2 to 3 tablespoons sugar, and spread cream over chocolate. Garnish with gratings of chocolate bar.

Serves 8

Marbelous

Crust:

½ cup brown sugar

¼ cup butter, softened

½ cup peanut butter

1 cup flour

Cream brown sugar, butter, and peanut butter until light. Add flour; blend until crumbly. Press half of mixture in 9- by 13-inch pan. Bake at 350 degrees 10 to 15 minutes.

Filling:

8 ounces cream cheese

½ cup sugar

¼ cup peanut butter

1 teaspoon vanilla

2 eggs, beaten

1 cup non-dairy whipped topping

6 ounces semisweet chocolate chips

Beat cream cheese, sugar, peanut butter, and vanilla at medium speed. Add eggs; fold in whipped topping. Spread filling over crust in pan. Melt chocolate chips and drizzle over filling. Use knife to marble it with filling. Sprinkle remaining crust on top. Freeze several hours. Remove from freezer about 15 minutes before serving, and slice into small pieces.

Serves 12 to 24

Ice Cream Torte

20 moist macaroons

1 quart chocolate ice cream, soft

1 quart coffee ice cream, soft

6 tablespoons chocolate syrup

6 Heath Bars, frozen and crushed

Freeze macaroons, then crush by hand. In a 10-inch spring-form pan place half the crushed macaroons. Spread the softened chocolate ice cream over the macaroons. Drizzle 3 tablespoons chocolate syrup over ice cream. Add another layer of macaroon crumbs, the coffee ice cream, and remaining chocolate syrup. Sprinkle crushed Heath Bars on top. Freeze at least 4 to 5 hours. Remove from pan to serve.

Serves 10

Ice Cream Puffs with Chocolate Sauce

Cream Puff Shells:

1 cup water	⅛ teaspoon salt
½ cup butter (no substitutions)	1 cup all-purpose flour

4 eggs

Preheat oven to 425 degrees. Bring water, butter, and salt to a boil in medium saucepan. Add flour and stir vigorously until mixture is smooth, forms a ball, and separates from sides of pan. Remove from heat, and cool. Add eggs one at a time, beating with electric mixer after each addition. Use an ice cream scoop to drop pastry onto a well-greased cookie sheet, leaving 2 inches between puffs. Bake for 20 minutes; reduce heat to 325 degrees and bake 20 minutes. Remove from oven when firm to the touch. Slit puffs, and fill with coffee or vanilla ice cream. Spoon chocolate sauce liberally over ice cream.

Semisweet Chocolate Sauce:

8 ounces semisweet chocolate squares	½ cup sugar
	4 tablespoons sour cream
8 tablespoons water	4 tablespoons butter

Melt chocolate over low heat or in top of double boiler, stirring occasionally until smooth. Add sugar, and stir until dissolved. Boil gently for 4 minutes, stirring constantly. While stirring, add sour cream 1 tablespoon at a time. Remove from heat and add butter. Stir until smooth.

Note: Start cream puffs first, and make sauce while baking them. All can be made in the morning, and sauce reheated before serving.

Serves 8 to 10

Chocolate Shells

6 ounce package semisweet chocolate chips	Seafood baking shells and aluminum foil

OR miniature muffin papers and muffin tins

Melt chocolate in top of double boiler over boiling water. If making shells, wrap aluminum foil around outside of a shell. Be careful to make foil smooth as you mold foil to contours of shell. Leave a small amount of foil overlapping edges of the shell. Paint aluminum foil with chocolate, covering completely and making it about ⅛-inch thick. Let shells harden in the freezer. When hard, carefully remove the shell and then aluminum foil. Fill shells with ice cream balls topped with a fruit sauce or liqueur which works well with chocolate.

To make miniature chocolate cups, place muffin papers inside tins. Using a butter knife, or other small blunt-edged knife, smooth a dollop of melted chocolate inside the papers. Work chocolate around the edges and bottom of the paper, leaving no holes in bottom. Work chocolate as far up the sides of paper as possible. Chocolate should be approximately ⅛-inch thick. Place pan of filled cups in freezer until chocolate is very hard. Carefully work papers off cups, and store cups in freezer in airtight containers or plastic bags. Fill cups with your favorite dessert soufflé or mousse.

Yield: 18 small cups
4 to 6 5-inch shells

Pots au Chocolat

8 ounces German sweet chocolate	⅛ cup orange liqueur or brandy
¼ cup sugar	5 eggs, separated
⅛ cup strong brewed coffee	Sweetened whipped cream, for garnish

In double boiler over hot, not boiling, water, combine the chocolate, sugar, coffee, and liqueur. Stir to melt chocolate and sugar. Cool to tepid, and add the beaten egg yolks. Beat the egg whites at room temperature until stiff. Stir ⅓ of the egg whites into chocolate mixture, and then fold the rest into chocolate mixture. Put in pots de creme or demitasse cups. Chill several hours. Serve with sweetened whipped cream.

Serves 8

Pot de Framboise

1 cup boiling water	¾ cup heavy cream
3 ounce package lemon-flavored gelatin	Fresh strawberries for garnish
	Whipped cream for garnish
10 ounce package frozen strawberries, partially defrosted	

Place boiling water and gelatin in a blender. Blend at lowest speed to the count of 15. Pour into glass bowl, and refrigerate for 10 minutes. It will set in 3 layers. Return to blender, and add cream and strawberries. Blend at lowest speed to the count of 5. Remove cover and stir to distribute berries. Blend again for 2 seconds. Pour into sherbet glasses. Refrigerate until serving time. Garnish with fresh strawberries and whipped cream.

Serves 6

Amaretto Chocolate Mousse

8½ ounce package plain chocolate wafers	6 eggs, room temperature, separated
6 tablespoons butter, melted	1 tablespoon vanilla
12 ounces semisweet chocolate chips	¼ cup Amaretto liqueur
	½ cup heavy cream, whipped

Crush wafers and combine with butter. Generously grease sides and bottom of spring-form pan with butter. Press crumb mixture into pan.

Melt chocolate chips in top of double boiler. Remove from heat and gradually add slightly beaten egg yolks, vanilla, and Amaretto. Beat egg whites until stiff, and fold into mixture. Fold in whipped cream. Spoon into crust, and refrigerate 5 hours before serving. Before removing from pan, arrange extra wafer crumbs around rim.

Serves 10

Frozen Raspberry Mousse

2 packages ladyfingers
2 10-ounce packages frozen
  raspberries, defrosted
1–2 tablespoons orange-flavored
  liqueur

4 egg whites
¼ cup sugar
1 pint whipping cream

Line 8- or 9-inch spring-form pan with ladyfingers, rounded sides out, on sides and bottom of pan. Put raspberries through food mill or strainer to remove seeds. Add liqueur to raspberries. Beat egg whites until soft peaks form, and then add sugar, 1 tablespoon at a time, beating until stiff. Whip cream until stiff peaks form. Fold together cream, egg whites, and raspberries. Pour into spring-form pan. Smooth top and cover with plastic wrap. Freeze 8 hours or overnight. Before serving, let stand at room temperature for 15 minutes to make cutting easier.

Serves 10 to 12

Frozen Grand Marnier Soufflé

2 egg whites
  Pinch salt
6 tablespoons sugar
1 cup whipping cream

2 tablespoons Grand Marnier
  Strawberries or raspberries for
  garnish

Beat egg whites with salt until softly peaked. Gradually beat in sugar until egg whites are stiff and shiny. In another bowl, whip cream until stiff. Gently blend in Grand Marnier. Fold in egg whites. Turn mixture into 1-quart mold or serving dish, and freeze until firm, 4 hours or longer. Serve with strawberries, raspberries, or a mixture of the two whole or puréed.

Serves 4 to 6

Lemon Cream Soufflé

6 ounce package lemon-flavored gelatin	¼ cup sugar
2 cups boiling water	¼ cup cold water
8 ounces cream cheese, softened	½ cup lemon juice
	1 cup heavy cream, whipped

Dissolve gelatin in boiling water. Combine cream cheese and sugar, mixing until well blended. Gradually add gelatin, cold water, and lemon juice. Blend well, and chill until slightly thickened, about 1½ to 2 hours. Fold in whipped cream. Wrap a 3-inch collar of foil around the top of a 1-quart soufflé dish. Secure with tape or rubber band. Spoon in lemon mixture. Chill about 4 hours or until firm. Remove foil before serving.

Note: Good topped with strawberries and cream.

Serves 8 to 10

Orange Bavarian Cream

Butter	½ cup sugar
1 cup orange juice	6 eggs, separated
1 envelope unflavored gelatin	¼ teaspoon cream of tartar
2 teaspoons orange zest	1 cup heavy cream

Butter bottom and sides of 1½- or 2-quart soufflé dish. If using 1½-quart dish, make aluminum foil collar as soufflé will rise above dish. In medium saucepan combine orange juice, gelatin, and orange zest, and let stand 1 minute. Cook over low heat about 5 minutes, stirring constantly until mixture boils and gelatin dissolves completely. Stir in sugar.

In small mixing bowl beat egg yolks at high speed until thick and lemon colored. Blend a little hot gelatin mixture into yolks, and then return all to gelatin mixture. Chill, stirring occasionally, until mixture mounds slightly when dropped from spoon. Beat egg whites and cream of tartar until stiff, but not dry. In another bowl, beat heavy cream until stiff. Fold beaten cream and gelatin mixture into egg whites. Carefully pour into prepared soufflé dish. Chill several hours or overnight. Remove foil collar immediately before serving.

Serves 8

Daiquiri Bavarian

1¾ cups graham cracker crumbs
¼ cup sugar
8 tablespoons butter, melted
1 envelope unflavored gelatin
½ cup sugar
½ cup light rum
2 teaspoons grated lime peel
1 cup whipping cream
2 teaspoons grated lemon peel
½ cup lime juice
4 egg yolks, beaten
16 ounces cream cheese, cubed
and softened
4 egg whites
½ cup sugar

Combine the graham cracker crumbs, ¼ cup sugar, and butter. Remove 2 tablespoons crumbs and set aside. Press remaining crumbs in bottom and 1¾ inches up sides of 9-inch spring-form pan. Chill while preparing filling.

In medium saucepan combine gelatin and ½ cup sugar. Stir in rum, citrus peels, lime juice, and egg yolks. Cook over medium heat, stirring constantly, until slightly thickened, 8 to 10 minutes. Remove from heat. Beat in cream cheese until smooth.

In another bowl, beat egg whites until soft peaks form. Add ½ cup sugar; beat until stiff. In a separate bowl, whip cream to soft peaks. Fold egg whites and whipped cream into gelatin mixture. Pour into prepared crust. Sprinkle crumbs around edge. Cover and chill overnight.

Note: Must make 1 day ahead. Much lighter than traditional cheesecake.

Serves 12

Crème Marron

2 egg whites
½ pint whipping cream
8¾ ounce can chestnut spread

Beat egg whites until they are stiff. In a separate bowl, beat whipping cream. Reserve a very small amount of whipped cream for garnish. Fold remaining whipped cream into egg whites. Then fold in chestnut spread. Spoon mixture into sherbet glasses. Top each with a dollop of reserved whipped cream. Chill a few hours before serving.

Note: Doubles easily. Purchase chestnut spread from gourmet grocery.

Serves 6

Kahlua Trifle

1 package chocolate cake mix
1 large box chocolate pudding
½ cup Kahlua

12 ounces frozen whipped
  topping
½ cup walnuts, chopped

Bake cake according to directions, either in 2 layers or 1 pan and slice in half. Prepare pudding according to package. Crumble half the cake in large trifle bowl. Pour half the Kahlua over it. Put half the pudding and half the whipped topping over cake. Crumble remaining cake, and repeat Kahlua, pudding, and whipped topping. Top with walnuts.

Strawberry Trifle

8 or 9 inch round layer cake, baked
3¼ ounce package vanilla pudding, not instant, prepared as directed
2 pounds frozen strawberries with juice, thawed

1 cup chilled whipping cream
¼ cup confectioners' sugar
¼ cup toasted almonds, slivered or sliced for garnish
8 whole strawberries for garnish

Have cake and pudding slightly warm for best results. Split cake layer horizontally, and then into eight wedges. Arrange half the pieces in 2-quart glass or crystal serving bowl. Pour half the strawberries with syrup over cake; spread with 1 cup pudding. Repeat with rest of cake, strawberries, and pudding. Cover, and refrigerate at least 4 hours. Can be refrigerated up to 24 hours.

Approximately 1 hour before serving, beat whipping cream and sugar until stiff. Spread over trifle. Sprinkle with almonds. Garnish with whole strawberries. Cover and refrigerate until serving time.

Note: Good with a little cream sherry sprinkled over top.

Serves 8 to 10

Strawberries with Amaretto Creme

2 pints strawberries
½ cup whipping cream

1 tablespoon confectioners' sugar

1 tablespoon Amaretto liqueur

Hull, wash, and drain strawberries. Place strawberries in balloon-shaped wine glasses or dessert dishes. Chill cream, bowl, and beaters. Whip cream until slightly stiff. Fold in confectioners' sugar and Amaretto. Place generous dollop of whipped cream on strawberries, and serve with almond macaroons.

Serves 4 to 5

Raspberry Wonder

1 cup all-purpose flour
½ cup pecans, chopped
½ cup butter or margarine, melted
¼ cup brown sugar, firmly packed
10 ounce package frozen raspberries, thawed and juice

1 cup sugar
2 teaspoons fresh lemon juice
2 egg whites
1 cup whipping cream
1 teaspoon vanilla
Fresh raspberries

Combine flour, pecans, butter, and brown sugar in an 8-inch square baking dish; stir well. Bake at 350 degrees for 20 minutes, stirring occasionally; cool.

Combine raspberries, sugar, lemon juice, and egg whites in a large mixing bowl. Beat at high speed, using an electric mixer for 10 to 12 minutes or until stiff peaks form. Whip cream. Add vanilla. Fold into raspberry mixture.

Press two-thirds of the crumb mixture into a 9-inch spring-form pan; spoon in raspberry mixture. Sprinkle remaining crumbs on top; cover and freeze until firm. Garnish with fresh raspberries.

Note: Best if made a day ahead to give it plenty of time to become firm.

Serves 8 to 10

Blueberry Bliss

2 cups graham cracker crumbs
½ cup sugar
¾ cup walnuts, chopped
½ cup margarine, melted
4 egg whites
1 cup sugar

16 ounces cream cheese,
    softened
2 cups blueberries
8 ounces frozen whipped
    topping, thawed

Preheat oven to 350 degrees. To make crust, combine graham cracker crumbs, ½ cup sugar, walnuts, and margarine. Press into 9- by 13-inch baking dish.

For filling, beat egg whites until soft peaks form. Beat in remaining sugar 1 tablespoon at a time. Then add cream cheese, and mix thoroughly. Spread over crust, and bake 20 minutes. Remove from oven, and cool 2 hours. Spoon blueberries over cooled filling, and top with whipped topping. Refrigerate for 6 hours. Slice into small portions to serve.

Serves 8 to 12

Pavlova

2 egg whites at room
    temperature
1½ cups superfine sugar
½ teaspoon vanilla
1 teaspoon white vinegar
1 teaspoon cornstarch

4 tablespoons boiling water
1 pint whipping cream
1–2 cups of fresh, sliced
    strawberries, kiwi, or
    bananas
Grated chocolate

Preheat oven to 350 degrees. Beat together first six ingredients at high speed until very stiff. Grease and lightly dust with flour a 12-inch ovenproof round plate or tray. Spread mixture onto plate and push up at sides into a crater shape. Bake at 350 degrees for 10 minutes. Reduce heat to 250 degrees, and bake for 45 minutes. Turn oven off, and allow to cool in oven. When ready to serve, top with whipped cream, choice of fruit, and grated chocolate.

Serves 8

Mrs. Posey's Cheesecake

Crust:

1½ cups graham cracker crumbs
4 tablespoons butter or margarine

1½ tablespoons cinnamon
¼ cup sugar

Bring all ingredients to room temperature. Blend, and line the bottom and sides of a spring-form pan evenly.

Filling:

1¾ cups sugar
3 8-ounce packages cream cheese, softened

4 eggs
1 teaspoon vanilla
16 ounces sour cream

Cream sugar and cream cheese. Add eggs one at a time. Add vanilla and sour cream. Pour filling into spring-form pan. Bake at 300 degrees for 60 minutes. Turn off oven, and leave cheesecake in oven for 3 hours. Chill overnight, and serve.

Note: To vary crust, increase sugar to ½ cup and add 4 tablespoons powdered cocoa; garnish cake with chocolate curls. Or sprinkle cake with cinnamon, and garnish with stick cinnamon in center. This is the family recipe of a favorite commercially sold cheesecake.

Serves 12 to 16

Mandarin Cheesecake

1½ cups graham cracker crumbs	16 ounces cream cheese
⅓ cup butter, melted	½ pint sour cream
3 tablespoons sugar	1 teaspoon vanilla
2 eggs	11 ounce can mandarin oranges
1 cup sugar	¼ cup sugar
2 teaspoons cornstarch	

Combine crumbs, butter, and sugar. Press into 9-inch spring-form pan, and bake at 325 degrees for 7 to 10 minutes. Cool. Beat eggs, 1 cup sugar, cream cheese, sour cream, and vanilla until smooth. Pour into crust, and bake at 350 degrees for 25 minutes. Turn the oven off. Do not open door, and leave cake in oven 1 hour. Chill.

To make glaze, drain mandarin oranges saving syrup. Combine liquid from oranges, sugar, and cornstarch in saucepan. Heat, stirring until thickened. Arrange oranges on cake, spoon glaze over oranges, and chill until serving.

Serves 10

Wholesome Apple Crisp

5 cups apples, sliced and pared	¼ cup sunflower seeds
¾ cup whole wheat flour	¼ cup walnuts, chopped
¾ cup rolled oats	⅛ cup wheat germ
1 teaspoon cinnamon	½ cup butter or margarine
½ cup honey	

Preheat oven to 350 degrees. Arrange apples in pie plate. Combine all remaining ingredients except butter and honey. Cut in butter until crumbly. Add honey, and mix with spoon. Mixture should be sticky. Spread and press mixture over apples. Bake 45 to 50 minutes or until top has browned.

Serves 8 to 10

Baked Apple Dumplings

Pastry:

2¼ cups flour   ¾ cup shortening

¾ teaspoon salt   7 to 8 tablespoons ice water

In a medium bowl mix together flour and salt. Use a pastry blender to cut in shortening; then add enough water to make dough stick together. Roll pastry to ⅛-inch thickness between two sheets of waxed paper; cut in six 7-inch squares. Reserve leftover dough to make leaves.

Filling:

6 medium-sized, tart, juicy   ½ cup sugar

  apples, pared and cored   1½ teaspoons cinnamon

1 tablespoon butter

Place an apple on each pastry square. In a small bowl combine sugar and cinnamon; fill the cavity of each apple with this mixture. Dot apple tops with butter. Use a small amount of water to moisten points of pastry squares, bring together, and seal well. Use reserved dough, and make leaves to hide seams at top of apple. Place 2 inches apart in an 8- by 12-inch baking pan. Chill thoroughly.

Syrup:

1 cup sugar   ¼ cup butter

¼ teaspoon cinnamon   2 cups water

Preheat oven to 500 degrees. Mix all ingredients together in a saucepan. Boil for 3 minutes; pour hot syrup around chilled dumplings. Bake immediately for 5 to 7 minutes; reduce heat to 350 degrees and bake for 30 to 35 minutes more.

Serves 6

Apple Turnovers with Nutmeg Sauce

2 cups flour
2 tablespoons shortening
1 teaspoon baking soda
2 teaspoons cream of tartar
Milk

4 cups tart apples, peeled, cored,
and sliced
1 cup sugar
2 cups water
Red food coloring

Combine flour, shortening, baking soda, and cream of tartar. Add small amounts of milk to make a soft dough. Roll out on pastry cloth, and cut into 8-inch rounds. Place apples in each round, fold in half, and pinch tight. Put in loaf pans or deep baking dish.

Preheat oven to 375 degrees. Make a syrup of the sugar, water, and coloring. Pour around dumplings. Bake 45 minutes. Remove from oven, and place on dessert plates. Serve with hot nutmeg sauce.

Serves 6

Nutmeg sauce:
1 tablespoon flour
1 cup sugar
¼ teaspoon salt
2 cups boiling water

1 tablespoon butter
1 teaspoon freshly grated
nutmeg

Mix flour, sugar, and salt together in small saucepan. Add boiling water gradually, whisking constantly. Add butter, bring to a boil, and cook for 5 minutes. Remove from heat. Add nutmeg and serve.

Yield: about 3 cups

Bavarian Apple Torte

Crust:

½ cup butter or margarine,   ⅓ cup sugar
  softened   ¼ teaspoon vanilla
                    1 cup flour

Cream butter and sugar. Stir in vanilla with flour, and mix well. Spread in a 9-inch spring-form pan. Cover bottom and up 2 inches of sides.

Filling:

8 ounces cream cheese,   ¼ cup sugar
  softened   ½ teaspoon vanilla
                    1 egg

Mix all ingredients until smooth. Spread over crust.

Topping:

4 cups apples, pared and grated   ⅔ cup sugar
  or sliced   ½ teaspoon cinnamon
                Pecans or other nuts

Mix ingredients together. If it seems too runny, drain some juice. Arrange over filling. Sprinkle with pecans. Bake at 450 degrees for 10 minutes. Reduce heat to 400 degrees, and bake an additional 25 to 30 minutes.

Serves 12

Fresh Blueberry Crunch Cake

Cake:

1 cup butter
2 cups sugar
4 eggs
1 teaspoon vanilla
½ teaspoon almond extract

3 cups flour
1 teaspoon baking powder
1 teaspoon baking soda
½ teaspoon cream of tartar
1 cup buttermilk

1 pint blueberries dusted with flour

Cream butter, sugar, and add eggs. Mix in flavorings. Combine dry ingredients, and blend with creamed mixture alternately with buttermilk. Mix well. Stir in blueberries, and pour batter into 9- by 13-inch greased pan.

Topping:

6 tablespoons butter, softened
1 cup sugar
½ cup brown sugar

½ cup flour
1 teaspoon cinnamon
½ cup coconut

½ cup nuts, chopped

Combine butter with sugars and flour. Add cinnamon and coconut, blending well. Stir in chopped nuts. Sprinkle on batter and bake at 350 degrees for 55 minutes.

Cherry Rhubarb Cobbler

1 cup sugar
2 tablespoons cornstarch
⅓ cup water
16 ounce can pitted sour red cherries, drained
OR 2½ cups fresh sour red cherries, drained
1½ cups rhubarb, sliced
2 tablespoons butter

2 tablespoons lemon juice
1 teaspoon grated lemon peel
1½ cups sifted flour
3 tablespoons sugar
3 teaspoons baking powder
½ teaspoon salt
⅓ cup shortening
½ cup milk
1 egg, beaten well

2 tablespoons sugar

Combine 1 cup sugar, cornstarch, water, cherries, and rhubarb in large saucepan, and bring to a boil. Stir constantly. Cook 1 minute, and stir in butter. Pour into 8-inch square baking dish. Add lemon juice, and sprinkle peel over fruit.

Sift together flour, 3 tablespoons sugar, baking powder, and salt. Cut in shortening until mixture is crumbly. Add milk and egg at once, stirring only until ingredients are moistened. Spoon dough over fruit. Sprinkle with 2 tablespoons sugar. Bake at 400 degrees for 35 to 40 minutes. Serve warm with cream or ice cream.

Serves 6 to 8

Peach Cobbler

3 to 4 fresh peaches, peeled,
       pitted, and sliced (2 cups)
½ cup margarine, melted
½ cup sugar
½ cup milk
1 cup flour

1 teaspoon baking powder
¼ teaspoon salt
½ teaspoon vanilla
OR ½ teaspoon almond extract
1 cup sugar
½ cup water

Preheat oven to 350 degrees. Place peaches in a two-quart baking dish. Combine margarine, sugar, milk, flour, baking powder, salt, and vanilla in a medium bowl. Pour over peaches. Mix together remaining sugar and water. Pour over batter. Do not stir. Bake for 1 hour.

Note: To make blueberry cobbler, substitute 2 cups blueberries for the peaches. Sprinkle 1 tablespoon lemon juice, ¼ teaspoon nutmeg or cinnamon over berries. Continue with recipe.

Serves 8 to 10

Baked Pears in Cream Sauce

2 tablespoons unsalted butter,
      divided
2 tablespoons sugar, divided

2 Bosc or Bartlett pears,
      unpeeled, halved, and cored
1 cup heavy cream

Preheat oven to 400 degrees. Butter a shallow baking dish with one tablespoon butter. Sprinkle one tablespoon sugar over bottom of pan. Place pears, cut side down, in baking dish. Sprinkle pears with remaining sugar. Dot pears with remaining butter. Bake for 10 minutes. Pour cream over pears, and bake 18 to 20 minutes longer. If necessary, brush sugar from the sides of baking dish. Serve the pears warm on dessert plates with sauce surrounding them.

Serves 4

Crêpes

2 eggs
5 tablespoons butter, melted
1½ cups flour

½ teaspoon salt
¾ cup milk
¾ cup water

Butter, softened

Combine all ingredients, except the softened butter, in a blender at medium speed. Blend until mixture is smooth. Let mixture stand for 2 hours before using. With a pastry brush, cover a hot 5-inch crêpe pan or small skillet with the softened butter. Add about 3 tablespoons batter to coat bottom of pan. Tilt pan to coat evenly. Cook each crêpe quickly, turning once, until crêpe is golden brown. Drain on paper towel while preparing other crêpes.

Note: To freeze, wrap each crêpe in plastic wrap. Thaw completely at room temperature before using.

Yield: 18 crêpes

Lemon Filling for Crêpes

Use your favorite crêpe recipe to make 6-inch crêpes

Granulated sugar
Fresh lemon juice

Cook crêpes, and turn darker side up. Sprinkle with 1 teaspoon sugar; then sprinkle with 2 teaspoons of lemon juice. Roll and serve crêpes, sprinkling additional sugar on top if desired.

Lemon Sauce for Crêpes

½ cup superfine sugar
2 teaspoons lemon zest

¾ cup butter, melted
2 tablespoons lemon juice

Make basic crêpe recipe. Combine lemon sauce ingredients, roll crêpes and pour sauce over immediately before serving.

Yield: 8 to 10 crêpes

Fresh Fruit and Cream Crêpe Filling

1 cup fresh strawberries,
peaches, blueberries, or
raspberries
Sugar, if desired

1 cup heavy cream
1 tablespoon confectioners'
sugar
¼ teaspoon vanilla
1 teaspoon Grand Marnier

Prepare fruit by washing, then slice or quarter if necessary. Sweeten to taste. Whip cream with confectioners' sugar, vanilla, and liqueur. Fold in prepared fruit. Fill crêpe with 2 to 4 tablespoons of fruit mixture. Roll and serve garnished with additional fruit.

Yield: 8 to 10 crêpes

Brown Sugar and Sour Cream Crêpes

Use your favorite recipe for
crêpes

Granulated brown sugar
Sour cream

After cooking each crêpe, sprinkle with ¾ teaspoon granulated brown sugar. Then spread a heaping teaspoon sour cream evenly over crêpe. Roll each crêpe and serve.

Chocolate Crêpes

2 eggs
2 egg yolks
¼ cup vegetable oil
⅓ cup milk
6 tablespoons flour
2 tablespoons cocoa powder

¼ teaspoon salt
1 tablespoon sugar
1 cup heavy cream
2 tablespoons confectioners' sugar

Make batter by placing eggs, yolks, oil, milk, flour, cocoa, salt, and sugar in blender. Mix at medium speed until smooth. Refrigerate 1 hour to allow flavors to blend. Thin with milk if too thick. Batter should be consistency of light cream.

Use a crêpe pan or 5-inch skillet covered with a small amount of butter. Add 3 tablespoons batter to pan, and tilt pan to coat evenly. Cook crêpe quickly, turning once. Drain on paper towel while preparing other crêpes.

Beat heavy cream; add sugar. Continue beating until stiff peaks form. Place a heaping tablespoonful on each crêpe, and roll.

Note: Top with chocolate fudge sauce. Substitute 2 tablespoons Grand Marnier for confectioners' sugar to flavor whipped cream if desired.

Yield: 12 crêpes

Chocolate Fudge Sauce for Crêpes

½ cup cocoa powder
1 cup sugar
1 cup light corn syrup

½ cup light cream
3 tablespoons butter
¼ teaspoon salt

1 teaspoon vanilla

Put all ingredients except vanilla into small saucepan, bring to boil, and boil 5 minutes and no more. Remove from heat, and stir in vanilla. Mixture should be thin. Sauce will thicken in refrigerator, and will keep two weeks. Serve over chocolate crêpes.

Yield: about 2 cups

Palacsinta (Hungarian Crêpes)

2 cups flour
1 teaspoon salt
2 teaspoons sugar
4 eggs, beaten well
2 cups milk

Cottage cheese filling
Butter
Powdered sugar
Sour cream
Strawberry preserves

Mix the flour, salt, and sugar. Combine eggs and milk. Add the egg and milk mixture gradually to the flour mixture, beating to a thin, smooth batter. Spoon 3 tablespoons of the batter on a hot buttered or greased 5-inch skillet. The crêpes will be very thin. Brown the crêpes lightly on both sides. Stack the crêpes on a warmed plate. Spread each with cottage cheese filling. Roll the crêpes up, and place in a buttered baking dish. Sprinkle with powdered sugar. Heat thoroughly in a 350 degree oven. Serve with sour cream and strawberry preserves on top.

Cheese filling:
1 pound dry cottage cheese
1 egg, well beaten

¼–½ cup sugar
Few drops vanilla

Mix all the ingredients well, adding the sugar to taste.

Yield: 24 crêpes

Chocolate Sauce

½ cup butter
1 ounce square unsweetened
  baking chocolate
¼ cup unsweetened cocoa
  powder

Dash salt
¾ cup sugar
5 ounce can evaporated milk
1 teaspoon vanilla

In a saucepan over low heat, melt butter and baking chocolate. When melted, add cocoa, salt, sugar, and evaporated milk. Bring to a boil, stirring constantly. When boiling, remove from heat, and add vanilla.

Yield: about 2 cups

Grand Marnier Sauce

4 egg yolks
1 cup milk

¼ cup sugar
2–4 tablespoons Grand Marnier

Combine egg yolks, milk, and sugar in top of double boiler. Cook over simmering water, stirring constantly, until mixture coats a metal spoon, approximately 10 to 20 minutes. Do not let mixture boil when cooking. Mixture should be thin. Remove from heat. Add Grand Marnier and chill. Mixture will thicken when chilled. Serve over fresh fruit.

Yield: about 1½ cups

Peanut Butter Sauce

¼ cup margarine   ½ cup water
½ teaspoon cornstarch   ⅓ cup peanut butter
        1½ cups confectioners' sugar, sifted

Melt margarine in saucepan. Stir in cornstarch. Gradually stir in water until smooth. Stirring constantly, bring to boil over medium heat, and boil 1 minute. Remove from heat. Stir in peanut butter. Add sugar, and beat until smooth. Store in covered jar in refrigerator. Will last several weeks if hidden!

Note: Serve warm or cold over ice cream. Or make your own ice cream parlor sundae with vanilla ice cream, chocolate and peanut butter sauces, whipped cream, and candy-coated peanut butter pieces!

Yield: 1⅓ cups

Pies & Pastries

Cruising the Chesapeake

The Chesapeake Bay, with its 1,726 square miles of water and 46 principal tributaries, is home to countless boating enthusiasts. Thousands of pleasure boats converge on the bay each summer from marinas dotted along the Magothy, Severn, Rappahannock, and other rivers that feed into the largest estuary in the United States. From wind-surfers to magnificent schooners and whalers to luxurious cabin cruisers, Marylanders take to the helm from April through October. The 4,000 miles of shoreline afford many sheltered harbors for swimming, picnicing, and overnight anchorage. Several Eastern Shore points, such as St. Michael's and Oxford are popular weekend boat trips from Baltimore. Annapolis, the capital of Maryland, is called the "Sailing Capital of the East Coast." Not only is it a scenic seaport, it's an historic port of entry dating from the 17th Century. With the waves lapping against the hull, the gulls crying overhead, and the sun slowly slipping into the Chesapeake, you have the ingredients of a perfect evening in Maryland.

Classic Apple Pie

1 double recipe pie crust	Dash nutmeg
7–8 firm Granny Smith apples	Juice of ½ lemon
⅔–¾ cup sugar	2–3 tablespoons bourbon
¼ cup flour	2–3 tablespoons butter
¼ teaspoon cinnamon	1 egg, to glaze crust

Prepare pie crust and chill until ready to use. Pare, core, and slice apples. Add sugar, flour, spices, lemon, bourbon, and mix well. Roll out bottom crust, and fit into pie plate. Arrange apple filling in pastry, and dot with butter. Roll out top crust, place over filling, and crimp edges.

Make egg wash by beating egg with 1 tablespoon of water. Brush generously over pie crust. Dust with sugar. Cut slits for steam. Bake at 450 degrees for 10 minutes. Reduce heat to 350 degrees, and bake 30 minutes longer. Serve with ice cream or heavy cream poured over slice of pie.

Glazed Peach Pie

3 fresh peaches	2 tablespoons butter
½ cup water	¼ teaspoon almond flavoring
1 cup sugar	1 9-inch pie shell, baked
3 tablespoons cornstarch	4–6 fresh peaches

Whipped cream or vanilla ice cream

Peel three peaches, and crush to equal one cup. Place in a saucepan and add water. In a small bowl, combine sugar and cornstarch; add to saucepan and mix well. Cook, stirring constantly, until thick and clear. Add butter and flavoring; let cool.

Slice four to six peaches into pie shell in a decorative manner, and cover with the cooled glaze. Place pie in the refrigerator until it is well chilled. Spread whipped cream or ice cream over top of pie before serving.

Fresh Peach 'n Blueberry Pie

1 double recipe pie crust
5–6 large firm peaches
1–2 cups blueberries
½–⅔ cup sugar
Egg wash

¼ cup flour
¼ teaspoon cinnamon
Dash nutmeg
Butter

Blanch peaches in boiling water. Peel, pit, and slice peaches. Rinse and pick over berries. Combine with peaches in large bowl. Add sugar, flour, spices, and mix together well. Roll out bottom crust, and fit into 10-inch pie plate. Add filling to shell. Roll out top crust, place over filling, and crimp edge. Cut slits for steam.

Make egg wash by beating egg and 1 tablespoon water with fork. Brush heavily on top crust and dust with sugar. Bake at 450 degrees for 10 minutes, reduce heat to 350 degrees, and bake 30 minutes longer.

Blueberry Tarts

1 cup sugar
3 tablespoons cornstarch
1 cup water
4 cups blueberries
2 tablespoons butter

Pinch salt
½ pint whipping cream
1 tablespoon superfine
   granulated or powdered sugar
10 3-inch tart pastries

Mix sugar and cornstarch together. Add water and stir to dissolve in top of double boiler. Add 1 cup blueberries. Cook for 1 hour or until clear and very thick, stirring often. Remove from heat, and add remaining blueberries, butter, and salt.

Before serving, fill pastries. Whip cream until stiff, adding sugar to sweeten. Garnish each tart with a dollop of whipped cream. These tarts can be made a day or two ahead of time and refrigerated.

Note: This recipe fills 3 dozen miniature tarts or one 9-inch pie pastry.

Strawberry Pie

1 9-inch pie crust, baked and
   cooled
3 pints fresh strawberries

2 cups water
1½ cups sugar
6 tablespoons cornstarch
1 cup whipping cream

Wash and slice strawberries, placing tops in a saucepan. To make glaze, add water to strawberry tops, and bring to a boil. Boil for 3 to 4 minutes, crushing strawberry tops with a fork or spoon. Strain liquid into bowl. Mix cornstarch and sugar together, and place in clean saucepan. Stir in strawberry liquid and bring to a boil, stirring constantly. Boil vigorously for 2 to 3 minutes until thick and clear. Remove from heat, and let cool while finishing pie.

Place half the sliced strawberries in baked pie shell. Add half the glaze. Add remaining berries and glaze. Chill pie. When pie cools, whip cream and cover top of pie with cream. This pie should be made and served the same day, as it does not hold well for the next day.

Ritzy Fruit Pie

20 RITZ® Crackers, crushed
½ cup walnuts, chopped
1 cup sugar
½ teaspoon baking powder

1 teaspoon vanilla
3 egg whites
   Fresh fruit
   Whipping cream

Thoroughly mix crackers, walnuts, sugar, baking powder, and vanilla. Beat egg whites until stiff, and fold into pastry mixture. Place in a greased pie plate, and bake 20 minutes in a 350 degree oven. Cool. Fill crust with fresh fruit. Serve topped with whipped cream.

Upside-Down Apple Pecan Pie

6 tablespoons butter, softened	¼ cup cold milk
¾ cup pecan halves	6 cups apples, pared and sliced
¾ cup brown sugar	2 tablespoons lemon juice
2 cups flour	⅓ cup brown sugar
1 teaspoon salt	2 tablespoons flour
½ cup light oil	½ teaspoon cinnamon
½ teaspoon nutmeg	

Spread butter evenly over bottom and half way up sides of 12-inch deep dish pie plate. Place pecans 1 inch apart around sides of plate, rounded side toward plate. Arrange remaining pecans in bottom of pie plate to make a design. Refrigerate 10 minutes.

To make crust, mix flour and salt with fork. Pour milk and oil into measuring cup. Do not stir. Pour into flour and blend. Form dough into ball, and divide in half. Roll out half into 13-inch circle between two sheets of waxed paper. Peel top piece. Carefully invert dough over pie plate leaving overhang. Remove waxed paper.

Combine apples with remaining ingredients. Arrange filling evenly in pie plate, being careful not to mound. Roll out the remaining dough using waxed paper. Place dough over apples leaving an overhang. Trim both crusts to ½-inch overhang, fold to top of pie, and flute.

Bake at 450 degrees for 10 minutes. Lower heat to 350 degrees, and bake 30 minutes. Remove pie from oven when crust is brown. When syrup stops bubbling, 30 seconds to 1 minute, place serving plate over pie and invert. Very carefully remove pie plate.

Chocolate Pecan Pie

½ cup butter	1 teaspoon vanilla
1 cup sugar	1 cup pecans, chopped
1 cup light corn syrup	6 ounces chocolate chips
4 eggs, slightly beaten	1 9-inch pastry shell, unbaked

Melt butter, and combine with remaining ingredients. Mix well. Pour filling into pie shell. Bake in 350 degree oven for 45 to 50 minutes. May serve warm or chilled. Refrigerate any leftovers.

My Mama's Pecan Pie

½ cup sugar
2 tablespoons butter
2 eggs, beaten
¼ teaspoon salt
1 cup light corn syrup
2 tablespoons flour

1 teaspoon vanilla
1 cup pecans, chopped
1 9-inch pie shell, unbaked
Sweetened whipped cream
(optional)

Cream sugar and butter. Add remaining ingredients, and blend well. Pour into pie shell, and bake at 350 degrees for 45 minutes. Serve warm or cool; may top with sweetened whipped cream.

Chocolate Mousse Pie

Meringue Crust:
1 cup sugar
4 egg whites

¼ teaspoon cream of tartar

Combine sugar and cream of tartar. Beat egg whites until stiff. Add sugar and cream of tartar to egg whites, and beat until stiff, glossy peaks form. Spread 1-inch thick in a well-greased 9-inch pie plate. Bake in 275 degree oven 1 hour or until light brown and crisp. Do not over bake.

Filling:
1 cup semisweet chocolate chips
1 egg
2 egg yolks
½ ounce unsweetened chocolate, shaved

2 teaspoons rum
2 egg whites
1¼ cups heavy cream

Melt chocolate chips in top of double boiler. Remove from heat, and beat in whole egg and yolks one at a time. Add rum. Beat egg whites until stiff peaks form. Fold chocolate into egg whites. Fold in 1 cup heavy cream, which has been whipped. Spoon into crust and refrigerate 12 to 24 hours.

Before serving, whip remaining ¼ cup heavy cream. Spread over pie, and garnish with chocolate shavings.

Chocolate Silk Pie

1 9-inch graham cracker crust, baked
¾ cup butter
1 cup sugar
1 pint whipping cream
3 ounces unsweetened baking chocolate, melted
2 teaspoons vanilla
3 eggs

Cream butter and sugar until smooth. Add melted chocolate squares and mix well. Add vanilla and continue to mix until light and airy. Using an electric mixer on medium speed, add eggs one at a time. Beat 2 minutes after each addition. Pour into baked pie shell, and chill for 2 hours. Whip cream, and spread over pie immediately before serving.

Chocolate Chess Pie

2 eggs
1 cup white sugar
½ cup margarine
1 9- or 10-inch unbaked pie shell
3 ounces semisweet chocolate squares
1 teaspoon vanilla

Preheat oven to 325 degrees. Beat eggs and sugar together. Add vanilla. Using double boiler, melt chocolate and margarine together. Remove from heat, and combine chocolate mixture with eggs and sugar. Pour into pie shell. Bake at 325 degrees for 30 minutes or until firm.

Chocolate Peanut Butter Pie

Crust:

½ cup graham cracker crumbs
6 tablespoons butter, melted

½ cup sugar
1–2 teaspoons cinnamon

Combine all ingredients, and press into a 9-inch pie plate. Chill approximately 1 hour.

Filling:

½ gallon chocolate ice cream,
  softened

6 ounces peanut butter
½ cup peanuts, chopped
  (optional)

Mix softened ice cream with peanut butter, and pour into pie shell. Garnish with chopped peanuts. Place in freezer until ice cream hardens.

Butterscotch Cream Pie

1 pie shell, baked
¾ cup dark brown sugar
¼ cup cornstarch
⅛ teaspoon salt
3 cups milk

3 egg yolks
1½ tablespoons butter
1 teaspoon vanilla
3 egg whites
⅜ teaspoon cream of tartar

¼ cup plus 2 tablespoons sugar

Combine brown sugar, cornstarch, and salt in heavy saucepan. Blend in milk and egg yolks. Gradually stir in sugar. Cook over medium heat, stirring constantly until mixture boils. Boil for 1 minute. Stir in butter and vanilla. Immediately pour into baked pie shell, and cover with waxed paper. Beat egg whites and cream of tartar on high speed for 1 minute. Gradually add sugar, and beat until stiff. Remove waxed paper. Spread egg whites over hot filling to edge of pastry. Bake at 350 degrees for 12 to 15 minutes. Cool and serve.

Lemon Chess Pie

1 9-inch pie shell, unbaked
1½ cups sugar
⅓ cup butter, melted

Juice of 3 lemons
Zest of 3 lemons
5 eggs, slightly beaten

Preheat oven to 425 degrees. Thoroughly mix all ingredients, and pour into pie shell. Bake at 425 degrees for 5 minutes. Reduce oven temperature to 325 degrees, and bake for 35 to 40 minutes or until filling is golden brown and set. Remove from oven and cool. Filling will set more as it cools. Refrigerate any leftovers.

Sherried Pumpkin Chiffon Pie

1 9-inch pie crust, baked
3 eggs, separated
1 cup pumpkin, cooked and
  strained, or canned
½ cup cream sherry
1 cup sugar

¼ teaspoon salt
¼ teaspoon cinnamon
¼ teaspoon nutmeg
¼ teaspoon ginger
1 envelope plain gelatin
¼ cup cold water

Whipped cream

Beat egg yolks slightly in top of double boiler. Stir in pumpkin, sherry, ½ cup sugar, salt, and spices. Cook, stirring constantly, for 5 minutes. Remove from heat.

Soften gelatin in cold water, and add to pumpkin. Stir until dissolved. Beat egg whites until stiff. When pumpkin mixture begins to thicken, fold in egg whites. Add the remaining sugar and mix. Pour into baked pie shell. Chill several hours, and serve topped with whipped cream.

Lemon Sponge Pie

2 tablespoons flour
1½ tablespoons butter, softened
1 cup sugar
1 cup milk

1 lemon, juice and zest
2 eggs, separated
¹⁄₁₆ teaspoon salt
1 deep dish pie crust, unbaked

Cream flour and butter in electric mixer. Add sugar, milk, juice and zest of lemon, well-beaten egg yolks, and salt. Beat egg whites until stiff. Fold the egg whites into lemon mixture, and pour into pie plate lined with unbaked pastry. Bake in preheated oven at 425 degrees for 10 minutes. Reduce the heat to 350 degrees, and bake for 30 to 45 minutes. Pie is done when knife blade inserted in center comes out clean.

Raspberry Paradise Pie

Crust:
3 egg whites
¼ teaspoon baking powder
¼ teaspoon salt
¼ teaspoon cream of tartar

1 cup sugar
¾ cup rolled oats
½ cup walnuts, finely chopped
½ teaspoon vanilla

Preheat oven to 325 degrees. Beat egg whites with baking powder, salt, and cream of tartar until almost stiff. Gradually add sugar, and beat until very stiff. Combine rolled oats and walnuts, and fold into egg whites. Fold in vanilla. Spoon into an 8- or 9-inch pie plate, and bake 25 minutes. Remove from oven and cool.

Filling:
10 ounces frozen raspberries, thawed
1 tablespoon cornstarch
½ pint whipping cream
¾ cup shredded coconut

Drain raspberries, and place juice in small saucepan over medium heat. Gradually blend in cornstarch. Cook, stirring constantly, until smooth and sauce thickens. Cool and add raspberries. Spoon mixture into pie shell. Whip cream until stiff, and spoon over raspberry filling. Garnish with coconut. Refrigerate pie several hours before serving.

Coffee-Raspberry Ice Cream Pie

⅓ cup melted butter
¼ cup sugar
⅛ teaspoon nutmeg or
   cinnamon

1½ cups chocolate wafer crumbs
1 quart coffee ice cream
1 pint raspberry sherbet
1 pint whipping cream

Chocolate curls for garnish

Mix melted butter, sugar, nutmeg or cinnamon, and chocolate wafer crumbs. Press into 9-inch pie pan. Bake 10 minutes at 350 degrees. Cool crust. Soften ice cream and sherbet. Spread layer of coffee ice cream in crust, then layer of raspberry sherbet, then another layer of coffee ice cream. Top with whipped cream and garnish with chocolate curls.

Ozark Pie

¾ cup sugar
1 teaspoon vanilla
1 egg, well beaten
3 tablespoons flour
¼ teaspoon baking powder

½ teaspoon salt
½ cup nuts, chopped
½ cup apples, finely chopped
1 quart ice cream
1 Heath Bar

Whipped cream, optional

Mix sugar, vanilla, egg, flour, baking powder, and salt. Add nuts and apples. Stir and pour into buttered 9-inch pie pan. Bake at 325 degrees for 25 to 30 minutes. Cool. Press to make rim to hold ice cream. Fill with ice cream of choice. Top with grated candy bar. Decorate with peaks of whipped cream if desired. Freeze. Place pan on hot towel 5 minutes before serving to facilitate cutting.

Fruit 'n Ice Cream Pie

Crust:

1½ cups graham cracker crumbs ⅓ cup butter, melted

3 tablespoons sugar

Combine all ingredients and mix well. Press into a 9-inch pie plate, and bake at 350 degrees for 8 to 10 minutes. Remove from oven and cool for 30 minutes.

Filling:

1 kiwi	¼ cup Grand Marnier
¼ cup strawberries	1 tablespoon sugar
¼ cup blueberries	1 quart vanilla ice cream, softened

Wash, peel, and thinly slice kiwi, yielding 8 to 10 slices. Clean strawberries and slice lengthwise in halves or quarters. In a bowl toss all fruit with Grand Marnier and sugar.

Spread ice cream in prepared crust, and arrange fruit over ice cream. Place pie in freezer until serving time.

Cakes

The Booming Port

By the mid-1800's, Baltimore was bustling with world trade, and at the turn of the century, it was an active point of immigration. During World War II shipbuilding was a major activity of the port.

Today, the Port of Baltimore is the second largest container port on the East Coast, moving nearly 60 million tons of cargo every year. Major imports include raw sugar, cars, furniture, and wines; major exports include grain, coal, and industrialized manufactured products—26 million tons of cargo crossing its docks each year. The port of Baltimore is closer to the industrial midwest than any East Coast seaport, a valuable advantage to shippers and manufacturers. Every year more than 4,000 ships voyage between Baltimore and 300 ports of call in 125 far-off lands. The Port of Baltimore is truly the economic heart of Maryland, pumping a supply of raw materials and manufactured items to and from factories, merchants, and consumers.

Almond Cake

3 eggs
1 cup sugar
1 cup cake flour, sifted
1 cup melted butter
1 tablespoon milk

½ cup slivered almonds
½ cup sugar
½ cup butter
1 tablespoon all-purpose flour

Combine eggs with 1 cup sugar and beat until frothy. Add cake flour and melted butter. Pour into greased 9- by 13-inch pan and bake at 350 degrees for 20 minutes. Combine remaining ingredients in sauce pan and heat until melted. Pour the sauce ingredients over the warm cake, and place under broiler until top is a light golden brown.

Apple Nut Cake

Cake:
1½ cups vegetable oil
1 cup sugar
1 cup brown sugar
3 eggs
3 cups flour
¾ cup flaked coconut

1 teaspoon baking soda
1 teaspoon salt
3 cups apples, pared and diced
1 cup walnuts
2 teaspoons vanilla

Preheat oven to 350 degrees. Cream oil and sugars. Add eggs one at a time, beating well after each addition. Sift dry ingredients, and add to apples and nuts; then add all to oil mixture. Add vanilla. Stir in coconut. Bake in a large tube pan, lined with waxed paper, which has been greased on both sides. Bake 1½ hours at 350 degrees. Do not open door during baking. Cool and remove waxed paper before spreading icing on cake.

Icing:
4 tablespoons margarine
2 tablespoons evaporated milk

½ cup dark brown sugar
½ teaspoon vanilla

Combine all ingredients in a saucepan over low heat. Stir until well blended and sugar dissolves. Boil approximately 3 minutes. Cool before spreading on cake.

Sugar Top Apple Cake

1 cup margarine	½ teaspoon salt
2 cups sugar	1 teaspoon cinnamon
3 eggs	¼ teaspoon mace
3 cups flour, sifted	2 teaspoons vanilla
1½ tablespoons baking soda	3 cups chopped apples

2 cups chopped walnuts

Cream margarine and sugar until fluffy. Add eggs one at a time, beating well after each addition. Sift together flour, baking soda, salt, cinnamon, and mace. Gradually add to egg mixture. Stir in vanilla, apples, and walnuts. This batter should be stiff. Spoon into greased and floured 10-inch tube pan, and bake at 325 degrees for 1½ hours. Let cool 10 minutes before removing from pan.

Carrot Cake

Cake:

3 eggs	2 cups carrots, grated
2 cups sugar	1½ cups pecans or walnuts,
1½ cups oil	chopped
3 cups flour	8 ounces crushed pineapple
½ teaspoon salt	with juice
2 teaspoons baking soda	½ cup flaked coconut
1 teaspoon cinnamon	2 teaspoons vanilla

Beat eggs slightly, and blend with sugar and oil. Gradually add flour, salt, soda, and cinnamon. Add carrots, nuts, pineapple, coconut, vanilla, and mix well. Bake in a greased and floured tube pan at 350 degrees for 1 hour or until done. Cool, remove from pan, and frost.

Icing:

8 ounces cream cheese, softened	1 teaspoon vanilla
4 ounces butter, softened	2½ cups confectioners' sugar

Blend cream cheese and butter until smooth. Add vanilla. Gradually add confectioners' sugar, blending until frosting is thick enough to spread over cake. Garnish cake with pineapple or some grated carrot.

Coconut Cream Cake

Cake:

3 cups sugar	¾ cup butter
6 eggs	1½ cups milk
3 cups flour	1½ teaspoons vanilla
¾ teaspoon salt	1½ teaspoons baking powder

Cream sugar and eggs until light. Gradually add flour and salt. Melt butter in milk, and add to cake mixture. Beat until smooth. Blend in vanilla and baking powder. The batter should be thin. Pour into a greased and floured 10-inch tube pan. Bake 1 hour at 350 degrees.

Icing:

8 tablespoons margarine	3 tablespoons flour
1 cup sugar	⅔ cup milk
½ cup shortening	1 teaspoon vanilla

1 7-ounce package coconut

Combine all ingredients except coconut in saucepan. Cook over medium heat until thick. Chill frosting until thick enough to spread. Spread over cooled cake. Pat coconut on top and sides of cake. Refrigerate several hours before serving to allow coconut flavor to blend.

Note: Garnish cake with fresh flowers and tinted coconut on top. To tint coconut, put ½ cup coconut in plastic bag with 1 drop food coloring and 1 teaspoon water. Shake bag.

Cranberry Swirl Cake

¼ pound butter or margarine, softened	2 cups flour, sifted
1 cup sugar	½ teaspoon salt
2 eggs	1 cup sour cream
1 teaspoon baking powder	1 teaspoon almond extract
1 teaspoon baking soda	1 7-ounce can whole cranberry sauce

1 cup chopped walnuts

Combine butter and sugar. Add eggs, one at a time. Using mixer at medium speed, add dry ingredients alternately with sour cream, ending with dry ingredients. Add almond extract. Grease and flour a tube pan. Place a layer of batter in bottom of pan, swirl around, add cranberry sauce in spoonfuls, add more batter. Layer several times, ending with batter on top. Sprinkle with chopped nuts. Bake at 350 degrees for 50 to 55 minutes. Cool cake and glaze if desired.

Glaze:

½ cup confectioners' sugar	1 tablespoon warm water

½ teaspoon almond extract

Orange-Zucchini Cake

1 cup butter, softened	4 eggs
2 tablespoons grated orange rind	3 cups flour, sifted
1¼ teaspoons cinnamon	3 teaspoons baking powder
½ teaspoon nutmeg	½ teaspoon salt
¼ teaspoon ground cloves	⅓ cup orange juice
2 cups brown sugar, firmly packed	1 cup shredded zucchini

Grease and flour a 10-inch tube pan. Cream together butter, orange rind, cinnamon, nutmeg, cloves, and brown sugar until fluffy. Add eggs one at a time, and beat well after each addition. Sift together dry ingredients. Blend into creamed mixture alternately with the orange juice. Stir in zucchini. Pour batter into tube pan. Bake 55 minutes in 350 degree oven. Cool for 10 minutes in pan before removing to wire rack.

Pumpkin Roll

Cake:

3 eggs
1 cup sugar
⅔ cup solid pack pumpkin
1 teaspoon lemon juice
¾ cup flour

1 teaspoon baking powder
2 teaspoons cinnamon
1 teaspoon ginger
½ teaspoon nutmeg
½ teaspoon salt

1 cup walnuts, finely chopped

Beat eggs on high speed for 5 minutes. Gradually add sugar. Stop beaters, and stir in pumpkin and lemon juice. Set aside. Stir together dry ingredients, except nuts. Fold dry mixture into pumpkin. Spread in jelly roll pan, which has been lined with waxed paper on bottom and then greased. Top with walnuts. Bake at 375 degrees for 15 minutes.

Filling:

6 ounces cream cheese
4 tablespoons butter

1 cup confectioners' sugar
½ teaspoon vanilla

To prepare filling, combine confectioners' sugar, softened cheese, butter, and vanilla. Turn cake out onto tea towel sprinkled with powdered sugar. Roll cake up with waxed paper, and leave 20 minutes. Unroll, remove wax paper, and roll again to allow the cake to cool. When cool, unroll, and spread filling on side of cake without nuts. Roll back up and chill. Sprinkle with powdered sugar.

Rhubarb Cake

1¼ cups brown sugar
¼ cup sugar
½ cup shortening
1 egg
1 teaspoon vanilla
1 teaspoon baking powder

1 teaspoon baking soda
2 cups sifted flour
1 cup buttermilk
1½ cups chopped rhubarb
¼ cup sugar
1 teaspoon cinnamon

Whipped cream

Cream sugars with shortening until light. Add egg and vanilla, and mix thoroughly. In separate bowl combine baking powder, baking soda, and flour. Blend buttermilk and dry ingredients alternately into creamed mixture until batter is smooth. Fold chopped rhubarb into batter.

Pour batter into a greased 9- by 13-inch pan. Mix sugar with cinnamon and sprinkle over batter. Bake in 350 degree oven for 30 to 40 minutes. Serve with whipped cream.

Real Lane Cake

Cake:

6 egg whites
2 cups sugar, divided
3 cups flour
1 cup milk

1 cup butter
1 tablespoon baking powder
1 teaspoon salt
1 teaspoon vanilla

Preheat oven to 375 degrees. Generously grease and flour two 9-inch cake pans. Beat egg whites until soft peaks form. Slowly add 1 cup sugar, and continue beating until stiff peaks form. Combine remaining cake ingredients, including 1 cup sugar, in a large mixing bowl. Beat on medium speed for 4 minutes. Fold in egg whites. Pour batter into prepared pans, and bake 35 minutes. Remove from oven; cool. Cut each layer in half horizontally.

Filling:

⅓ cup bourbon
¾ cup white raisins, chopped
1 cup candied cherries, chopped

8 egg yolks
1¼ cups sugar
8 tablespoons butter
4 ounces coconut

1 cup pecans

Soak cherries and raisins in bourbon overnight. In top of double boiler combine yolks, sugar, and butter. Stir over medium heat about 5 minutes or until thick. Add soaked fruit, coconut, and pecans. Spread filling between layers.

Frosting:

1 tablespoon maple or corn syrup
1⅓ cups sugar

⅓ cup water
½ teaspoon salt
2 egg whites

1 teaspoon vanilla

In saucepan over medium heat, combine corn syrup, sugar, water, and salt. Boil until soft ball stage, 240 degrees. Remove from heat, and let cool. Beat egg whites until soft peaks form; then slowly pour syrup over the egg whites beating constantly. Add vanilla and beat. Spread frosting over top and sides of cake.

Note: This can be made partially ahead of time. Soak fruit and prepare layers the day before making the filling and frosting.

Strawberry Shortcake

1¼ cups cake flour, sifted	1 cup egg whites (7 or 8)
1½ cups sugar	1 teaspoon cream of tartar
¼ cup egg yolks (6)	1 teaspoon salt
¼ cup water	1 pint whipping cream
1 tablespoon lemon juice	2 tablespoons sugar
1 teaspoon vanilla	2 teaspoons vanilla

1 quart strawberries, cleaned and hulled

Mix together flour and ¾ cup sugar. Add egg yolks, water, lemon juice and vanilla. Beat until smooth. In a large bowl beat egg whites, cream of tartar, and salt until foamy. Gradually add ¾ cup sugar to egg white mixture until meringue is firm and stands in peaks. Pour batter over meringue and fold gently just until blended. Line a 9- by 13-inch sheet cake pan with waxed paper. Gently spoon batter into prepared pan and bake at 350 degrees for 30 to 35 minutes until top springs back when touched. When cake is cool, remove from pan, and cut into two 9- by 6½-inch rectangles. Whip cream, sugar, and vanilla until stiff peaks form. Arrange half of strawberries on the cake. Spread remaining cream on top and sides of cake. Decorate with remaining berries.

Premier Pound Cake

2 cups sugar	3 cups cake flour, sifted
1 teaspoon vanilla	3 teaspoons baking powder
1 cup cooking oil	¼ teaspoon mace
4 eggs, separated	½ teaspoon salt

1 cup milk

Cream together sugar, vanilla, oil, and egg yolks. Beat well. Sift together cake flour, baking powder, mace, and salt. Add to mixture alternately with milk. Beat egg whites until stiff. Gently fold egg whites into batter. Pour into a large greased tube pan. Bake for 45 minutes to 1 hour at 350 degrees. Serve unfrosted. Serve with fresh fruit and ice cream. It can be frozen.

Pineapple-Banana Pound Cake

Cake:

3 cups all-purpose flour
2 cups sugar
1 teaspoon baking soda
1 teaspoon salt
1 teaspoon cinnamon

1 cup almonds, chopped
3 eggs, beaten
1½ cups vegetable oil
1 teaspoon almond extract
2 cups bananas, chopped

1 8-ounce can crushed pineapple, undrained

Mix flour, sugar, baking soda, salt, and cinnamon together in a large bowl. Stir in almonds. Combine beaten eggs, vegetable oil, and almond extract with chopped bananas and undrained pineapple in small mixing bowl. Add to dry ingredients, mix thoroughly by hand. Pour into greased 10-inch tube pan, and bake in preheated 325 degree oven for 1 hour and 20 to 25 minutes. After baking let cake cool 10 to 15 minutes on wire rack before removing from pan.

Icing:

8 ounces cream cheese, room temperature
½ cup butter or margarine, room temperature

1 teaspoon vanilla
1 box confectioners' sugar

Beat together cream cheese and butter until smooth. Add vanilla and then gradually add powdered sugar. Spread over cake after it has completely cooled. Store cake in refrigerator.

Oatmeal Chocolate Chip Cake

1¾ cups boiling water	1¾ cups flour
1 cup rolled oats	½ teaspoon salt
1 cup brown sugar	1 teaspoon baking soda
1 cup sugar	1 tablespoon cocoa powder
½ cup margarine	12 ounces chocolate chips
2 large eggs	¾ cup nuts, chopped

Pour boiling water over rolled oats, and let stand for 10 minutes. Add sugars, margarine, and stir. Add eggs and beat well. Blend in flour, salt, soda, and cocoa. Add 6 ounces of the chocolate chips. Pour the batter into a greased and floured 9- by 13-inch pan. Sprinkle the nuts and remaining chocolate chips over the top. Bake at 350 degrees for 35 to 40 minutes. Slice into small squares to serve.

Banana-Chocolate Chip Cake

8 tablespoons butter, softened	1 cup bananas, mashed (2
1¼ cups sugar	large bananas)
2 eggs, beaten slightly	1½ cups all-purpose flour
1 teaspoon baking soda	¼ teaspoon salt
¼ cup sour cream	6 ounces chocolate chips
1 teaspoon vanilla	Confectioners' sugar

Grease and flour a 9- or 10-inch tube pan or 2 loaf pans. Preheat oven to 350 degrees. In mixing bowl, cream butter and sugar together. Add eggs. Stir baking soda into sour cream, and add to butter mixture. Beat well. Stir in vanilla and mashed bananas. Add flour and salt. Mix well. Stir in chocolate chips, and turn batter into prepared pan. Bake for 50 to 60 minutes, or until cake tests done. Remove from pan, and sprinkle with confectioners' sugar.

Chocolate Midnight Cake

Cake:

1 cup butter	¾ cup cocoa powder
2½ cups sugar	2 teaspoons baking powder
3 eggs	2 teaspoons baking soda
3 cups flour	2 cups hot water

1 teaspoon vanilla

Cream butter and sugar until light and fluffy. Add eggs, one at a time, beating well after each addition. Sift dry ingredients together. Gradually add dry ingredients to butter mixture alternately with the hot water. Add vanilla and mix very well. Pour batter into two 8- or 9-inch pans. Bake at 350 degrees for 30 minutes.

Frosting:

1½ cups sugar	1 cup boiling water
3 tablespoons cornstarch	1 teaspoon vanilla
2 ounces unsweetened chocolate squares	Small piece of butter

Mix sugar and cornstarch well. Add chocolate squares. Add boiling water over medium heat. Boil mixture until thick, approximately 20 minutes. Add vanilla and butter. Stir well. Frost cooled cake.

Chocolate Irish Mist Cake

Cake:

2 eggs, slightly beaten
½ cup oil
2 cups sifted flour
2 cups sugar
2 teaspoons baking soda

1 cup cocoa powder
1 teaspoon baking powder
¾ cup milk
¼ cup Irish Mist liqueur
½ cup hot coffee

1½ teaspoons vanilla

Combine eggs and oil in a large bowl. Sift together flour, sugar, baking soda, cocoa, and baking powder. Add to eggs and mix well. Stir in milk and liqueur. Add hot coffee and vanilla. Blend well. Pour cake mixture into greased tube pan. Bake in 350 degree oven for about 40 minutes. Cool, remove from pan, and frost.

Frosting:

8 ounces cream cheese,
   softened
½ cup coffee, cooled
¾ cup brown sugar

2 tablespoons Irish Mist liqueur
1 cup heavy cream
¼ teaspoon salt
½ cup sugar

3 tablespoons chocolate, grated

Beat cream cheese until soft. Add coffee a little at a time. On low speed blend in brown sugar and liqueur. In a separate bowl beat cream until soft peaks form. Slowly add salt and sugar. Whip until stiff. Add this mixture to cream cheese mixture, and blend well. Frost cake and garnish with grated chocolate. The icing is thin, but firms in refrigerator.

Broiled Coconut Chocolate Cake

Cake:
2 cups sugar
½ cup vegetable oil
2 eggs
2 tablespoons cocoa powder

¼ teaspoon salt
2 cups flour
½ cup buttermilk
1 cup boiling water
1 teaspoon baking soda

Combine sugar and oil until fully mixed. Add eggs, cocoa, salt, flour, buttermilk, and mix well. Beat in boiling water mixed with baking soda. The batter will be thin. Pour into a greased 9- by 13-inch pan. Bake at 350 degrees for 35 to 45 minutes.

Icing:
6 tablespoons margarine,
  softened
¾ cup coconut

½ cup evaporated milk
1 cup brown sugar, packed
1 cup nuts, chopped

Combine all ingredients, and mix well. Spread over cooled cake. Broil iced cake until the icing is bubbly and slightly brown.

Sinful Chocolate Creole Cake

Cake:

8 tablespoons butter
½ cup salad oil
3 ounces unsweetened
chocolate squares
2 cups flour
1 teaspoon baking soda

2 cups sugar
2 eggs, beaten
½ cup sour milk (place 1½
teaspoons vinegar in
measuring cup, and fill to ½
cup with milk)

1 teaspoon vanilla extract

Combine butter, oil, and chocolate in saucepan over low heat. Stir until chocolate melts, and add 1 cup water. Cool. Sift together flour and baking soda. Add sugar, eggs, sour milk, and vanilla. Mix well. Blend in cooled chocolate mixture. Bake in two greased and floured 8-inch square pans at 350 degrees for 30 to 35 minutes. Cool 5 minutes before removing from pans.

Filling:

1 5-ounce can evaporated milk
¾ cup sugar
¼ cup raisins, chopped

½ cup dates, chopped
1 teaspoon vanilla extract
½ cup pecans, chopped

½ cup heavy cream, chilled and whipped

In saucepan combine milk, sugar, and ½ cup water. Stir over medium heat to dissolve sugar. Add raisins and dates. Cook 5 minutes, stirring until mixture thickens. Add vanilla and nuts. Cool completely, or sauce will run off layers. Spread filling over one layer. Then spread whipped cream over filling. Put second layer on top.

Frosting:

6 ounces semisweet chocolate
chips

½ cup sour cream
Dash of salt

Melt chocolate in top of double boiler. Remove from heat, and stir in sour cream and salt. Beat until smooth. Cool 5 minutes, or until frosting is spreading consistency. Frost top and sides of cake. Refrigerate 1 hour before serving.

Chocolate Pound Cake for Trifle

2 ounces unsweetened chocolate squares	5 eggs
1 cup butter or margarine	⅛ teaspoon salt
1⅔ cups sugar	1½ cups flour
	1 teaspoon vanilla

Melt chocolate in top of double boiler. Cream melted chocolate, butter, and sugar together. Beat in eggs, one at a time. Fold in salt, flour, and vanilla. Bake 1½ hours at 300 degrees in lightly greased loaf pan.

Chocolate Trifle

Chocolate pound cake (see recipe above)	12 ounce jar cherry jam or preserves
4–6 ounces whiskey, liqueur, or rum	1 package vanilla pudding or egg custard mix
1 pint whipping cream	

Make chocolate pound cake. Cool, slice in ½-inch slices. Lay slices in shallow pan, and sprinkle with liqueur. Let stand overnight. Next day, spread slices with cherry jam. Using milk, make pudding according to package directions. Spoon pudding over slices. Just before serving, top with whipped cream, and put in individual serving dishes or arrange in layers in glass bowl.

Serves 10 to 15

Cookies & Candy

All Aboard!

Railroading in America began in Baltimore. America's first railroad, the Baltimore and Ohio, began with the laying of its first stone on July 4, 1828, and reached the Ohio River by 1853. A group of 25 local merchants turned to the railroad idea because they were fearful their city was losing its lucrative trade with the pioneer settlements west of the Allegheny Mountains, and they wanted to remain competitive with New York, Philadelphia, and Washington, all of which were building canals to the Midwestern territories.

In 1830, Peter Cooper built the Tom Thumb, America's first steam locomotive. Although it lost its famous race with a horse due to a slipped fan belt, the locomotive was still cheaper to run than the horse, thereby opening up a new era in transportation.

Currently, on the site of the B & O's birthplace is the Mount Clare Station, the country's first railroad station, housing the nation's largest exhibit of historic railroad memorabilia.

Mina's Almond Crescents

1 cup butter
½ cup sugar
2 cups flour

1 cup almonds, finely chopped
1 cup confectioners' sugar
½ teaspoon vanilla

Cream butter. Add granulated sugar. Blend in flour gradually, then stir in almonds. Form dough into crescent shapes, and bake at 350 degrees for 10 to 12 minutes, or until cookies are just barely starting to brown. Let set for 2 or 3 minutes after removing from oven to harden. Combine confectioners' sugar and vanilla. Gently roll cookies in the flavored confectioners' sugar.

Note: These can be frozen. If you handle them when they first come from the oven, they will break.

Yield: 5 to 6 dozen

Coconut Almond Macaroons

8 ounces almond paste
1 cup, less 1 tablespoon, sugar

3 egg whites
⅓ cup confectioners' sugar
1⅓ cups flaked coconut

Preheat oven to 350 degrees. Crumble almond paste into bowl. Add sugar and mix with fingers. Beat in egg whites until well blended. Stir in confectioners' sugar, and then fold in coconut.

Line cookie sheet with brown paper. Drop cookie mix by rounded teaspoonfuls onto brown paper. Bake for about 12 to 15 minutes or until golden. Remove from oven. Slide paper onto a damp cloth, and let stand 1 or 2 minutes or until cookies can be removed easily from paper.

Yield: 4 dozen

Chocolate Snowballs

2 cups sifted flour
½ teaspoon salt
¾ cup sweet butter, softened
½ cup sugar
2 teaspoons vanilla

1 egg
1 cup walnuts or pecans, chopped
6 ounces semisweet chocolate chips
Confectioners' sugar

Preheat oven to 350 degrees. Sift together flour and salt. Blend and beat together butter, sugar, and vanilla. Add egg, and stir in flour mixture, nuts, and chocolate chips. Shape into 1-inch balls, and bake on ungreased cookie sheet for 15 to 20 minutes. While snowballs are still warm, roll in confectioners' sugar.

Yield: 6 dozen

Chocolate Cracked-Tops

4 ounces unsweetened chocolate
2½ cups sifted flour
2 teaspoons baking powder
½ teaspoon salt

½ cup vegetable oil
2 cups sugar
4 eggs
2 teaspoons vanilla
1 cup confectioners' sugar

Melt chocolate in top of double boiler. Sift together flour, baking powder, and salt. In a large bowl, combine oil, chocolate, and sugar. Add eggs one at a time, beating well after each addition. Add vanilla. Add dry ingredients and blend well. Chill several hours or overnight. Lightly grease cookie sheets. Drop by rounded teaspoonfuls into cup of confectioners' sugar, and roll around to shape into balls. Place 2 inches apart on cookie sheets. Bake at 350 degrees for 10 to 12 minutes.

Yield: 6 dozen

Chocolate Madeleines

2 eggs, separated
½ cup sugar
½ cup Dutch cocoa powder
½ cup sifted all-purpose flour

1 teaspoon baking powder
Pinch salt
4 ounces sweet butter, softened
1 teaspoon vanilla

Preheat oven to 425 degrees. Beat egg yolks, sugar, and cocoa powder together. Fold in flour, baking powder, and salt. Add butter and vanilla extract. Beat egg whites until stiff and fold into batter. Brush madeleine molds with butter. Fill each ⅔ full. Bake 10 to 15 minutes until risen and firm. You may find your oven's temperature will dictate a baking time of only 5 to 8 minutes.

Reprinted with permission from Williams-Sonoma.

Yield: 22 to 24

Halloween Monster Cookies

3 eggs
1 teaspoon vanilla
1 teaspoon light corn syrup
2 teaspoons baking soda
½ cup butter
12 ounce jar creamy peanut
butter

4½ cups uncooked rolled oats
1 cup brown sugar
1 cup sugar
¼ pound miniature chocolate
chips (optional)
¼ pound raisins (optional)
Nuts (optional)

"M&M's" Plain Chocolate Candies°

Preheat oven to 350 degrees. Combine all ingredients except "M&M's" in a large mixing bowl. Using an ice cream scoop, put 6 balls of dough on an ungreased cookie sheet. Flatten slightly. Bake 15 minutes. Do not over-bake. If desired, create monster faces with candies as soon as cookies are removed from oven. Children love these very chewy cookies all year!

Yield: 24 large cookies

° *"M&M's" is a registered trademark of Mars, Incorporated.*

Williamsburg Gingersnaps

¾ cup butter
1 cup sugar
¼ cup molasses
1 egg, beaten
2 cups flour
¼ teaspoon salt

2 teaspoons baking soda
1 teaspoon ginger
1 teaspoon cinnamon
1 teaspoon ground cloves
1 teaspoon nutmeg
1 cup raisins, preferably golden

½ cup sugar, for coating

Cream butter and sugar. Add molasses and egg. Beat well. Sift dry ingredients. Add to butter mixture and mix well. Add raisins if desired. Roll in small balls. Put ¼ to ½ cup sugar in small paper bag. Drop in 2 to 4 balls of dough, and shake to coat the balls. Place 2 inches apart on greased cookie sheet. Bake at 350 degrees for approximately 10 minutes.

Yield: 4 dozen

Lace Cookies

2¼ cups rolled oats
3 tablespoons flour
2¼ cups light brown sugar
1 teaspoon salt

1 cup butter or margarine,
  melted
1 egg, slightly beaten
1 teaspoon vanilla

Preheat oven to 375 degrees. Mix rolled oats, flour, sugar, and salt. Stir in butter, egg, and vanilla. Cover cookie sheets with heavy duty foil and drop dough 2 inches apart by half teaspoonfuls onto sheets. Bake 6 minutes or until light brown. Let cool completely on racks and cookies slip off foil. Watch carefully as these burn easily.

Yield: 12 dozen

Mocha Balls

12 ounces semisweet chocolate chips	4 egg yolks
2 rounded teaspoons instant coffee	1½ cups powdered sugar
4 tablespoons brandy	1 cup butter, softened
	2 teaspoons vanilla
	2 cups pecans, finely chopped

Melt and slightly cool chocolate chips. Dilute instant coffee in the brandy. Beat egg yolks, and mix all ingredients. Chill. Shape into balls; then roll in nuts. Must be kept refrigerated.

Yield: 2 to 3 dozen

Mandel Bread

¾ cup sugar	2 eggs
¾ cup oil	2 cups flour
1½ teaspoons vanilla	1½ teaspoons baking powder
¾ cup walnuts, chopped	¾ teaspoon salt
Cinnamon sugar	

Preheat oven to 350 degrees. Mix sugar, oil, and vanilla in bowl. Add the remaining ingredients except the cinnamon sugar, and stir well. Divide dough in half. Shape into 2 long bars on cookie sheet. Sprinkle with cinnamon sugar. Bake 25 minutes. Remove from oven and cut into ½-inch slices immediately. Place each piece on its side. Bake 5 more minutes.

Note: This recipe doubles easily.

Yield: 2 to 3 dozen

Pizzelles

3 eggs, beaten well	1 teaspoon baking powder
¾ cup sugar	2 teaspoons vanilla
¾ cup butter or margarine, melted	1 teaspoon anise extract or anise oil
1½ cups sifted flour	

Beat together ingredients in order listed. Drop by rounded spoonfuls, approximately the size of a large walnut, onto the center of a preheated grid of a pizzelle iron. Close the lid, clip handles together. Allow to cook 30 to 60 seconds. Cool on racks. Sprinkle with confectioners' sugar when cooled. Store in cookie tins in dry place.

Note: These cookies are very light and airy, and look like snowflakes after the sugar has been sprinkled on them.

Yield: 3 dozen

Sugar-Rolled Kolacky

5 cups flour	Granulated sugar
2 yeast cakes	Powdered sugar
1 pound margarine	Pineapple preserves or favorite
4 egg yolks	nut filling
½ pint sour cream	

Sift flour and crumble yeast cakes into flour. Cut in margarine until very fine crumbs are formed. Add yolks and sour cream. Mix together until flour is mixed in and a solid ball is formed. Dough should leave sides of bowl. Separate into 5 balls, and chill for at least 2 hours before using.

When ready, sprinkle granulated sugar thinly onto pastry board. Take each ball and roll it out until paper thin, but not thin enough to tear when handling. Cut into 2-inch squares. Fill each square with 1 teaspoon nut filling or pineapple preserves. Fold over the sides lengthwise, and press the ends together with a fork to seal. Bake in 350 degree oven for 15 minutes or until golden brown. These burn easily. Sprinkle with powdered sugar while still warm.

Yield: 3 dozen

Kieflies (A Hungarian Cookie)

Dough:

6 cups flour
1½ teaspoons salt
1 pound butter

12 egg yolks, whites reserved
1 cup sour cream
1 teaspoon vanilla

Mix flour and salt together. Cut butter into flour mixture until completely blended. In a separate bowl, mix egg yolks, sour cream, and vanilla. Add to flour-butter mixture. Blend and knead until it is the consistency of pie dough. Form into 1-inch balls. Refrigerate at least four hours or overnight.

Filling:

1½ cups egg whites (about 8 large)
¼ teaspoon cream of tartar

4 cups confectioners' sugar
½ teaspoon lemon juice
2 pounds walnuts, finely chopped

Beat egg whites and cream of tartar until stiff. Add sugar and beat well. Stir in lemon juice and nuts. Refrigerate overnight or until dough has chilled.

Preheat oven to 350 degrees. To assemble, roll each ball into a thin, 3-inch circle on well-floured surface. Place a heaping teaspoon of filling on each circle. Roll up, shape like a crescent, and pinch ends. Bake on a lightly greased cookie sheet for 12 minutes. Cool slightly and sprinkle with confectioners' sugar.

Yield: 10 to 12 dozen

Scottish Shortbread

1 cup butter, softened
¾ cup confectioners' sugar

1½ cups sifted flour
¼ teaspoon salt

Preheat oven to 325 degrees. In a large mixing bowl, cream butter and sugar together. Sift flour with salt, and add slowly to the butter mixture. Mix and knead well until ingredients take on a putty consistency. Press firmly into a 9-inch glass pie plate, being sure dough fits into every part of the plate. Bake 30 to 40 minutes or until lightly browned.

Note: This is rich, buttery, and sweet, and is good served with morning coffee or with fresh fruit as a dessert.

Serves 6 to 8

Caramel Ice Box Cookies

1 cup butter
2 cups brown sugar
2 eggs, beaten
3½ cups flour

Dash salt
1 teaspoon cream of tartar
1 teaspoon baking soda
1 teaspoon vanilla

Pecan halves

Mix all ingredients thoroughly. Shape into rolls about 1 inch in diameter. Wrap in waxed paper. Place in freezer until firm but not frozen. Preheat oven to 350 degrees. Slice ¼-inch thick; decorate with pecan halves if desired. Bake on ungreased cookie sheet for 4 to 5 minutes for chewy cookies or 7 minutes for crisp cookies. May be frozen.

Yield: varies with diameter of roll

Date Swirl Cookies

Dough:

1 cup margarine	¼ teaspoon almond extract
2 cups light brown sugar, packed	3½ cups flour
	½ teaspoon baking powder
2 eggs	½ teaspoon salt
½ teaspoon baking soda	

Mix margarine, sugar, eggs, and almond extract in large bowl. Combine dry ingredients, and add to margarine mixture. Divide into thirds, wrap each in waxed paper, and chill at least 2 hours.

Filling:

8 ounces pitted dates, chopped	¼ cup sugar
1 cup water	⅛ teaspoon cinnamon
1 cup finely ground walnuts	

Cook dates, water, and sugar to boiling. Reduce heat and cook until thick, about 10 to 12 minutes. Remove from heat, and add cinnamon and nuts. Keep at room temperature. Working with a third of the dough at a time, roll out between two sheets of waxed paper into 12- by 18-inch rectangles. Dough will be very thin.

Remove top sheet of waxed paper. Spread evenly with ⅓ of the date nut filling. This will also be thin. Lift 12-inch edge to roll dough; pick up bottom of waxed paper, and draw it along parallel to counter to make a neat roll. Repeat with the remaining dough and filling. Wrap roll and chill for at least 3 hours.

Cut into ¼-inch slices, and place 1 inch apart on greased cookie sheets. Bake at 350 degrees for 10 to 12 minutes. Remove from cookie sheets and cool before storing.

Yield: 8 dozen

Fruitcake Cookies

2½ cups sifted all-purpose flour
¼ teaspoon cream of tartar
1 cup butter
1 cup confectioners' sugar
1½ cups pecan halves

1 egg
1¼ cups candied pineapple, coarsely chopped
1¼ cups candied cherries, whole

Sift together flour and cream of tartar. Set aside. Cream the butter in a large bowl. Add sugar and mix well. Add egg and beat well. On low speed add the dry ingredients gradually. Beat only until ingredients are mixed. Add the fruits and nuts, and mix with a large wooden spoon. Shape dough on waxed paper into 2 rolls 2 inches in diameter and 9 inches long. Wrap each roll in paper and freeze on a cookie sheet overnight.

Preheat oven to 375 degrees. Lightly grease cookie sheet or line with parchment paper. Place cookies on cookie sheets ½ inch apart. Bake 12 to 14 minutes, or until edges and bottoms are golden. Transfer cookies to cooling racks. Cool before storing, and put waxed paper between layers to prevent sticking.

Yield: 6 dozen

Humdingers a la Hall

½ cup butter
1 cup sugar
8 ounces chopped dates
Confectioners' sugar

1 teaspoon vanilla
1½ cups crisped rice cereal
1 cup pecans, chopped

In 2-quart saucepan, melt butter, and add sugar and dates. Cook for 5 minutes. Add remaining ingredients, except confectioners' sugar. Press ¼-inch thick onto a cookie sheet. Chill 10 to 15 minutes. Cut into bars and dust with confectioners' sugar.

Yield: 30 cookies

Melt-In-Your-Mouth Yummmmms

½ cup margarine
5 tablespoons cocoa powder
¼ cup sugar
1 teaspoon vanilla
1 egg
2 cups graham cracker crumbs
½ cup coconut
½ cup walnuts, chopped

¼ cup margarine, softened
3 tablespoons milk
2 tablespoons instant vanilla
  pudding mix
2 cups confectioners' sugar
3 1-ounce squares semisweet
  chocolate
3 tablespoons margarine

Combine ½ cup margarine, cocoa, sugar, vanilla, and egg in 2-quart saucepan. Boil over medium heat, stirring constantly for 2 minutes. Add graham cracker crumbs, coconut, and nuts. Spread in ungreased 9- by 13-inch pan. Pat down flat. Chill. Combine ¼ cup margarine, milk, pudding mix, and sugar. Spread on bottom layer. Cover with waxed paper, and rub to make it smooth. Chill.

Melt chocolate and margarine over hot water. Spread on top of white layer. Chill. Cut into 1-inch squares and store in airtight container in refrigerator. Serve at room temperature for best flavor, but if you are craving chocolate, they are great cold. These freeze well.

Yield: 100 squares

Toffee Bars

1 cup butter
1 cup brown sugar, packed
1 egg yolk

1 cup flour
6 milk chocolate bars, 1.45
  ounces each

⅔ cup crushed nuts

Preheat oven to 350 degrees. Cream butter, brown sugar, and egg yolk. Add flour gradually, stirring until well blended. Spread dough on lightly greased jelly roll pan. Bake until medium brown, about 15 to 25 minutes. Remove from oven and lay chocolate bars on top. Spread when melted, and sprinkle with nuts. Cut into squares, then place pan in freezer for easy removal of cookies. Serve frozen, cold, or at room temperature.

Yield: 3 dozen

Lemon Pecan Squares

6 tablespoons butter
⅓ cup light brown sugar
1 cup plus 3 tablespoons flour, divided
½ cup pecans, finely crushed

2 eggs
1 cup sugar
2 tablespoons fresh lemon juice
2 teaspoons lemon rind, grated
½ teaspoon baking powder
Confectioners' sugar

Preheat oven to 350 degrees. Cut butter into bits. Blend with brown sugar, 1 cup flour, and nuts until coarse. Put all except ½ cup into bottom of a 9-inch square pan, and press down. Bake at 350 degrees for 15 to 20 minutes.

Beat eggs and stir in sugar, 3 tablespoons flour, lemon juice, grated rind, and baking powder. Pour over baked crust. Sprinkle top with rest of crumb mixture. Bake for 25 to 30 minutes. Cool and cut into squares. Sift confectioners' sugar over top.

Yield: 1 dozen

Raspberry Ripples

Dough:
2 cups flour
½ cup sugar

⅛ teaspoon salt
1 cup sweet butter
1 egg yolk, beaten

Combine flour, sugar, and salt in large bowl. Cut in butter. Add beaten egg yolk, and form dough into a ball. Divide dough into thirds. Make three 12- by 1-inch strips on cookie sheets. With a wooden spoon, make a slight depression lengthwise in the center of each strip.

Filling:
½ cup seedless raspberry jam
¼ cup sliced almonds
½ teaspoon vanilla

Preheat oven to 350 degrees. Combine filling ingredients in a small bowl. Spoon filling into depression. If depression is too deep, cookies will crumble when cut. Chill at least 30 minutes. Bake 20 to 25 minutes. Cool completely; then cut into 1-inch diagonal slices. Can be frozen.

Yield: 3 dozen

Orange-Coconut Bars

Crust:

½ cup butter, softened   1 cup sifted flour

Preheat oven to 350 degrees. Thoroughly blend butter and flour. Press firmly into greased 9-inch square pan. Bake 20 minutes.

Filling:

1½ cups light brown sugar   2 eggs, slightly beaten
2 tablespoons flour   1½ teaspoons vanilla
¼ teaspoon baking powder   1 cup walnuts, chopped
½ teaspoon salt   ½ cup coconut

Combine brown sugar, flour, baking powder, and salt. Mix well. Add remaining ingredients and blend. Spread evenly over baked crust. Return to oven for 25 minutes. Cool.

Frosting:

1½ cups confectioners' sugar   2 tablespoons frozen orange
2 tablespoons butter, melted   juice concentrate
             2 teaspoons lemon juice

Combine frosting ingredients until smooth. Spread on cooled filling. Cut into small bars.

Note: To curb sweetness, you may want to halve frosting.

Yield: 16 bars

Peanut Butter Bars

Base:

½ cup butter or margarine
½ cup sugar
½ cup brown sugar
1 egg
⅓ cup chunky peanut butter

½ teaspoon baking soda
¼ teaspoon salt
½ teaspoon vanilla
1 cup flour
1 cup rolled oats

Preheat oven to 350 degrees. Mix all above ingredients and spread in ungreased 9- by 13-inch pan. Bake for 20 to 25 minutes until lightly browned.

Topping:

6 ounces semisweet chocolate chips
½ cup confectioners' sugar

¼ cup chunky peanut butter
4 tablespoons milk
Chopped peanuts

Immediately sprinkle chocolate chips over base and allow to melt. Spread evenly over top. Mix confectioners' sugar, peanut butter, and milk; and drizzle over chocolate. Garnish with chopped peanuts. Cool and cut into small bars.

Yield: 2 dozen

Chocolate Pecan Pie Bars

1⅓ cups all-purpose flour
2 tablespoons brown sugar
½ cup butter, softened
½ cup brown sugar
2 eggs
½ cup dark corn syrup

2 tablespoons butter, melted
⅛ teaspoon salt
¾ cup pecans
6 ounces semisweet chocolate chips
4 ounces golden raisins

Combine flour and 2 tablespoons brown sugar. Cut in butter until mixture has the texture of corn meal. Press into 9-inch square pan. Bake at 350 degrees for 15 to 17 minutes. Combine remaining ingredients, and pour over baked crust. Bake at 350 degrees for 25 minutes. Let cool several hours or overnight before cutting into bars.

Yield: 2 dozen

Williamsburg Pecan Bars

Crust:

¾ cup butter
¾ cup sugar
2 eggs
Zest of 1 lemon, about 2 teaspoons
3 cups flour
½ teaspoon baking powder

Preheat oven to 375 degrees. Grease and flour two 9-inch square pans. Cream butter and sugar. Add eggs and lemon zest. Beat well. Sift dry ingredients and add to creamed mixture. Beat well. Chill until firm. Press dough ⅛-inch thick into bottom and halfway up sides of pan. Prick with fork. Bake 12 to 15 minutes or until very lightly browned. Remove from oven and spread with filling.

Filling:

1 cup butter
1 cup light brown sugar, firmly packed
1 cup honey
¼ cup heavy cream
3 cups pecans, chopped

Boil butter, sugar, and honey in a heavy 3-quart saucepan for 5 minutes. Cool slightly. Add cream and pecans. Mix well. Pour into center of partially baked dough and spread toward edges. Return to oven. Bake 30 to 35 minutes. Filling will be bubbly but will set while cooling. Cut into bars when completely cool.

Yield: 50 bars

Brownies Amaretto

8 ounces unsweetened chocolate	1 tablespoon vanilla
1 cup butter or margarine	1–1½ teaspoons almond extract
5 eggs	2 teaspoons cinnamon
3 cups sugar	1½ cups unsifted flour

2 cups walnuts, chopped

Preheat oven to 375 degrees. Melt chocolate and butter in saucepan over low heat, stirring constantly. In a large bowl, beat eggs, sugar, vanilla, cinnamon, and almond extract on high speed about 10 minutes. Blend in chocolate mixture on low speed. Add flour, beating just enough to blend. Stir in nuts. Spread in greased 9- by 13-inch pan. Bake for 35 to 40 minutes. Do not overbake.

Yield: 24 brownies

Brownies au Chambord

1 cup sugar	2 cups confectioners' sugar
1 cup flour	½ cup margarine, softened
½ cup margarine or butter	4 tablespoons Chambord
4 eggs	liqueur
16 ounce can chocolate syrup	1 cup semisweet chocolate chips
½ teaspoon baking soda	6 tablespoons butter
¼ teaspoon baking powder	Red food coloring (pleasing pink)

Preheat oven to 350 degrees. Grease and flour 9- by 13-inch pan. Mix first seven ingredients in a bowl until smooth. Pour in pan and bake for 25 minutes. Let cool. Mix confectioners' sugar, margarine, and liqueur until smooth. Spread on top of brownies and chill until set. Melt chocolate chips and butter over low heat. Remove from heat. When it is cool, but spreadable, spread a thin layer on top of liqueur mixture. Chill until firm. Slice into squares.

Note: Any liqueur whose flavor complements chocolate can be used in the frosting layer. Try mint, orange, or strawberry.

Yield: 12 to 16 brownies

Grandma Beeman's Brownies

4½ ounces unsweetened
   chocolate
1 cup butter
4 eggs
2 cups sugar

2 tablespoons instant coffee
1 teaspoon vanilla
1 scant cup flour
1 cup semisweet chocolate chips
1 cup walnuts (optional)

Preheat oven to 350 degrees. Melt chocolate squares in top of double boiler and set aside. In separate pan, melt butter and pour into a large bowl. Combine butter, eggs, sugar, instant coffee, and vanilla, and beat until thoroughly blended. Add melted chocolate. Fold in flour.

Pour batter into a greased 9- by 13-inch pan. Top with chocolate bits and walnuts. Bake for 30 minutes. For chewier brownies, underbake slightly. These are very rich. Cut into small pieces!

Yield: 32 brownies

Cocoa-Caramel Brownies

14 ounces light caramels
⅔ cup evaporated milk, divided
   Chocolate cake mix
1 cup semisweet chocolate chips

¾ cup butter, melted
1 cup pecans or walnuts,
   chopped

Melt caramels and ⅓ cup evaporated milk in the top of a double boiler. Keep warm. Combine cake mix, butter, and remaining ⅓ cup evaporated milk. Mix thoroughly; mixture will be crumbly. Press half the dough into bottom of a greased 9- by 13-inch pan. Bake at 350 degrees for 6 minutes. Remove from oven and cool slightly. Sprinkle nuts then chocolate chips over baked dough.

Working quickly, spread caramel mixture on top. Finely crumble remaining dough over caramel mixture and press lightly with a spoon. Bake at 350 degrees for 14 to 18 minutes or until mixture pulls away from sides of pan. Cool 60 minutes. In warm weather, refrigerate until set. Cut into small squares.

Yield: 24 brownies

All-Natural Fudge

1 cup honey
1 cup peanut butter
1 cup carob powder
½ cup raisins or dates

1 cup sesame seeds
1 cup sunflower seeds
½ cup coconut

Blend honey and peanut butter together in mixing bowl. Quickly add carob powder and blend. Add remaining ingredients. Pour into a greased 8- by 8-inch pan. Refrigerate to harden.

Yield: 40 squares

Walnut Fudge

2 4-ounce bars German sweet chocolate
2 ounces unsweetened chocolate squares
12 ounce bag semisweet chocolate chips

7 ounce jar marshmallow fluff
1 can sweetened condensed milk
1 teaspoon vanilla extract
2 cups walnut pieces

Melt German chocolate, cooking chocolate, and semisweet chocolate chips in top of a double boiler or in the microwave. Stir to combine; then mix in marshmallow fluff and sweetened condensed milk. Blend in vanilla extract and walnuts. Spread in a greased 9- by 13-inch dish, and refrigerate until firm. Cut when solidified. Keep refrigerated.

Yield: 32 squares

Almond Truffles

3 tablespoons butter, softened	1 egg yolk, slightly beaten
½ cup powdered sugar, sifted	2 tablespoons white creme de
6 squares semisweet chocolate,	cacao
finely grated	24 whole almonds

½ cup almonds, finely chopped

Cream butter in large mixing bowl. Gradually add sugar, beating well. Add grated chocolate, egg yolk, and creme de cacao. Beat until blended. Chill one hour. Meanwhile, toast almonds. Shape dough into 1-inch balls, and insert one whole almond in each. Roll in finely chopped almonds. Cover and refrigerate overnight before serving. Store in refrigerator.

Yield: 2 dozen

Easter Eggs (Two Variations)

Butter Cream Easter Eggs:	Coconut Cream Easter Eggs:
½ pound butter	1 quart fresh coconut
2 pounds confectioners' sugar	2 pounds confectioners' sugar
2 tablespoons vanilla	1 teaspoon vanilla
2 tablespoons cream	

1 pound semisweet or unsweetened chocolate, for coating

Combine all ingredients, except chocolate, for either variation in food processor bowl, and mix with steel blade until well mixed. Shape with hands into egg-sized ovals. Melt chocolate over very low heat in small pan or the top of a double boiler. Keep chocolate warm enough to stay melted. Dip eggs in chocolate. Place on waxed paper to dry. Should be kept cool or refrigerated.

Note: Dipping eggs is easier when handled with toothpicks. Turn around in chocolate using toothpick in egg.

Yield: 20 to 25 eggs

Chocolate Turtles

14 ounce package caramels   2 cups pecan pieces
3-4 tablespoons milk   Butter or margarine
    12-ounce package semisweet chocolate chips

In saucepan, melt caramels in milk over low heat. Add pecans. Drop by teaspoonfuls onto generously buttered waxed paper or aluminum foil. Chill for 1 hour. Melt chocolate in top of double boiler. Dip candy into warm chocolate, and return to waxed paper. Refrigerate.

Choco-Peanut Butter Balls

8 tablespoons butter   4 cups crispy rice cereal,
1 pound smooth peanut butter   crushed
1 box powdered sugar   12 ounces chocolate chips
1 teaspoon vanilla   ⅓ bar paraffin (optional)
    100 paper bonbon cups

Melt butter in saucepan or microwave. Mix with peanut butter, powdered sugar, vanilla, and cereal. Make little balls, and place on large sheet pan, being careful that they do not touch. Wrap pan with plastic wrap. Place in refrigerator for at least 4 hours.

After 4 hours has passed, remove peanut butter mixture from refrigerator; melt chocolate chips and optional paraffin in top of a double boiler. Dip 3 balls at a time in chocolate-paraffin mixture. Place each ball in paper bonbon cup. After cooled, put in airtight containers, and store in cool place. Do not refrigerate.

Yield: 100 balls

Ye Old Kentucky Bourbon Balls

1⅓ 16-ounce boxes confectioners' sugar	5 tablespoons bourbon
½ cup butter, no substitutes	5 ounces unsweetened chocolate squares
1 cup pecans, chopped	1 heaping tablespoon paraffin wax

Soften butter at room temperature and cream with sugar in mixing bowl. The mixture will be stiff. Add pecans and bourbon. Form into walnut-sized balls and refrigerate overnight.

Melt chocolate and paraffin in a double boiler. Keeping chocolate mixture over hot water, dip the chilled balls quickly, coating thoroughly. Dip quickly so sugar won't melt, but do not immerse. Place dipped balls on waxed paper on cookie sheets. When all balls are dipped, place cookie sheets in refrigerator. When thoroughly chilled and chocolate is firm, put balls in covered tin, and store in refrigerator. Will keep for weeks if well sealed with thin coat of chocolate.

Note: The best way to dip the refrigerated balls is to put ball on spoon and drip chocolate over it with another spoon. These make a delicious gift at holiday time.

Yield: approximately 4 dozen

English Toffee

1 cup pecans, chopped	2 cups sugar
2 cups butter	6 chocolate candy bars

Cover the bottom of a 9- by 13-inch baking pan with pecans. In a saucepan, melt butter and sugar together. Bring to a boil. Cook stirring constantly for 8 to 9 minutes until color turns from yellow to light brown. Pour over pecans in pan. Break chocolate bars into pieces and lay over top of mixture. Let stand 5 minutes, then spread chocolate over entire surface. Cool; break into pieces.

Glazed Pecans

1 cup pecans
½ cup granulated sugar

2 tablespoons butter
½ teaspoon vanilla

1–2 teaspoons salt

Stir pecans, granulated sugar, and butter in medium saucepan over medium heat until glaze will coat a wooden spoon. Have ready a large sheet of foil sprayed with vegetable oil spray. Add vanilla to cooking mixture. Stir constantly. Pour onto foil, spread, and separate very quickly. Sprinkle with salt. Allow to cool. Store in airtight container.

Yield: 1 cup

Glazed Nuts

¾ cup margarine
3 egg whites
1½ cups granulated sugar

2 12-ounce cans mixed salted nuts

Preheat oven to 325 degrees. Grease edged cookie sheet, and place in oven until butter is melted. Beat egg whites until stiff peaks form. Add sugar, then add nuts. Mix thoroughly. Spread on cookie sheet. Bake for 30 minutes, turning every 10 minutes. Remove from oven. Spread on cloth towel. Dry. Store in glass jar or tin.

Yield: 3 cups

Chocolate Leaves

Leaves   Milk chocolate pieces (optional)
Semisweet chocolate squares

Use leaves from non-poisonous plants such as roses or geraniums. Wash and pat dry with paper towels. Melt semisweet chocolate squares in top of double boiler. Add milk chocolate pieces if desired. Using a narrow spatula or knife, spread melted chocolate on veined side of each leaf until ⅛-inch thick. Do not let any chocolate spill to other side of leaf. Wipe edges with fingertip. Place on flat pan or tray. Chill until firm. Carefully peel off leaves starting at stem end to decorate cakes or other desserts.

Chocolate Strawberries

½ pound sweet, semisweet, or   12–16 strawberries at room
   bittersweet chocolate   temperature, wiped clean

Line the bottom of a tray with waxed paper or aluminum foil. Coarsely chop the chocolate, and place it in top of a small double boiler over warm water on low heat. Cover until the chocolate is partially melted. Then uncover and stir until the chocolate is all melted and very smooth. If melted chocolate is too thick, add 2 scant tablespoons vegetable shortening, not butter or margarine. This will thin the chocolate and also make it glossy.

Make sure the berries are very dry. Hold each one by the hull and dip it to about three-quarters of its length (leaving some red showing at the top). Wipe off excess chocolate on the rim of the pan. Place dipped berry on its side on the lined tray. If chocolate begins to thicken, replace it over warm water.

Place the tray of dipped berries in the refrigerator only until the chocolate is firm, no longer. Then gently lift the berries off the waxed paper by the hull. Do not refrigerate again. Serve at room temperature within 24 hours.

Note: Try dipping orange or tangerine sections, making sure membranes are intact. Or place toothpicks in 1-inch pieces of banana or seedless green grapes and dip.

Pickles & Relishes

The Hometeam

Any sports enthusiast can find a team to cheer for in the greater Baltimore area. The Baltimore Orioles have become a permanent fixture in professional baseball by consistently winning divisional and national pennants. The Blast continues to draw soccer fans to sell-out games from surrounding cities and suburbs. The Baltimore Skipjacks play a tough game of ice hockey at the Civic Center to partisan crowds. The Stars, professional football's newest addition to Baltimore, bring a championship record to uphold. There are several club lacrosse teams in the area, as well as semiprofessional teams in other sports. There are almost as many types of sports as there are players in Baltimore from youth teams to the professional teams, all with a winning spirit!

Jerusalem Artichoke Pickle

½ peck Jerusalem artichoke
  roots
6 whole sweet red peppers (or
  bottled peppers with juice)
2 quarts vinegar
2 pounds sugar
2 tablespoons dry mustard

2 tablespoons turmeric
2 tablespoons mustard seed
1 teaspoon celery seed
6 sticks cinnamon
4–6 onions, sliced
Salt to taste
Garlic cloves

Wash artichokes with steel brush and soak in cold water overnight. Drain well. Combine the red peppers, vinegar, sugar, dry mustard, turmeric, mustard seed, celery seed, and cinnamon. This makes the mustard dressing. Bring to a boil, add the onions, and boil for 15 minutes. Add salt to taste. Sterilize jars. Cut artichokes into bite-sized pieces. Pack artichokes into jars, and pour hot mustard dressing over the artichokes, insert one clove of garlic in each jar and seal immediately.

Pregnant Pickles

2 cups onions, sliced
2 cups cucumbers, sliced
1 cup sugar
1 cup vinegar

1 tablespoon salt
½ teaspoon dry mustard
⅓ teaspoon celery seed
⅓ teaspoon turmeric

If cucumbers have been waxed, peel before slicing. Fill half a 1-quart jar with sliced onions and half with sliced cucumbers. Combine remaining ingredients. Pour over cucumbers and onions, and cap jar. Refrigerate. Shake jar occasionally. Let stand a few days before serving. These keep indefinitely in refrigerator.

Yield: 1 quart

Betty McKimmon's Squash Pickles

4 quarts yellow squash, thinly
   sliced
4 quarts white onions, thinly
   sliced
½ cup salt

3 cups white vinegar
3 cups sugar
1½ teaspoons turmeric
1 teaspoon celery seed
1 teaspoon mustard seed

Mix squash, onions, and pour salt over; then cover with cracked ice or ice cubes. Let stand at room temperature for 3 hours. Drain and rinse with cold water.

To make pickling juice, combine remaining ingredients. Bring to a boil. Drop in squash and onion. Bring to boiling point, but do not boil. Pack in hot, sterilized jars, and seal.

Yield: 8 pints

Sliced Green Tomato Pickle

1 peck very green tomatoes (16
   pounds)
8 onions, sliced
½ cup salt
1 pint cider vinegar
1 pint water

2 teaspoons whole cloves
2 teaspoons cinnamon pieces
2 teaspoons whole allspice
1½ quarts cider vinegar
2 pounds brown sugar
2 pounds white sugar

Salt tomatoes and onions very well, and let stand overnight. Drain thoroughly, but do not rinse. Add 1 pint vinegar and water, and boil for 5 minutes. Drain again. Tie 1 teaspoon each cloves, cinnamon, and allspice in cheesecloth to make 2 bags. Add 1½ quarts vinegar, the sugars, and spices to tomatoes. Cook until tomatoes are tender. While cooking, sterilize jars. Ladle cooked tomato pickle into hot jars and seal immediately.

Yield: 10 pints

Hot Pepper Jelly

6 large bell peppers	6 cups sugar
3 large Cayenne or other hot peppers	3–4 dashes hot pepper sauce
	Red or green food coloring
1½ cups vinegar	6 ounces liquid fruit pectin

Purée peppers and place in large pot. Add vinegar, sugar, and bring to rolling boil. Allow to boil 5 to 10 minutes. Add hot sauce to taste and red or green food coloring. Add liquid fruit pectin, and boil exactly 1 minute. Pour into hot sterile jars, and seal with paraffin. Serve with cream cheese and crackers or as an accompaniment to roast beef.

Note: May need to skim boiled mixture if it is foamy on surface. Use red and green bell peppers for color, and omit food coloring if desired. Do not double recipe, but it may be halved.

Yield: 10 8-ounce jars

Rhubarb Conserve

1 quart rhubarb (32 ounces frozen rhubarb)	1 pint dried currants
2 lemons	1 pound raisins, ground
2 oranges	4 pounds sugar
1 pint fresh red raspberries (or frozen raspberries in light syrup)	1 pound walnuts, ground into 3½ cups

Cut rhubarb in small pieces. Slice lemons and oranges very thin, removing seeds. Mix in raspberries, currants, and raisins. Weigh fruit, and add an equal amount of sugar. Cook until as thick as jam. Add nuts. Pour into hot sterilized jars, and seal with paraffin.

Yield: 7 pints

Chunky Tomato Relish

2½ pounds tomatoes, seeded	⅔ cup sugar
1 medium onion, cut up	½ cup white vinegar
1 medium sweet red pepper, chopped	1 teaspoon celery seed
	1 teaspoon paprika
1 small clove garlic	⅛ teaspoon pepper
⅛ teaspoon allspice	

Put tomatoes in blender and process until chunky. Place in saucepan, reserving ½ cup. Purée reserved chunks with onion, pepper, and garlic. Add to saucepan with remaining ingredients. Cook 1 hour and 15 minutes to thicken, or cook until desired consistency. Store in refrigerator for 1 month, freeze, or process for canning.

Note: Sweet, low-sodium relish. Good with grilled meats and sandwiches.

Yield: 2 cups

Coolidge Tomato Marmalade

4 quarts tomatoes (about 8 pounds)	7 sticks cinnamon
3 oranges	1 heaping tablespoon whole cloves
2–3 lemons	5 pounds sugar (approximately)

Peel and dice tomatoes. Cut the oranges and lemons into fine strips. Place cinnamon and cloves in cheese cloth and tie. Pour off most of the juice from the sliced tomatoes, and weigh them. Place in pot, and add strips of orange and lemon and seasonings. Add sugar equal to the weight of the tomatoes. Cook over high heat until rapidly boiling; then reduce to medium heat, and cook approximately 2 hours. Test for doneness by putting a teaspoon of marmalade in a saucer. When the surface crinkles, it is ready. While marmalade is cooking, sterilize jars. When marmalade is done, ladle into hot jars and seal immediately.

Note: This is President Calvin Coolidge's recipe.

Yield: 6 to 8 ½-pint jars

Pepper Relish

12 green peppers
12 red peppers
7 medium onions

2 tablespoons salt
2 tablespoons mustard seed
3 cups vinegar

3 cups sugar

Coarsely grind peppers and onions, saving liquid. Combine liquid, peppers, onions, and remaining ingredients in large pot. Simmer uncovered for 30 minutes. Ladle into sterilized jars and seal.

Yield: 8 to 10 pints

Marguerite McKee's Green Tomato Relish

6 green tomatoes, peeled
4 onions
2 green peppers
3 cups brown sugar

3 cups vinegar
1 ounce mustard seed
¼–½ cup salt
1 cup seedless raisins

6 sour apples

Grind tomatoes, onions, and peppers. Add other ingredients except apples. Add the raisins if desired, and simmer for 1 hour. Peel, core, and finely chop apples. Add to tomato mixture, and cook until tender. While cooking, sterilize jars. When relish is done, ladle into hot jars and seal immediately.

Yield: 6 pints

Celebrities

The Star Spangled Banner

Sitting in a corner of a rowhouse in Baltimore's Old Town, Mary Pickersgill sewed the massive 30 by 42 foot Star Spangled Banner by hand. This most famous of all American flags is the one that was "still there" over the ramparts of Fort McHenry in the dawn of September 14, 1814, during the War of 1812. A lawyer named Francis Scott Key was so moved by the sight of the flag still flying after the intensive 25-hour bombardment of Baltimore by the British that he penned the emotional words that became our national anthem.

Bittersweet Chocolate Bourbon Cake

1 cup seedless raisins	¾ cup butter, room temperature
¾ cup bourbon	6 egg yolks
1 cup sugar	1 cup almonds, blanched and
¼ cup water	ground
10 ounces unsweetened	½ cup flour
chocolate	6 egg whites

Soak raisins in bourbon. In a saucepan bring sugar and water to a boil. Add chocolate. Remove from heat and stir until chocolate melts; cool. Cream softened butter; then add egg yolks one at a time. On low speed add half the chocolate mixture and half the almonds. Repeat. Blend in bourbon, raisins, and flour. Beat egg whites until stiff and fold them into batter.

Pour batter into greased 9-inch fluted or plain tube pan lined with waxed paper and greased on sides. Bake for 30 minutes in 375 degree oven. Ice with your favorite milk or sweet chocolate frosting.

Sylvia H. Badger
Columnist for the NEWS-AMERICAN

My Father-In-Law's Barbecue Sauce

1 onion, finely chopped	Cayenne pepper
2 cloves garlic, minced	2 bay leaves
½ cup butter	⅔ bottle (10-ounce)
Salt	Worcestershire sauce
Pepper	Juice of 2 lemons

In an ovenproof skillet, sauté the onion and garlic in 4 tablespoons butter until soft. Add remaining butter, salt, pepper, and Cayenne to taste. Add the bay leaves. Bring the mixture just to a boil. Remove skillet from heat and add Worcestershire sauce and lemon juice. Put pan of sauce on grill to keep warm as you cook fish, chicken, or beef, basting the meats with the sauce often. Serve any remaining sauce as a gravy.

Note: You may also use your oven or broiler to cook the meats. Keep the sauce warm on very low heat on your range.

Vince Bagli
Sports Director, WBAL-TV

Apple Cake

5 tablespoons sugar	1 cup vegetable oil
2 teaspoons cinnamon	4 eggs, beaten lightly
4 medium apples, pared and	⅓ cup orange juice
sliced	1½ teaspoons vanilla
3 cups flour	3 teaspoons baking powder
2¼ cups sugar	¼ teaspoon salt

Confectioners' sugar

Mix sugar and cinnamon with apples and set aside. In a large bowl, combine the remaining ingredients. Place half the cake mixture in a greased and floured fluted tube pan. Spoon the apple mixture over batter, and pour in remaining batter. Bake at 325 degrees for 1 hour and 15 minutes. Remove cake from oven, cool, and remove from pan. Dust with confectioners' sugar before serving.

The Honorable Benjamin L. Cardin
Speaker, Maryland House of Delegates

Oven French Toast

2–3 eggs, beaten	1 teaspoon vanilla extract
½ pint light cream	4–5 thick slices of dense French
2½ tablespoons Grand	or Italian bread
Marnier, to taste	

Mix the first four ingredients well, and pour the mixture into a shallow baking pan. Poke holes in the bread with fork. Turn the bread several times in the mixture, cover, and refrigerate overnight. Turn occasionally.

Remove bread slices from mixture and butter the pan. Return the bread slices to the pan and broil until golden brown, turning once.

Yield: 5 slices

Dr. Milton Eisenhower
President Emeritus, Johns Hopkins University

Winter Soup

3 onions, chopped	1 cup carrots, diced
2 tablespoons butter	1 cup celery, diced
1 pound lean ground beef	1 cup potatoes, diced
1 garlic clove, minced	1 cup green beans, diced
3 cups beef stock	1 cup dry red wine
2 16-ounce cans of tomatoes,	2 tablespoons parsley, chopped
undrained and roughly	½ teaspoon basil
chopped	¼ teaspoon thyme

Salt and pepper to taste

In a soup kettle, cook onions in butter until they are tender and golden. Stir in ground beef and garlic and cook, separating the ground beef with a fork until it is brown. Add the beef stock, tomatoes, carrots, celery, pota- toes, green beans, red wine, parsley, and all of the seasonings. Bring to a boil, reduce the heat, and simmer for 1½ hours.

Serves 6 to 8

The Honorable Benjamin R. Civiletti
Former United States Attorney General under President Carter. Presently, a partner with the Baltimore law firm, Venable, Baetjer, Howard and Civiletti

Ave Avocado

3 ripe avocados	Dash of hot pepper sauce
2 10-ounce cans of beef	
consommé	

In a blender, purée avocados, one can of consommé, and hot pepper sauce. Divide mixture equally into 6 individual glass bowls. Chill in refrigerator for 45 minutes. When set, gently spoon contents of remaining can of consommé over mixture in equal amounts. Do not pour to achieve a layered effect. Chill 2 hours before serving.

Serves 6

Sister Kathleen Feeley, S.S.N.D.
President, College of Notre Dame of Maryland

Thornhill Broccoli Soufflé

6 tablespoons butter or margarine	½ teaspoon salt
	¼ teaspoon pepper
6 tablespoons flour	2 cups broccoli cooked, finely
2 cups milk	chopped and well drained
6 large eggs, separated	

Over low heat melt butter in saucepan; stir in flour. Add milk; cook, and stir constantly over moderately low heat until thickened and bubbly. Remove from heat. Gradually and vigorously stir milk mixture into slightly beaten egg yolks. Mix in salt, pepper, and broccoli. Beat egg whites until peaked; fold in broccoli mixture. Turn into ungreased 2-quart soufflé dish. Bake at 325 degrees for 45 minutes.

Note: This soufflé is tested and true and delicious. But like all soufflés, you can't fool around with the cooking time.

Serves 8

Dee Hardie
Contributing Editor for HOUSE BEAUTIFUL, "View from Thornhill Farm"

Government House Crab Dip

4 tablespoons unsalted butter
4 shallots, minced
1 pound crab meat
  Salt
  White pepper
½ tablespoon lemon juice

½ cup Béchamel sauce (see below)
1 teaspoon Worcestershire sauce
½ cup heavy cream
½ tablespoon sherry

½ tablespoon cognac

Melt butter in a medium-sized skillet. Sauté shallots over moderate heat until transparent. Add crab meat, salt, pepper, and lemon juice. Cook until warm. Add Béchamel sauce. Mix thoroughly. Taste for seasoning and add the Worcestershire sauce and heavy cream. Ten minutes before serving, add the sherry and cognac. Taste the dip again for proper seasoning. Serve very warm from a chafing dish with hard crackers. Too much heat will cause the dip to separate.

Béchamel Sauce:
1½ tablespoons unsalted butter
1½ tablespoons flour
½ cup milk

2 tablespoons grated Swiss cheese

Melt the butter in a small saucepan. Add the flour and stir well. Gradually add the milk, stirring constantly. When sauce is thickened, add the grated Swiss cheese.

The Honorable Harry Hughes
Governor, State of Maryland

Canapé Lorenzo

This lavish hors d'oeuvre descends from Lorenzo Delmonico who founded the American restaurant industry before the Civil War. It is an ideal formal appetizer for Maryland dinners or dressy buffet events.

1 pound lump crab meat, picked over
½ pound plus 5 tablespoons butter, at room temperature
4 tablespoons onion, finely diced
1 tablespoon flour
1 pint light cream
pinch of salt

¼ teaspoon Cayenne pepper
¼ teaspoon white pepper
¼ teaspoon nutmeg
1 cup fresh Parmesan cheese, grated
40 2-inch toast rounds or 20 4-inch toast rounds sliced in half
½ teaspoon paprika

Preheat the oven to 400 degrees. Sauté crabmeat in 3 tablespoons butter until lightly browned. Set aside. Sauté chopped onion in 2 tablespoons butter until transparent, but not browned. Add flour to cooked onions and moisten with cream. Add salt, Cayenne, white pepper, and nutmeg. Simmer over very low flame, stirring until thickened. Add mixture to the crab sauté. Work together with fingers the remaining ½ pound of butter and grated Parmesan. Spread the crab mixture on each of the toast rounds, and then spread a dollop of the Parmesan butter over each canapé. Put the assembled canapés on a greased cookie sheet. Dust with a little paprika and lightly brown in oven.

Note: Make half the amount of butter and Parmesan mixture and use less on each canapé to produce a wonderful canapé, which is less rich.

Yield: 30 to 40 pieces

Carleton Jones
Restaurant Reviewer, THE SUN

Corn Bread Pie

1 pound ground beef	¾ teaspoon pepper
1 large onion, chopped	1 tablespoon chili powder
1 can tomato soup	1 cup whole kernel corn,
2 cups water	drained
1 teaspoon salt	½ cup green pepper, chopped

Preheat oven to 350 degrees. Brown beef and onion in skillet. Add soup, water, seasonings, corn, and green pepper. Simmer for 15 minutes. Fill greased pie pan or baking dish three quarters full with this mixture, leaving room for topping.

Topping:

¾ cup corn meal	1½ teaspoons baking powder
1 tablespoon sugar	1 egg, beaten
1 tablespoon flour	½ cup milk
2 tablespoons bacon fat or shortening	

Sift together the corn meal, sugar, flour, and baking powder. Add egg and milk. Stir lightly, and fold in bacon fat. Cover the meat mixture with corn meal topping and bake for 18 to 20 minutes. The corn bread will sink to the bottom and rise again as a crusted topping.

Note: An old Indiana recipe, but served on the diners of the Baltimore & Ohio Railroad a half century ago and more.

Serves 6

Carleton Jones
Restaurant Reviewer, THE SUN

Kahlua Cordial

2 cups water	9 teaspoons instant coffee
2 cups sugar	3 cups 100-proof gin

Bring the water to a boil. Dissolve the sugar and instant coffee in boiling water. Remove the saucepan from heat. Add the gin and refrigerate in a tightly capped bottle. This recipe only works well with 100-proof gin.

Note: Use this cordial to season cakes, pastries, sundae sauces, or ice cream, or serve it as a dinner cordial.

Yield: 1½ quarts

Carleton Jones
Restaurant Reviewer, THE SUN

Mint Julep

For each Julep:	2 teaspoons club soda
6 mint leaves	Crushed ice
2 teaspoons powdered sugar	Bourbon

Late at night plunge a 10-ounce glass or a silver julep cup into a pot filled with ice. Work the glass into the ice until the ice almost touches the top of the glass. Put one glass in the ice for each julep drinker.

Pluck six mint leaves from the top of a sprig of mint and drop them into each glass. Now muddle. Muddling means crushing the mint leaves against the side of the glass with a short, blunt, wooden stick. A wooden spoon may be used. Add the sugar and club soda to the glass; muddle a minute more. Now let the happy liquid sit overnight, in the cooling shed or in the refrigerator.

The next day when the guests arrive, fill each glass with crushed ice. Pour the bourbon to the top of the glass. At the top of glass put a decorative sprig of mint.

Position the straw: This is very important—

Push the straw to the bottom of the glass. This insures that the juleper does not sip straight bourbon. Instead the bourbon flows down over the ice, sugar, and mint and up the straw.

At the top of the glass, place the other end of the straw near the decorative sprig of mint. Snip off the top of the straw so that it barely sticks out over the edge of the glass.

Now gently pull each glass from its ice bath. Ice should stick to the outside of the glass. This makes the drink look inviting and less potent.

Wrap the bottom of the glass in a napkin and serve it.

You can have some reserved mint base made and stored in the refrigerator for brave souls willing to risk another julep. Reserve can be made as follows:

The night before snap off extra mint leaves and put them in that great muddler of the North, the electric blender.

The blender, with the help of a little club soda, chops the mint into a green liquid.

Pour the green liquid into a mixing bowl and add the correct proportions of club soda and powdered sugar (6 mint leaves, 2 tablespoons soda, 2 tablespoons sugar).

The bowl should be refrigerated. To serve, put about 2 ounces of the liquid in a glass, adding crushed ice and bourbon and positioning decorative mint and straw.

Rob Kasper
Columnist for "A La Carte" section, THE SUN

Fourteen Layers Cake

Cake:

12 egg yolks
2 cups sugar

2 teaspoons vanilla
12 egg whites

1½ cups flour

Preheat oven 400 degrees. Beat egg yolks until light in color. Gradually add sugar and beat well. Blend in vanilla. In separate bowl beat egg whites until very stiff but not dry. Generously grease and flour two 8-inch cake pans, preferably those with removable bottom. Spread 1 cup of batter in each pan. Bake for 4 to 5 minutes. Remove from pan and place on waxed paper. Repeat layers in freshly greased and floured pans until you have 14 layers.

Icing:

1 pound semisweet chocolate
¾ cup water

2 cups confectioners' sugar
1 pound sweet butter

Cook first 3 ingredients in double boiler until soft-ball stage. Remove from heat. Add butter. Beat very well. Ice sides and tops, assembling layers.

Andrea Leand
Baltimore's world-ranked tennis professional

Crab Cakes

1 egg, beaten
½ cup mayonnaise
½ teaspoon Worcestershire
  sauce
1 tablespoon parsley flakes
1 teaspoon Old Bay Seasoning

½ teaspoon salt
½ teaspoon ground black pepper
½ teaspoon dry mustard
6 finely crumbled saltines
1 pound crab meat
  Butter

Mix all ingredients except crab and butter. Add crab meat and blend in with a fork. Brown crab cakes in a hot skillet with butter.

Yield: 6 medium crab cakes

The Honorable Barbara A. Mikulski
U.S. House of Representatives 3rd District, Maryland

Maryland Kidney Stew

1 pair beef kidneys	3 tablespoons flour
4 tablespoons butter	2 quarts hot water
1 chopped onion	Salt and pepper

Waffles or hotcakes

Soak kidneys in cold salted water for an hour. Remove gristle and cut meat into small pieces. Place butter in skillet to melt. Add onions and flour and cook, stirring constantly, until golden brown. Add the water and chopped kidneys. Simmer from early morning until evening, allowing two hours to first come to a boil. On the following morning, again bring to a boil, season to taste, and serve over waffles or hotcakes. More water may be required on the first day of cooking if the gravy thickens too much.

Note: For a milder flavor substitute 2 pair veal kidneys for the beef kidneys.

Serves 6

The Honorable Charles McC. Mathias, Jr.
U.S. Senator, Maryland

German Butter Cake

1 pound sweet butter, softened	6 eggs
3 cups sugar	3 cups flour
8 ounces sour cream	¼ teaspoon baking powder

1½ teaspoons vanilla

Cream butter. Add sugar, sour cream, and eggs. Mix well. Add dry ingredients and vanilla. Mix well. Pour into well-greased and floured plain or fluted tube pan. Bake for 1 hour and 20 minutes at 325 degrees or until cake tester inserted in center comes out clean.

Rudy Miller
Anchorperson, WBAL-TV News 11

Rouse Family Rum Punch

1 part sour (lemon or lime juice)	5 parts pineapple juice
2 parts sweet (1½ parts sugar and ½ part grenadine)	8 parts dark rum

Measure all ingredients in ounces or cups. Combine all ingredients and serve over ice. Freezes well.

Jim Rouse
Chairman of the Board and Chief Executive Officer of the Enterprise Foundation and the Enterprise Development Company

Oyster Stew

1 quart oysters	Salt and pepper to taste
2 tablespoons butter	Dash mace
1 quart half-and-half	½ cup celery, finely chopped

Drain oysters thoroughly in colander. Melt butter in large skillet and add oysters. Cook over medium heat until the edges of the oysters begin to curl; do not overcook. Add half-and-half. Bring just to a boil, and remove from heat. Add salt and pepper to taste and a dash or two of mace. Add finely chopped celery and serve.

Serves 4

Jim Rouse
Chairman of the Board and Chief Executive Officer of the Enterprise Foundation and the Enterprise Development Company.

Diamondback Terrapin Soup

Let swim in warm water to clean. Put in boiling water about 5 minutes or until skin looks white and free. Take from water. Pull off skin from feet and exposed body. Pull skin from head and neck. (You may want to do this with a paper towel to prevent burning fingers.)

Return to fresh water. Cook until you can easily squeeze through foot with fingers. Top and bottom shells should part when pulled. If knife is necessary, terrapin is not cooked.

When you take shell off, be sure to dump juice into bowl or pan and reserve. Pick meat from bones. Watch for gallbladder. Cut gall from liver while holding under running water over sink. If gall breaks, water will wash it away. Toss bones into water terrapin was cooked in. Simmer for stock, while picking. Then drain through sieve. Add reserved juice from picking terrapin.

To each quart of meat add 1 quart of stock. Season to taste with Cayenne pepper, black pepper, and salt. Will taste saltier and hotter night before than next day. To serve, add ¼ pound butter to a chafing dish of hot terrapin. Melt and stir butter throughout.

On the subject of sherry: Real terrapin eaters serve terrapin without adding dry sherry. Simply pour dry sherry from glass at table into terrapin as desired. Some, however, prefer to add sherry to taste before serving. Madeira is also a nice wine to serve with terrapin.

Terrapin tips: Don't use hearts or entrails or lungs.
Get rid of all bones.
Get strips of meat on top shell.
Don't be in a hurry. Let terrapin cool before picking meat.

To freeze: Fill up jars with meat. Then add stock. It freezes well.
Take thin skin off eggs. Add to top of meat when freezing.
Take out eggs when meat thaws; hold on side and add when serving, so they don't disintegrate.

Yield: 10 small or 1 large terrapin (8-inch) make 2 quarts soup.

Jim Rouse
Chairman of the Board and Chief Executive Officer of The Enterprise Foundation and The Enterprise Development Company

Mock Terrapin Soup

My mother served this often as a substitute for diamondback terrapin, perhaps Maryland's most elegant dish—served for generations at grand banquets. Always carefully, but quietly, she called it "mock" terrapin. Few could tell the difference. Most people, if they don't know what it is, find it better than terrapin.

When serving you will perhaps want to give your own camouflage name, like "marsh rabbit" because people are turned off by its true name. But in fact, it would be difficult to find an animal better nourished for the table. It is cleansed by the water of the marsh where it lives, eats tender shoots, and is the most tender of meats.

Purchase 4 muskrat at Lexington or Cross Street Market—very inexpensive. Soak muskrat in salted water for several hours or overnight. Discard water. Wash muskrat. Cover and parboil in new salted water for 30 to 40 minutes until tender, depending on size of muskrat. While boiling, melt ¼ pound butter. Add ½ cup flour. Hardboil 6 eggs. Chop yolks fine or push through sieve.

Pick meat off bones, remove any leathery skin-like layer and set aside. Put bones in cooking water. Simmer for stock. Strain. Add chopped yolks to butter and flour. Add 2 cups of stock. Then add stock as necessary for sauce, to thickness of heavy cream. Add meat. Salt and pepper to taste. Add ½ to 1 cup sherry before serving.

Note: This will be a thick meat dish to eat with a fork. More stock makes soup texture like terrapin and many people think it is better than terrapin. So do I. For best flavor, it should be made two days before serving and re-heated. Muskrat is only available from January through mid-March. Can be frozen.

Yield: With sauce, about two quarts

Jim Rouse
Chairman of the Board and Chief Executive Officer of the Enterprise Foundation and the Enterprise Development Company

Chocolate Brownies

½ cup margarine
2 cups sugar
4 eggs
1 cup cake flour, sifted

4 ounces unsweetened
  chocolate, melted
1 teaspoon vanilla
1 cup pecans, chopped

Preheat oven to 325 degrees. Cream margarine and sugar. Add eggs and continue to cream. Slowly add flour while stirring. Blend in melted chocolate and vanilla. Stir in nuts. Bake in greased 9- by 13-inch pan for 30 minutes. Cool for half an hour. Cut into two-inch squares while still warm.

Yield: 20 brownies

The Honorable Stephen H. Sachs
Attorney General, State of Maryland

Al Sanders' Scrumptious Surprise (Individual Cheesecakes)

2 8-ounce packages cream
  cheese, softened
¾ cup sugar
2 eggs
1 teaspoon vanilla extract

1 teaspoon lemon juice
1 box vanilla wafers
16 ounce can strawberry,
  cherry, pineapple,
  or blueberry
  pie filling

Cream cream cheese and sugar. Add eggs and beat well. Add vanilla extract and lemon juice and blend thoroughly. Place 1 vanilla wafer (flat side up) in each regular muffin-sized paper cup. Fill each cup ¾ of the way up with cheese mixture. Bake for 15 minutes at 350 degrees. Let cool for ½ hour. Spoon on pie filling as a topping.

Yield: 2 dozen

Al Sanders
Anchor, WJZ-TV, Eyewitness News

Apple Crumble

5–6 cups apples	Pinch of ginger
Lemon juice	2 cups flour
1½ cups sugar, divided	½ cup butter
½ teaspoon cinnamon	Cream

Place peeled, cored, and sliced cooking apples in a deep dish. Sprinkle with lemon juice, ¾ cup sugar, cinnamon, and a pinch of ginger.

On top, place following crumble mix: flour, butter, and ¾ cup of sugar rubbed together until consistency of bread crumbs. Pat into place and mark with a fork. Cook in 375 degree oven for 30 to 35 minutes. Serve with pitcher of cream.

Christine Sarbanes
Wife of U.S. Senator, Paul S. Sarbanes, Maryland

Indonesian Green Beans

½ cup chopped onions	4 tablespoons peanut oil
1 clove garlic, minced	1 pound green beans (prefer
2 tablespoons grated lemon	fresh, or frozen thawed)
rind	1 teaspoon salt
½ teaspoon dried chili peppers	Pinch of sugar
1 bay leaf	

Chop onions fine, add garlic, lemon rind, and chili peppers. Heat oil and saute mixture for three minutes, stirring constantly. Add beans, salt, sugar, and bay leaf and mix thoroughly. Cover and cook over low heat until barely tender, adding oil if necessary.

Serves 4

Richard Sher
Co-Host, WJZ-TV's People Are Talking and Co-Anchor, Eyewitness News at Noon

Schaefer's Wafers

2 egg whites, at room
   temperature
⅔ cup sugar

½ teaspoon vanilla
6 ounces semisweet chocolate
   chips

Preheat oven to 375 degrees. Beat egg whites until stiff. Add ⅓ cup sugar and beat 3 minutes. Add remaining sugar and beat 3 more minutes. Add vanilla. Fold in chocolate chips. Drop by teaspoonfuls onto cookie sheet. Place in oven, and count to 10. Turn off oven. Leave cookies in oven overnight.

Yield: 50 cookies

The Honorable William Donald Schaefer
Mayor, City of Baltimore

Hot Fruit Mélange

10 dried figs, poached until
   soft, and sliced
2½ cups canned pears, thickly
   sliced
2½ cups fresh apples, pared,
   cored, and thickly sliced
2½ cups canned pineapple,
   thickly sliced
2½ cups fresh bananas, thickly
   sliced

2½ cups canned peaches or
   apricots, thickly sliced
½ cup unsalted butter
8 large macaroons, crumbled
1 cup slivered almonds
1 cup brown sugar
1 cup sweet sherry
   Whipped cream flavored
   with sherry, for garnish

Butter large, deep baking dish. Alternate layers of fruit, dotting each layer with butter, and sprinkling with crumbled macaroons, almonds, and brown sugar. Cover last layer with a generous amount of macaroon crumbs, and pour sherry over all. Dot with any remaining butter. Bake in 350 degree oven for 30 minutes. Serve hot or at room temperature with sherry-flavored whipped cream.

Note: Using rum instead of sherry will give a stronger flavor. Can be made a day ahead of serving.

Serves 12 to 18

Rita St. Clair
Interior Designer and Columnist

Fillet of Beef with Several Sauces

This fillet is served with dabs of one, two, or more sauces on one's plate. The pieces of meat are dipped in each sauce very much like for fondue Bourguignonne.

2 to 3 pounds fillet of beef, tenderloin or beef loin	Bouquet garni (bay leaf, thyme and parsley)
¼ pound fat back, thinly sliced or cut into thin strips	1 carrot, diced
5 tablespoons butter, softened	1 onion, diced
	Salt and pepper

Remove the fat and outside membrane from the fillet. Prick the roast with little strips of fat back (using a pricking needle), or wrap the fat back slices around the roast. Tie with a string to give it a nice shape. Smear the roast with 3 tablespoons butter.

Lay the bouquet garni, diced carrot, and onion on the bottom of a roasting pan. Set the meat on top. Season with salt and pepper. Bake in a preheated oven at 425 degrees, basting frequently. Count 8 minutes a pound for medium rare and 10 minutes for medium. When done, transfer to a platter and keep in a warm place, covered with foil, for 30 minutes.

Slice and serve with one or more of the following:

Raspberry sauce:

2 cups light red wine or dry white wine	¼ cup raspberry vinegar
4 shallots, finely chopped	OR 1 teaspoon raspberry preserve and 3 tablespoons vinegar
1 tablespoon mixed herbs (parsley, thyme, bay leaf, chervil)	1 cup heavy cream
	3 tablespoons butter, at room temperature

Pour off excess fat from roasting pan and deglaze with wine. Add shallots. Bring to a boil, scraping bottom of pan. Add the herbs and cook until the liquid is reduced to ½ cup. Strain through a chinois into a clean pan. Add the vinegar and then the cream. Boil until the sauce has reduced to a nice consistency. Remove from heat, whisk in butter.

Red wine sauce:

2 cups heavy red wine
1 garlic clove, minced
3 anchovies, crushed with a fork

1 cup brown sauce (home made or commercial)
Beurre manié (page 326)

3 tablespoons butter, at room temperature

Boil the wine until reduced to ½ cup. Add the garlic and anchovies. Cook until well blended. Add the brown sauce and boil until the sauce is a nice smooth consistency, adding some beurre manié, if too thin. Remove from heat, whisk in butter.

Butter with mustard and herbs:

8 tablespoons butter
Chopped herbs

1 teaspoon Dijon mustard

To butter, add Dijon mustard and some chopped herbs. Combine well to make sauce.

Tomato sauce with herbs:

⅛ pound fat back
½ carrot, chopped
½ medium onion, chopped
2 tablespoons butter, oil, or lard
½ tablespoon flour
Salt and pepper
1 teaspoon sugar

2 garlic cloves, crushed (optional)
1½ pounds tomatoes or 1 large can
½ cup white stock or water
Fresh tarragon, chopped
Fresh parsley, chopped
Fresh chives, chopped

Make a mirepoix with the fat back, carrot, and onion. Cook it slowly in the fat, stirring occasionally with a wooden spoon. Add the flour and cook a few minutes, stirring. Add the tomatoes, stock, sugar, salt, pepper, and the herbs and garlic. Simmer 1 hour. Use as is or strain.

The following are cooking terms you will find helpful in preparing this recipe:

Bouquet garni: Place the following herbs in folded cheesecloth and tie securely: 2 sprigs parsley, ⅓ bay leaf, and ⅛ teaspoon thyme.

Deglaze: To add wine (or stock or cream) to loosen browned particles from the pan in which food has cooked.

Chinois: Conical-shaped sieve with a fine mesh.

continued

Beurre manié: (or kneaded butter) Rub 2 tablespoons butter with 2 table-spoons flour. Form into small balls, drop into one cup hot liquid and stir to blend ingredients for a thickened sauce. Simmer, but do not boil, until there is no floury taste.

Germaine Sharretts

Instructor of French Cuisine, accredited by the International Association of Cooking Schools and a member of Les Dames d'Escoffier, Washington, D.C., Chapter

Sally's Szechuan String Beans

1½ pounds fresh string beans
3 ounces dried baby shrimp
5 cups oil
5 ounces ground lean pork
2 teaspoons ginger, chopped
2 ounces chopped szechuan
(preserved vegetable)
1 tablespoon soy sauce

½ teaspoon salt
1 teaspoon sugar
½ tablespoon sherry
2 tablespoons water
½ tablespoon vinegar
1 teaspoon sesame oil
2 tablespoons scallions, chopped

Cut string beans into 5-inch sections. Soak shrimp in warm water for 5 minutes and chop into small pieces. Heat oil in wok until very hot (315 degrees) and deep fry string beans until just wrinkled, about 1 minute. Remove beans and drain oil. Put 3 tablespoons oil back into skillet and stir fry pork. Add ginger, shrimp, szechuan, soy sauce, salt, sugar, sherry, water, and string beans. Stir well over high heat until sauce is gone. Add vinegar and sesame oil and sprinkle chopped scallions overall, stirring evenly. Remove from heat and serve.

Note: You can find the dried baby shrimp and szechuan in an Oriental grocery store.

Serves 6

Sally Thorner
Anchorwoman, WMAR-TV

Noodle Pudding

16 ounce can peach or cherry
   pie filling
1 pound medium noodles
6 eggs
½ cup sugar

1 teaspoon vanilla
20 ounce can crushed pineapple,
   drained
   White raisins
¼ pound margarine, melted
Cinnamon and sugar mixture

Grease glass 9- by 13-inch baking dish. Put pie filling in baking dish and distribute. Cook noodles per box instructions. Drain noodles and put in bowl or pot. Mix eggs, sugar, and vanilla with electric beater. Stir egg mixture through noodles. Then mix in crushed pineapple and raisins. Put noodles in baking dish and distribute evenly. Sprinkle margarine over noodles. Sprinkle cinnamon and sugar mixture over noodles. Bake uncovered at 325 degrees for 50 minutes.

Serves 8

The Honorable Melvin A. Steinberg
President, Maryland State Senate

Pumpkin Bread

2 eggs
½ cup salad oil
1½ cups sugar
1 cup solid pack pumpkin
1 cup flour
¼ teaspoon baking powder

1 teaspoon baking soda
¾ teaspoon salt
1½ teaspoons pumpkin pie spice
   (optional)
½ cup raisins
½ cup walnuts, chopped

With electric mixer, combine eggs, oil, sugar, and pumpkin. Combine dry ingredients then add to pumpkin mixture and mix together. Stir in raisins and walnuts. Grease and flour a 9- by 5-inch loaf pan and bake at 350 degrees for 1 hour.

Serves 12 to 15

Neela Ubriaco
Wife of Gene Ubriaco, Coach of the Baltimore Skipjacks

Bavarian Cream Pie

9 inch pastry shell, baked or
graham cracker crust
2 cups milk
½ cup sugar
4 egg yolks

1 envelope unflavored gelatin
dissolved in ¼ cup cold water
Pinch of salt
2 teaspoons vanilla
1 pint whipping cream

Pour 1½ cups milk into a heavy saucepan. Add sugar and stir. Place over medium heat. Beat egg yolks well, add remaining ½ cup milk, stir, and with the gelatin add to the hot milk-sugar mixture. Stir constantly over medium heat until mixture lightly coats a metal spoon. Add salt to the hot milk mixture.

Remove the cooked mixture from heat, add vanilla. Leave to cool, stirring now and then. When the mixture has cooled to the consistency of unbeaten egg whites, whip the cream until thick. Using the same beaters beat the cooked mixture until smooth; then add the whipped cream, folding in until well mixed.

Pour into prepared pie shell. This can be made the day before. Refrigerate until served.

Sandy Unitas
Wife of John Unitas, Star Quarterback of the Baltimore Colts

Australian Chicken

2 sweet red peppers, sliced	3 tablespoons butter
2½ cups mushrooms, sliced	Salt and pepper
1 onion, chopped	3 cups heavy cream
2 green peppers, sliced	3 tablespoons English mustard
½ cup cooked peas	3 tablespoons Worcestershire
½ cup celery, chopped	sauce
Meat of 2 cooked chickens, skinned, boned, and chopped	Paprika

Lightly sauté vegetables in butter. Mix vegetables and chicken in casserole dish. Salt and pepper to taste. Whip cream with mustard and Worcestershire sauce until very stiff. Spread cream mixture over top of chicken-vegetables. Sprinkle paprika over top of cream. Bake at 350 degrees for 20 to 25 minutes until cream is melting through casserole and is brown on top.

Note: Can be made ahead.

Serves 8

Mrs. David Zinman (Mary)
Wife of the Music Director of the Baltimore Symphony Orchestra

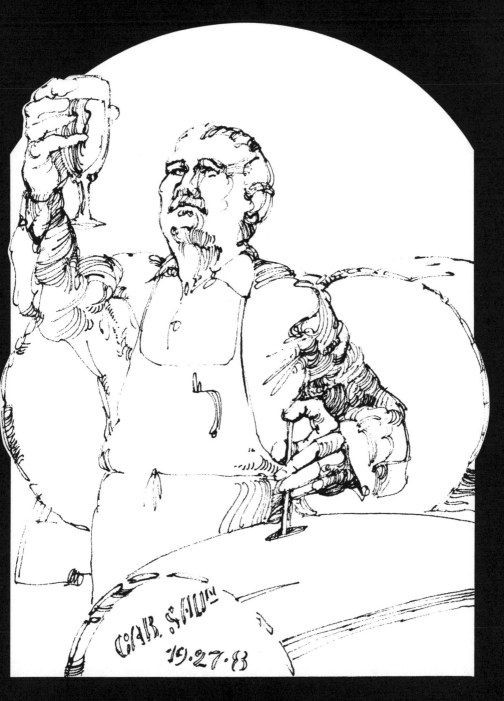

Restaurants,
Caterers, & Vineyards

Fruit of the Vine

Wine has been produced in Maryland since the time of the earliest settlers. Currently 10 wineries and 120 grape-growing facilities are located here. Our annual wine production exceeds 300,000 gallons and $1.5 million in sales. Frederick, Carroll, and Baltimore Counties are the leading wine producers. A great variety of wines is produced each year, from apple wine to Cabernet Sauvignon.

Potato Croquettes

5 pounds potatoes, peeled	Basil to taste
6 ounces butter	8 ounces flour, approximately
8 egg yolks	2 pounds bread crumbs
Salt and pepper to taste	4 eggs and 1 ounce milk, mixed
Nutmeg to taste	Oil

Cook potatoes in water until tender. Dry and pass through sieve. Work in butter, egg yolks and seasonings. Sprinkle flour on board and shape potato mix into desired shapes. Let rest 1 hour. Dredge in flour, egg wash, and finally bread crumbs. Fry in clear oil (375 degrees) until crisp and golden brown.

Yield: 20 to 30 croquettes

Gregory J. Wentz, Chef
Baltimore's International Culinary Arts Institute
19–21 South Gay Street, Baltimore, Maryland

Frikadellar

2–3 slices white bread	1 ounce green pepper, minced
3 ounces light cream	and cooked
3 tablespoons flour	2 eggs
Salt and pepper to taste	8 ounces minced pork
1 ounce onion, minced and	8 ounces minced veal
cooked	Clarified butter for frying

Soak bread in cream. Mix flour with spices, onion, and green pepper. Mix with meat and eggs. Combine all ingredients and shape into patties. Let rest one hour before cooking. Pan fry in clarified butter over medium heat. Serve with brown butter and parslied potatoes.

Serves 3

Gregory J. Wentz, Chef
Baltimore's International Culinary Arts Institute
19–21 South Gay Street, Baltimore, Maryland

Griessnockel

¾ cup butter, softened
3 eggs, room temperature
Salt and pepper
Nutmeg

12 ounces semolina flour (2 cups)
Consommé
Chives

Combine softened butter and beaten eggs. Add seasonings to taste. Fold in semolina flour. Form dumplings with teaspoon, and poach in boiling, salted water for 10 minutes. Serve in consommé with chives.

Yield: 15 to 20 dumplings

Gregory J. Wentz, Chef
Baltimore's International Culinary Arts Institute
19–21 South Gay Street, Baltimore, Maryland

Shrimp Nicola

Butter
Garlic, diced
2 lemons, sliced

4–7 shrimp per person
Parsley, chopped
2–3 tablespoons white vermouth

Put butter, garlic, lemon slices, and shrimp in a heavy skillet. Add chopped parsley and heat until butter is almost melted. Add vermouth and continue to cook until sauce becomes a little heavy. Serve on a plate garnished with a slice of garlic bread.

Chipiarelli's
237 South High Street, Baltimore, Maryland

Honey-Ginger Dressing

1 pound honey	1 tablespoon ginger, minced
2 ounces apple juice	1 ounce lemon juice
1 tablespoon mint leaves, finely chopped	

Put all ingredients in bowl and mix well. Chill one hour before serving. Serve with fresh fruit salad.

Note: Will keep almost indefinitely in refrigerator.

Yield: 2½ cups

Ethel's Place
1225 Cathedral Street, Baltimore, Maryland

Veal Biloxi

6 ounces veal cutlet, cut into three pieces	1 teaspoon capers
¼ cup clarified butter	2 tablespoons white wine
3 26–30 count shrimp, peeled and deveined	Fettucine
¼ cup mushrooms, sliced into quarters	2 tablespoons parsley, chopped
	Lemon wedge

Pound veal between two pieces of waxed paper. Heat clarified butter in a skillet and sauté veal with remaining ingredients, being careful not to overcook. Serve over fettucine with shrimp and mushrooms on top of veal. Sprinkle with parsley and accompany with lemon wedge.

Serves 1

The Inn at Perry Cabin
Post Office Box 359, Easton, Maryland

Breast of Chicken Dijonaise

2 boneless chicken breasts	3 mushrooms, sliced
Flour for dredging	1 ounce white wine
2 ounces clarified butter	1 teaspoon Dijon mustard
1 shallot, minced	2 ounces heavy cream

½ ounce parsley, chopped

Dredge chicken breasts in flour and sauté in hot clarified butter. After breasts are cooked, remove and sauté chopped shallots and sliced mushrooms in the same pan with remaining butter. Add white wine and Dijon mustard; let reduce for approximately 1 minute, add heavy cream and chopped parsley. After sauce is blended well, add chicken breasts and heat through. Place breasts on plate and pour sauce over top to serve.

Note: A nice garnish with this dish is strawberries and sliced kiwi fruit on a piece of endive. When served with rice pilaf and green vegetable, this is an inexpensive but elegant meal.

Serves 1 to 2

Clarified Butter:
1 cup (2 sticks) unsalted butter,
  cut into 1-inch pieces

Completely melt butter in a heavy saucepan over low heat. Remove from heat and let stand for 2 to 3 minutes, allowing the milk solids to settle to the bottom. Skim the butter fat (froth) from the top. Strain the clear yellow liquid through a sieve lined with a double thickness of rinsed and squeezed cheesecloth into a container. This clarified butter will keep indefinitely in the refrigerator stored in a covered jar or crock.

Yield: ¾ cup

Stephen T. Powell, Chef
The Manor Tavern
Manor and Monkton Roads, Monkton, Maryland

Scallops in Mustard Cream

½ cup heavy cream
2 tablespoons grainy Dijon
   mustard
2 tablespoons dried tarragon

1 teaspoon white pepper
1½ pounds bay scallops
1 tablespoon shallots, chopped
2 tablespoons sweet butter

8 puff pastry shells, prebaked

In a heavy saucepan, boil cream briskly until reduced slightly. Add mustard, tarragon, and pepper. Cook briskly until thickened (about 5 minutes). Keep warm. Pat scallops dry. In another pan, lightly sauté shallots in butter. Add scallops and cook about 2 minutes until slightly firm. Add sauce to scallop mixture and bring to a boil for one more minute. Arrange prebaked shells on warm plates or platter and divide scallops among them. Pour sauce over each shell.

Serves 4

Masthead Club
Post Office Box 490, Oxford, Maryland

Old Obrycki's Broiled Stuffed Hard Crabs

4 steamed hard crabs
1 egg
2 tablespoons mayonnaise

1 pound crab meat, picked over
½ cup seasoned bread crumbs
Mayonnaise for topping

Clean steamed crabs by removing bottom shell, discarding lungs and inedible portions. Place edible crab meat in the top crab shells. Cut off claws at joint where they meet body, and reserve. Beat egg and mayonnaise together in a small bowl. In another bowl, mix crab meat and bread crumbs together. Combine egg and crab meat mixtures. Mound ¼ of mixture on each crab shell. Spread thinly with mayonnaise to cover. Broil, together with claws, until golden brown and thoroughly heated. Serve with lemon wedges and drawn butter.

Serves 4

Obrycki's Crab House
1729 East Pratt Street, Baltimore, Maryland

Veal Audrey

12–14 ounces prime veal, cut and pounded into small thin pieces (1½ to 2 ounces each)	Salt and pepper to taste
	½ cup dry white wine
	2 teaspoons lemon juice
	1 teaspoon chopped shallots
Flour	3 ounces shelled, green pistachio nuts
6 tablespoons clarified butter	

Dust veal lightly with flour. Brown lightly in clarified butter. Salt and pepper to taste. Add white wine, lemon juice, shallots and pistachio nuts. Simmer over medium heat until the sauce thickens slightly. Remove to hot serving platter.

Serves 2

The Pimlico Restaurant
1777 Reisterstown Road, Baltimore, Maryland

Strawberries Romanoff

3 pints fresh strawberries, washed and hulled	4 ounces Grand Marnier
	4 ounces port wine
½ pint vanilla ice cream, softened	2 tablespoons melba sauce (available at gourmet stores)

1 pint whipping cream

Divide ¾ of strawberries among 6 wine glasses. Crush remaining strawberries in a bowl. Add softened vanilla ice cream, Grand Marnier, port wine and melba sauce. Mix to smooth texture. Whip cream until almost stiff. Fold into ice cream mixture, and pour over strawberries.

Serves 6

Rudy Paul
Rudy's 2900 Restaurant
2900 Baltimore Boulevard, Finksburg, Maryland

Scallops Hawaiian

2 pounds sea scallops
½ pound bacon
Fresh pineapple juice

1 fresh pineapple cut into
1½-inch cubes

Wrap scallops in bacon and place on skewers, alternating scallops with pineapple cubes. Pour juice over kabobs. Grill kabobs 3 to 4 inches from heat or bake at 350 degrees for approximately 30 minutes or until bacon is crisp.

Serves 6

John B. Allen, Jr.
Phillips Harborplace
301 Light Street, Baltimore, Maryland

Robert Morris Inn's Scallop Casserole

6 tablespoons butter
1 cup onions, chopped
1 cup celery, chopped
1 tablespoon basil leaves
1 teaspoon poultry seasoning
1 teaspoon salt

½ teaspoon black pepper
½ teaspoon seafood seasoning
1 pound scallops
1 cup milk
1 tablespoon parsley, chopped
3 cups bread crumbs

In a heavy skillet melt butter, setting aside 2 tablespoons. Sauté onions and celery until tender. Add all seasonings except parsley. Add scallops and sauté over medium heat, stirring constantly until tender, approximately 5 minutes. Add 1 cup milk and remove from heat. Pour into medium bowl, sprinkle with parsley and stir. Add 2 cups bread crumbs (reserving 1 cup) and mix well. Put into one 8- by 8-inch casserole dish or 4 individual casserole dishes. Mix remaining 1 cup bread crumbs with reserved 2 tablespoons melted butter and stir until moist. Sprinkle on top and bake in 350 degree oven for 7 minutes or until golden brown.

Note: Can be prepared in advance. Cover and refrigerate. Bake when ready for seven minutes or until hot. Serve with chilled Chardonnay.

Serves 4

Robert Morris Inn
Oxford, Maryland

Italian Dinner for Four

Prosciutto and Melon
Fettucine in White Broccoli Sauce
Veal Francese à la Sabatino
Italian Demitasse
Assorted Biscotti

Proscuitto and Melon:

1 ripe honeydew melon   Thinly sliced prosciutto

Remove seeds and rind from melon, and slice. Arrange on platter. Lay a
slice of prosciutto over each piece. Serve with lemon wedges.

Fettucine in White Broccoli Sauce:

1 pound broccoli	Salt
3 cloves garlic, chopped	Oregano
¼ pound butter	Crushed red pepper
½ cup olive oil	1 pound fettucine

Parmesan cheese

Boil and cook broccoli until tender; then chop into large pieces. Sauté
garlic in melted butter and olive oil. Add cooked broccoli. Season with salt,
oregano and red pepper. Sauté approximately 8 minutes over low heat.
Boil fettucine in lightly salted water until tender. Drain. Pour fettucine
into broccoli mixture. Cook 1 minute. Serve hot. Sprinkle with Parmesan
cheese.

Veal Francese à la Sabatino:

1 pound veal scallopini (thin slices)
4 eggs
¼ cup half-and-half
Salt, to taste
Parsley, to taste
Oregano, to taste
Parmesan cheese, to taste

Italian bread crumbs
¼ cup butter
½ cup olive oil
¼ cup flour
¾ cup cooking sherry
¼ cup marsala wine
Juice from ½ lemon

To prepare veal, make an egg batter by combining eggs, half-and-half and seasonings. Beat well. Dip veal slices into egg mixture and coat each piece with crumbs. In a skillet, heat oil and butter. Fry veal until crispy and lightly browned. Set aside. Save ½ of drippings in skillet. In a bowl combine flour, sherry, marsala and lemon juice and mix well. Add to drippings to make gravy. Strain hot gravy over veal. Garnish with thin lemon slices and fresh parsley.

Dessert:
Serve Italian biscotti (cookies) from a local Italian bakery along with demitasse cups of strong Italian coffee.

Serves 4

Sabatino's Restaurant
901 Fawn Street, Baltimore, Maryland

Chicken Adobo

2 pounds chicken thighs
¼ cup cider vinegar
2 tablespoons soy sauce
4 cloves garlic, minced
½ teaspoon salt

2 small bay leaves
⅛ teaspoon freshly ground black
  pepper
¼ cup water
2 tablespoons cooking oil

Combine all ingredients except cooking oil in a saucepan. Let stand for at least 1 hour, turning over once to season all pieces of chicken. Simmer covered for about 30 minutes or until meat is tender. Drain sauce from meat and reserve. Heat 2 tablespoons oil in a skillet. Add chicken. Brown on all sides until almost crispy and transfer to a serving dish.

Pour off half the oil in skillet. Add reserved sauce. Cook for a minute or two, scraping all browned bits sticking to pan. Pour sauce over browned chicken. Decorate with tomato wedges and spring onions. Serve.

Serves 6

Sony Robles-Florendo and Luis Florendo
Sony's Philippine-Asian Restaurant
324 Park Avenue, Baltimore, Maryland

Tod-Man-Pla

1 pound haddock, skinned and
  boned
½ pound shrimp, shelled and
  deveined
      Oil

4 ounce can Thai red curry
  paste
¼ pound fresh string beans,
  sliced very thin

Blend the haddock, shrimp and red curry paste together in a food processor. If the mixture is too sticky, add a small amount of water and mix well. Add the string beans and mix well with your hands for 5 minutes. Form the mixture into small patties about 2 inches in diameter. Heat the oil until very hot in a wok or deep frying pan. Fry the patties until lightly browned, about 2 to 3 minutes. Drain on paper towels. Serve with Cucumber Salad.

Yield: Approximately 18 patties

Thai Restaurant
3316 Greenmount Avenue, Baltimore, Maryland

Cucumber Salad

1 cup white vinegar
¼ cup sugar
1 teaspoon salt
1 cucumber, cut in fourths
lengthwise and sliced very
thin

¼ cup ground peanuts (unsalted
and unroasted)
1 tablespoon Chinese parsley
(coriander), optional

Boil the vinegar, sugar and salt for 20 minutes. Let cool. Roast the peanuts in a very slow oven until golden brown. Chop the peanuts in a food processor or blender. Add the cucumber, peanuts and coriander to the cooled vinegar mixture. Refrigerate until ready to serve.

Note: You can buy the Thai red curry paste, Chinese parsley (coriander) and unsalted, unroasted peanuts in an Oriental grocery store.

Serves 3

Thai Restaurant
3316 Greenmount Avenue, Baltimore, Maryland

Cream of Crab Soup

1 medium onion, minced
3 tablespoons butter
3 tablespoons flour
1 pint clam juice
Pinch of Old Bay Seasoning

Freshly ground pepper and
salt to taste
¼ cup dry white wine
1 pint half-and-half or cream
1 pound crab meat

Sauté onion in butter until very soft. Stir in flour and gradually add clam juice. Add seasonings, wine, and half-and-half. Simmer until flour is cooked, about 15 minutes. Add crab meat and heat. Do not boil.

Serves 4 to 6

The Tidewater Inn
Post Office Box 359, Easton, Maryland

Escalloped Oysters

3 cups crushed saltines	1 quart oysters
½ teaspoon salt	2 tablespoons butter
¼ teaspoon pepper	Milk
1 teaspoon chicken bouillon	Parsley, chopped
Paprika	

Mix crushed saltines with salt, pepper, and chicken bouillon. In a shallow, buttered casserole dish, alternate layers of cracker mixture and oysters, ending with crackers. Melt butter and add enough milk to cover oysters. Sprinkle with parsley and paprika. Bake at 325 degrees for 35 minutes.

Serves 4 to 6

The Tidewater Inn
Post Office Box 359, Easton, Maryland

Crab Imperial

4 tablespoons mayonnaise	Pinch each of thyme, oregano, and dry mustard
¾ teaspoon Worcestershire sauce	1 egg
¼ teaspoon salt	1 pound crab meat
Dash of hot pepper sauce	Paprika
Parsley	

Mix all ingredients except paprika and parsley, adding crab meat last. Coat a casserole lightly with mayonnaise and fill with crab mixture. Spread a thin layer of mayonnaise over top and sprinkle with paprika and parsley. Bake at 350 degrees for 15 to 20 minutes.

Serves 4

The Tidewater Inn
Post Office Box 359, Easton, Maryland

Tandoori Chicken

3 medium-sized chickens	½ teaspoon turmeric powder
2 teaspoons chili powder	2½ teaspoons salt
1½ teaspoons coriander powder	2 cups yogurt
2 inch piece ginger, peeled	2 fresh lemons
6 cloves garlic	1 egg yolk
4 bay leaves	4 tablespoons olive oil
6 cardamom pods	⅛ teaspoon saffron
2 tablespoons paprika	½ cup yogurt
1 teaspoon crushed black	Leaf coriander, chopped
pepper	Parsley for garnish

Remove skin and clean chickens. Cut 2 or 3 deep slits (to touch bone) on the legs, breasts and backs of chickens. Split each chicken into halves. Grind all listed ingredients from chili powder to salt in a blender or food processor to a fine paste. In a large bowl, mix the paste with 2 cups yogurt. Cut the lemons in half and squeeze the juice into the mixture. Leave the halved lemon pieces in the mixture. Add the egg yolk and olive oil. Soak saffron in the ½ cup yogurt for ½ hour. Add this to the mixture. Marinate the chicken overnight or preferably for 24 hours. Cook the chickens in a "tandoor" oven for about 7 to 10 minutes. If a tandoor is not available, cook the chicken on a grill (preferably) or under the broiler until done, about 20 to 30 minutes, turning once. Remove and serve hot with raw onion rings, lime wedges and tomato slices. Garnish with chopped leaf coriander and parsley.

Note: Purchase leaf coriander and cardamom pods from Indian or Chinese grocery store.

Serves 6, ½ chicken per person

Tandoor Restaurant
Pratt Street Pavilion
Harborplace, Baltimore, Maryland

Red Snapper Anise

½ cup white wine
1 teaspoon Worcestershire sauce
½ lemon, juiced
4 6-ounce red snapper fillets
1 cup flour

1 cup clarified butter
2 bulbs fresh fennel, finely julienned
1 tablespoon shallots or onion, finely chopped
½ cup Pernod

1 pint heavy cream

Combine the wine, Worcestershire sauce, and lemon juice. Dip the red snapper into this mixture, then dredge lightly in the flour. Shake off all excess flour. Heat a large fry pan and add enough butter to cover bottom. Sauté snapper until both sides are golden brown. Remove from pan and keep warm. In another pan, sauté the julienned fennel until tender and put on warmed plates. In the same pan sauté the shallots until clear and add the Pernod (watch for flambé). Reduce liquid by half, add cream, and reduce until thick. Put snapper on fennel and top with sauce.

Note: Orange sections (peel orange and cut section between each membrane) and green peppercorns (½ teaspoon) make an excellent garnish for this dish. Leeks can be substituted for fennel.

Serves 4

Joseph Hardtke, Sous Chef
Trellis Garden
Hyatt Regency, 300 Light Street, Baltimore, Maryland

Paupiette of Salmon

4 sheets parchment paper,
  24- by 16-inches
2 tablespoons olive oil
6 ounce fillets of fresh salmon
  Salt

Pepper
1 bunch basil, chopped
8 slices lemon
8 slices tomato
8 slices zucchini
2 egg yolks with some water

Fold parchment and cut as shown in Figure 1. Place parchment paper on working table. Put ½ tablespoon of olive oil on one side of paper with salmon on top as in Figure 2. Sprinkle salt, pepper, and basil on top, then add slices of lemon, tomato, and zucchini. Egg wash the side with a brush and fold the paper over and egg wash again. Seal the paper around the edges. Cook the salmon for 8 minutes at 425 degrees.

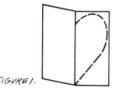
FIGURE 1.

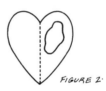
FIGURE 2.

Sauce:
2 tablespoons shallots, chopped
1 cup white wine
½ cup cream

½ pound butter
Salt
Pepper

Reduce chopped shallots and white wine almost completely. Add the cream and reduce by two-thirds. Add the butter slowly and mix it with a whip. Be careful not to overheat. Add salt and pepper.

This dish needs to be served at once. To do so, the dish should be prepared in the following order: Prepare the fish and vegetables in the parchment; preheat the oven. Chop the shallots and add to the white wine and reduce; put the fish, etc. into the oven. Add the cream, reduce. Add the butter (in small bits) while the fish is cooking. Take the fish out of the oven and remove it and the vegetables from the parchment. The sauce should be ready; pour the sauce over the fish and vegetables and serve.

This can be served as a first course by itself or as a main course with a salad or other vegetable.

Bluefeld Gourmet Caterer, Inc.
401 Reisterstown Road, Pikesville, Maryland

Crown Roast of Lamb

2 or more rib sections of crown   Ground lamb, if desired
  roast of lamb   Salt and pepper

Have butcher shape 2 or more rib sections of lamb into a crown. If you choose to fill the center with ground lamb, ask butcher to place in center of crown roast. Season ground lamb with salt and pepper.

Cover ends of crown with cubes of bread, salt pork or aluminum foil to prevent burning. Sprinkle crown with salt and pepper.

Place meat in open roast pan and roast at 350 degrees for 18 to 20 minutes per pound. Before serving remove bread, salt pork or aluminum foil from ends of crown and replace with frills for serving.

If ground lamb is not placed in center, before serving you may fill center with any of the following: mashed potatoes, buttered peas, buttered peas and carrots, buttered cauliflower, buttered peas and mushrooms.

Note: Be sure to check with your butcher in case you need to order this meat ahead of time.

Serves 9 to 12

Eddie's-Victor's Market
5113 Roland Avenue, Baltimore, Maryland

Marinated Vegetables

3 pounds fresh vegetables, any
combination:
Broccoli
Zucchini

Cauliflower
Mushrooms
Carrots
Green pepper

Cherry tomatoes

Marinade:
  1 cup cider vinegar
  1¼ cups vegetable oil
  ½–1 tablespoon pepper
  1 tablespoon sugar

  1 tablespoon dried dillweed
  ½–1 tablespoon salt
  1 tablespoon garlic salt
  1 tablespoon MSG

½ can pitted ripe olives (optional)

Clean and cut fresh vegetables. Separate the broccoli and cauliflower into florets. Slice zucchini, mushrooms and green pepper. Cut carrots on a diagonal and halve the cherry tomatoes. Combine marinade ingredients and pour over vegetables. Add olives, if desired. Marinate 12 hours, stirring occasionally. Keep in refrigerator, and serve cold. Will keep up to four days.

Serves 10 to 12

Sandy Spanos
Culinary Delight Caterers
12 Pemberly Lane, Reisterstown, Maryland

Herb Cheese Spread

11 ounces cream cheese, softened	½ teaspoon crumbled dried tarragon
3 tablespoons sour cream	1 small clove garlic, minced
3 tablespoons heavy cream	Salt and white pepper to taste
1 shallot or spring onion, finely chopped	Dash of hot pepper sauce

Place cream cheese in a bowl and mix with sour cream and heavy cream until smooth. Add remaining ingredients, mixing well. Cover and chill several hours. Make a few days in advance for best flavor.

Yield: 3 to 4 cups

Sandy Spanos
Culinary Delight Caterers
12 Pemberly Lane, Reisterstown, Maryland

Berrywine Roast Lamb à l'Orange

1 large clove garlic, slivered	OR 1 cup dry white wine (optional)
1 large leg of lamb	
1 cup Berrywine Plantations Allegre wine	1 cup orange juice
	1 cup orange marmalade

Make small slashes in leg of lamb. Insert clove of garlic in lamb and roast lamb in oven at 325 degrees until needle of meat thermometer indicates meat is nearly done. Twenty minutes before cooking is complete, mix wine, orange juice and orange marmalade together in small bowl and pour over lamb. Baste once before lamb is done. Remove lamb from pan when cooked. Skim lamb fat from drippings and add more wine to gravy. Thicken gravy with cornstarch if necessary. Serve with herbal rice.

Lucille Allen
Berrywine Plantations, Inc.
13601 Glisans Mill Road, Mt. Airy, Maryland

Berrywine Turkey Dressing

2 large onions, chopped	1 cup green olives, chopped
4 large stalks of celery	1 pound hard boiled eggs, chopped
2 pounds ground beef	
1 pound pork sausage	1 large apple, chopped
½ pound butter	1 cooked turkey liver, chopped
2 tablespoons parsley	1 large loaf of bread, sliced, soaked with a bottle of Berrywine Plantations Dry Vidal
2 tablespoons pine nuts	
½ pound cooked chestnuts, chopped	
½ pound walnuts, chopped	1 small can poultry seasoning

In large Dutch oven, brown onions, celery, beef and sausage in butter. Add all other ingredients and stir until well mixed. Use all leftover wine in bread mixture. Stuff bird and use leftover stuffing as extra side dish.

Lucille Allen
Berrywine Plantations, Inc.
13601 Glisans Mill Road, Mt. Airy, Maryland

Cherry-Wine Parfaits

1 pint vanilla ice cream	½ pound Bing cherries, pitted
½ cup Berrywine Plantations Cherry wine	

Put ice cream, all except 4 cherries, and wine in blender. Stir until desired thickness. Serve in parfait glasses garnished with reserved cherries as a simple dessert.

Note: Put parfaits in freezer before serving if mixture is too soupy.

Serves 4

Lucille Allen
Berrywine Plantations, Inc.
13601 Glisans Mill Road, Mt. Airy, Maryland

Boordy Wine Loaf

½ cup butter, softened
½ cup brown sugar
1 egg
¼ cup maple syrup
¼ cup dry red wine

1¼ cups whole wheat flour
1 teaspoon baking powder
¼ teaspoon baking soda
¼ teaspoon salt
½ teaspoon nutmeg

½ cup pecans or walnuts, chopped

In a bowl, cream butter with brown sugar, beat in the egg, then the maple syrup and wine. In another bowl, stir together the dry ingredients; beat into the maple mixture and add nuts. Pour into greased 9- by 5-inch loaf pan and bake at 350 degrees for approximately 35 to 40 minutes or until it tests done with a toothpick. Cool on a rack.

Yield: 1 Loaf

Boordy Vineyards
12820 Long Green Pike, Hydes, Maryland

La Soupe de la Vendange

4 carrots
4 potatoes
4 stalks celery with leaves
2 inch wedge of cabbage
1 onion
1 leek
1 clove of garlic, minced
2 quarts cold water

2 teaspoons salt
1 can kidney beans
2 tomatoes, chopped, or ¾ cup
    canned
1 teaspoon basil
1 tablespoon olive oil
½ teaspoon pepper
Mild cheese, grated

Coarsely chop vegetables. Put these into 2 quarts salted cold water, bring to a boil, and simmer for 1 hour. Remove from heat. Mash the vegetables with an electric mixer. Add kidney beans and tomatoes, basil, olive oil, and pepper. Return to heat and simmer for at least 1 more hour. To serve, pour into a tureen and garnish with grated cheese.

Note: Soup is better when reheated. Peas, string beans, turnips, or zucchini may be added, and rice, barley, noodles, or other herbs. Freezes well.

Serves 6 to 8

Montbray Wine Cellars
818 Silver Run Valley, Westminster, Maryland

Simmering Beef in Wine with Vegetables and Gravy

Vegetable cooking spray	4–5 potatoes
2½ pounds eye of round	4–5 carrots
Garlic powder	2 beef bouillon cubes
Salt and pepper	½ teaspoon or more browning
1 cup water	and seasoning sauce
1 cup Byrd Chardonnay (or	½ cup water
very dry white wine)	4 heaping tablespoons flour

Spray electric frying pan with vegetable cooking spray. Brown all sides of beef at 200 degrees. While browning sprinkle each side with a generous amount of garlic powder, salt, and pepper. Reduce heat to lowest setting, about 125 to 150 degrees. Add water and wine. Clean, pare and slice carrots and potatoes, and place around beef. Cover. Simmer for 5 to 6 hours. The longer it simmers the more flavorful and tender it becomes. Remove beef and vegetables. Reserve 2 cups of the liquid or add water to make 2 cups. Return to pan. Add bouillon cubes and browning and seasoning sauce. Combine flour and water, then stir into liquid. Heat to boiling stirring constantly. Boil one minute. Serve gravy with beef cut into half-inch slices lengthwise. Leftovers make a good stew.

Note: Suitable for buffet. Serve the remaining Chardonnay wine with dinner or serve Cabernet Sauvignon.

Serves 4

Sharon R. Byrd
Byrd Vineyards and Winery
Church Hill Road, Myersville, Maryland

Ethnic Festivals

Baltimore's International Flavor

Weekends from June through September attract a diverse population to Baltimore's famous ethnic festivals, collectively known as the Parade of Nations. Each festival features authentic ethnic costumes, dances, foods, and crafts as presented by each of the local nationality groups. They afford Baltimoreans and visitors an opportunity to learn one another's customs and explore each other's roots. Current festivals include Polish, Asian, Italian, Afram, Caribbean, Hispanic, German, American Indian, Indian, Korean, Jewish-American, Ukrainian, Irish, Lithuanian, Philippine, Estonian, and Greek.

After the diversity of the summer festivals, the city comes together again at the annual City Fair, a celebration of Baltimore's neighborhoods for everyone to enjoy.

Crab Soup

2 large onions, diced
1½ pounds beef cubes
1 large turnip, diced
1 small head of cabbage, shredded
1½ pints of any other mixed vegetables, fresh or frozen, such as peas, corn, carrots, string beans, lima beans
6 celery stalks
2 bay leaves

1 large can of tomatoes
1 tablespoon sugar
2 tablespoons salt
1 garlic clove, minced,
OR 1 teaspoon garlic salt
1½ tablespoons seafood seasoning
2 pounds claw crab meat
OR 12 steamed crabs which have been picked

Make a regular beef-vegetable soup by combining first 11 ingredients and simmering for 1½ to 2 hours. Add seafood seasoning and crab meat or crabs the last 20 minutes. Serve in large bowls.

Afram Festival
From the Afram Bicentennial Yearbook-1976

Crackling Bread

1½ cups self-rising corn meal
1 egg
1 cup cracklings

1 cup milk
¾ cup water

Preheat oven to 400 degrees. Grease one pie pan and set in oven while preheating. Mix corn meal, egg, milk, and water thoroughly. Stir in cracklings. Pour into heated pie pan. Bake for 15 to 20 minutes.

Afram Festival
From the Afram Bicentennial Yearbook-1976

Stuffed Ham

20 pound corned ham	20 small onions
1 bushel kale	OR 10 large onions
4 small heads cabbage	½ box red pepper flakes
	10 tablespoons salt

1½ bunches celery

Bone the ham. Chop all vegetables and combine with spices. Make incisions all over ham and pack in vegetable mixture. Pack any leftover vegetables around the ham. Wrap in cheesecloth. Place in large roasting pan half full of water. Cook for 4 hours on top of stove, adding water as needed. Store in refrigerator until thoroughly chilled. Serve cold.

Afram Festival
From the Afram Bicentennial Yearbook-1976

Pork and Sauerkraut with Barley

2 pounds sauerkraut	Enough water to cover
¾ cup barley	ingredients
2 pounds pork (marbled), cubed	2–3 tablespoons maple or corn
1 apple, cubed	syrup
½ teaspoon salt	1 small onion, chopped

1 tablespoon butter

Place the sauerkraut in a large kettle. Add the barley, pork, cubed apple, and salt. Add enough water to cover the ingredients. Simmer about 2 hours. Then add syrup and onion which has been sautéed in butter. Simmer about one more hour. Be sure to check moisture so the sauerkraut does not burn. Add a little water as needed.

Note: Can be made ahead and warmed up. It will stay in refrigerator for about 2 weeks. The more you reheat it, the better it tastes.

Serves 4 to 6

Estonian Festival
Submitted by Meeta Liiv

Liivakook-Sandtorte

6 cups flour	1 cup butter or margarine
2 cups sugar	1 lemon, juice and grated peel
1 teaspoon baking powder	2 eggs, beaten
¾ cup milk	

Combine flour, sugar, and baking powder. Using a pastry blender or knife, cut the butter into flour mixture until coarse. Add grated lemon peel and juice. Make a hole in the mixture and slowly add beaten egg; keep cutting and add milk. Use hands to form the dough, but do not knead. Roll out ⅕ of the dough on a floured board and cut a circle 10 to 12 inches in diameter (use a plate for a template). Carefully place the thinly rolled dough on a greased cookie sheet. Bake at 350 degrees for 12 minutes. Immediately after baking, cut one inch off edge to be used later for crumbs. Repeat the procedure 4 more times. Cool the layers.

Filling:

3 ounce package vanilla pudding	1 cup milk
and pie filling mix	1 cup sweet butter
1 pound damson plum preserves	

Combine pudding mix and milk in saucepan. Cook according to package directions. Cream butter and mix into pudding.

To assemble sandtorte: put one layer on the serving plate, spread with pudding, top with second layer. Spread damson plum preserves on second layer. Repeat until finished, alternating pudding and preserves between layers.

Frost the top and sides of the cake with a thin coating of pudding. Crush the reserved cake pieces. Press the crumbs ¼-inch thick onto top and sides of the cake. Chill for 24 hours before serving.

Serves 24

Estonian Festival
Submitted by Meeta Liiv

Marinated Fresh Smelts

2 pounds fresh smelts	2 cups water
1 tablespoon salt	1 cup vinegar
2 onions, thinly sliced	2 eggs
2 carrots, thinly sliced	2 tablespoons milk
10 peppercorns	1–1½ cups bread crumbs or
5 bay leaves	flour
1 tablespoon sugar	Butter for frying

Wash, clean, and season the smelts with salt. Boil the onions, carrots, peppercorns, bay leaves, and sugar in the water about 5 minutes. Add the vinegar and cool. Meanwhile, dry lightly-seasoned smelts with paper towel. Mix well-beaten eggs and milk. Dip the smelts into the egg mixture and then coat with breadcrumbs. Fry the fish in hot butter until light brown. Cool. Alternate the layers of cooled fish with vegetables in marinade. Pour any remaining marinade over the smelts.

Estonian Festival
Submitted by Meeta Liiv

Lumbee Sweet Potato Pie

4 tablespoons margarine, softened	3 eggs, well beaten
1½ cups sugar	1½ cups milk
2 teaspoons nutmeg	1½ pounds sweet potatoes,
1 teaspoon vanilla	cooked and mashed
	2 unbaked 9-inch pie shells

Cream margarine and sugar well. Add nutmeg and vanilla. Beat the eggs and milk and combine with sugar. Beat well. Blend in the sweet potatoes. Pour into pie shells and bake at 325 degrees for 45 minutes to an hour.

American Indian Festival
Submitted by Vonnie Oxendine, Jr., Lumbee

Fried Fresh Corn Cakes

½ pint grated fresh corn	1 egg
3 level tablespoons flour	½ cup milk
½ teaspoon salt	Butter

Scrape or grate the corn from the cob. Sift flour and mix into a batter with egg, salt and milk; stir the corn into the batter and drop by spoonfuls into a frying pan containing hot butter. When one side is brown, turn and cook the other side. Serve with wild honey.

American Indian Festival
Submitted by Kathy Dalrymple, Cherokee

Irish Porter Bread

11 ounces English ale	4 eggs
1 pound dark brown sugar	1 tablespoon lemon juice
1 cup butter	1 tablespoon vanilla extract
2 cups seedless raisins	1 teaspoon nutmeg
2 teaspoons baking soda	5 cups all purpose flour

Heavily grease three 9- by 5-inch bread tins or nine demi-loaf pans. Preheat oven to 350 degrees. Heat ale, brown sugar, butter, and raisins, but do not boil. When heated and sugar is dissolved, add baking soda. Place in large mixer bowl; add slightly beaten eggs, flavorings, and spice. Add flour. Beat on slow speed then increase to medium speed until well blended. Immediately fill heavily greased bread tins ¾ full with batter. Bake for 45 minutes to 1½ hours, depending on size of tin. Bread is done when a cake tester inserted in center of loaf comes out dry.

Note: If mixing by hand, make well in flour and work liquids in until batter is blended. Freezes well if wrapped properly. Suitable as dessert or breakfast bread, or for tea.

Yield: 3 9- by 5-inch tins or 9 demi-loaves

Irish Festival
Submitted by Robert P. Reilly, Chef-Owner Angelina's Restaurant

Jamaican Style English Plum Pudding

Fruit mixture:

1 cup seedless currants
1 cup seedless raisins
1 cup pitted prunes
1 cup unsalted cashews
1 cup maraschino cherries, drained

1 cup mixed fruit peel
2 cups overproof Jamaican white rum
4 cups sweet red wine or red port wine

Finely grind fruits and nuts in food grinder or food processor. Mix thoroughly, place in large container, and add white rum and red wine to mixture. Store covered as long as possible. Fruits are usually prepared several weeks or a month in advance of the traditional Christmas baking season in order to insure that fruits absorb the maximum flavor of the alcohol. Fruits tend to absorb the alcohol in which they are placed for soaking, so from time to time the mixture may be stirred, and more alcohol may need to be added prior to the baking period. Drain any excess liquid prior to using fruit.

Cake mixture:

1 cup butter
2 cups sugar
6 eggs, separated
1 cup flour
2 teaspoons baking powder
1½ cups unflavored bread crumbs

½ teaspoon cinnamon
2 teaspoons orange peel
2 teaspoons vanilla
2 teaspoons burnt sugar
3 cups prepared ground fruits, drained

In large mixing bowl, cream butter and sugar. Gradually beat in egg yolks. In small mixing bowl, beat egg whites until stiff. Combine flour, baking powder, and bread crumbs and add alternately with beaten egg whites to egg yolk mixture. Add cinnamon, orange peel, vanilla, and burnt sugar. Add prepared ground fruits and mix well. Pour in two greased 8-inch round cake tins, approximately 4 inches deep, lined with waxed paper. Cover top with aluminum foil before covering tightly with lid.

Place tin securely on a base inside a covered pot of boiling water with water line well below lid cover to prevent seepage into tin while water boils. Steam for approximately 1 to 1½ hours or until well done. Pudding is done when a knife inserted in center comes out clean. Let cool 15 minutes before turning pudding out of tin.

Note: Fruit mixture may be prepared and used at time of baking, although fermentation process would be excluded.

Caribbean Festival
Submitted by Heather D. A. Nugent-Charles

Chinese Barbecued Roast Pork

½ cup sugar
1½ tablespoons salt
⅓ cup sherry
½ cup vegetable oil
1½ teaspoons brown bean sauce
1 tablespoon hoisin sauce
  (spicy bean sauce)

2 teaspoons thin soy sauce
1 teaspoon red food coloring
1 teaspoon five spice powder
3 cloves fresh garlic, minced fine
5 pounds fresh Boston butt or
  fresh ham

Mix together sugar, salt, sherry, vegetable oil, brown bean sauce, hoisin sauce, thin soy sauce, red food coloring, five spice powder, and fresh garlic. Combine thoroughly. Cover and set aside.

Trim off visible fat from Boston butt or fresh ham. Debone pork with deboning knife; keep meat in whole pieces. Cut pork into strips about 8 inches long, 2 inches wide, 1 to 1½ inches thick. Place in baking pan. Uncover barbecue-marinade mixture and stir once again. Pour mixture over strips of raw pork. Use pastry brush and coat top and bottom of all pieces of pork. Cover and refrigerate for 6 to 7 hours. Remove marinated pork from refrigerator. Cover bottom of a shallow baking pan with aluminum foil. Place rack on baking pan and marinated pork on rack. Preheat oven to 350 degrees. Place marinated pork in oven; place a baking dish half full of water on oven rack below the pork. Total roasting time is 40 minutes. After first 20 minutes of roasting, turn pork over with tongs and complete cooking for the remaining 20 minutes. (Purpose for the pan of water on the bottom of the oven is to keep the pork moist.)

Remove pork from the oven. Allow to cool for 30 minutes; then slice on a diagonal in thin pieces. Arrange on platter, garnish with sprig of parsley. Serve with Chinese hot mustard and either plum or lemon sauce.

Note: If plum or lemon sauce is not available, use chutney. Other specialty ingredients may be purchased at a Chinese food store.

Asian Festival
Submitted by Katherine M. Chin

Lumpia Frito (Crispy Egg Roll)

1 pound lean ground pork	¼ cup fresh peas
1 pound raw shrimp, shelled and chopped	3 egg yolks
¼ cup fresh mushrooms, chopped	Salt and pepper to taste
	1 tablespoon soy sauce
½ cup onions, chopped	1 package lumpia wrappers (or spring roll wrappers)
¼ cup raisins	Oil

Mix all ingredients except lumpia wrappers and oil in a bowl. Line a large steamer with cheesecloth. Add the mixture to the lined steamer, cover and steam until meats are cooked.

Separate the lumpia wrappers. Place 2 tablespoons of cooked mixture near one corner. Fold the corner tightly over the mixture. Then fold the two side corners toward the center and roll the egg roll toward the remaining corner. Moisten the remaining corner with a little water. This will seal the egg roll. Cover the prepared egg rolls with a damp cloth. Keep them covered until ready to fry. Heat the oil in a wok or deep frying pan until very hot. Fry the egg rolls until golden and crispy. Serve with sweet and sour sauce.

Sweet and Sour Sauce:

1 cup white vinegar	1 tablespoon salt
2 cups water	1½ tablespoons cornstarch
1¼ cups sugar	Water
1 tablespoon ketchup or tomato sauce	1 hot pepper, sliced thinly
	1 clove garlic, chopped

Mix the first five ingredients in a pan. Bring the mixture to a boil. While it is boiling, add the cornstarch, which you have dissolved in a little water, to thicken the sauce. Add the hot pepper and garlic. Boil for about 20 minutes. Refrigerate before serving.

Note: You can find the lumpia wrappers in an Oriental grocery store. They are approximately 8-inch squares and are thinner, crispier wrappers than the regular egg roll wrapper.

Yield: 24

Filipino Festival
Submitted by Maria A. Inocencio

Chicken Arroz Caldo

6 cups water
1 small chicken, cut into pieces
2 tablespoons oil
2 cloves garlic, finely chopped
1 small onion, chopped

1 inch cube fresh ginger, peeled and chopped
2 green onions, chopped
Patis (fish sauce) to taste
1 cup rice, uncooked

Boil the chicken pieces in water until done. Remove pieces from water, reserving water. Remove the skin and bones and cut the chicken into bite-sized pieces. Skim the top of the chicken stock that you have reserved. Sauté garlic and onion in oil until just soft. Add the garlic, onion, ginger, green onions, and rice to reserved chicken stock and simmer for 15 minutes. Then add the chicken pieces and patis and simmer for another 30 minutes, covered. If the soup is too thick, add enough canned chicken stock to suit your taste.

Note: Patis is an Oriental substitute for salt that may be purchased in an Oriental grocery store. It is universally called fish sauce. You may want to make this soup a day ahead, refrigerate it, and then remove the fat from the top of the chilled soup before reheating.

Serves 4

Filipino Festival
Submitted by Maria A. Inocencio

Nani Torte (German Torte)

Torte:

7 extra large eggs
7 heaping tablespoons sugar
2 tablespoons water
1 teaspoon vanilla extract (1 tablespoon if extra vanilla flavor desired)

6 heaping tablespoons sifted flour
1 heaping tablespoon finely ground chocolate

Separate the seven eggs. In a small mixing bowl, beat the egg whites together with the sugar, adding the sugar little by little. Beat this mixture with an electric mixer at highest speed until the egg white mixture stiffens. In a separate bowl, stir the egg yolks with 2 tablespoons water and 1 teaspoon or tablespoon vanilla extract. Stir the egg yolk mixture slowly into the egg white mixture with a spoon. Then add the sifted flour and the ground chocolate gradually to the egg mixture. Stir slowly with a spoon until the mixture is smooth and thick. Grease three 8- or 9-inch round pans with butter. Place mixture, evenly divided, into pans. Bake at 350 degrees approximately 20 to 25 minutes.

Filling:

¼ cup milk
4 heaping tablespoons ground walnuts or hazelnuts
¾ cup sweet butter

1½ cups powdered sugar
1 large egg
1 teaspoon vanilla extract
Your choice of icing

Warm milk, gradually adding nuts, and bring to a boil for one minute. When the mixture has boiled, remove from heat, cover, and let stand to cool. In the meantime, beat butter and sugar together until fluffy. Then add the egg, vanilla extract, and the nut/milk mixture to the butter mixture, stirring them together slowly. This is the filling for the layers of the torte.

To assemble: Spread filling between the three cake layers. Then cover completely with icing.

German Festival
Submitted by Anna Steffen

Tiropites (Cheese Triangles)

8 ounces cream cheese,
softened
1 pound feta cheese, crumbled
¼ pound Danish bleu cheese,
crumbled

1 tablespoon parsley or dill,
minced
4 eggs
1 pound phyllo dough
½ pound sweet butter

Preheat oven to 350 degrees. Mix first five ingredients together until smooth. Melt butter in saucepan. Separate the phyllo into 2 halves. Refrigerate one half, and cover the other half with a slightly dampened cloth. This half you will use first.

Remove 1 sheet of dough. Place on cutting surface, and cut into four 4-inch strips. Fold each strip over lengthwise and brush with butter. Place 1 teaspoon of cheese mixture at bottom right corner of each strip. Fold into a triangle, as you would fold a flag. With each fold be sure the bottom edge is parallel to the alternate side edge. Butter the top and bottom of each finished triangle.

Continue with phyllo sheets until cheese mixture is used. Bake on cookie sheet for 20 minutes or until golden brown.

Note: These may be frozen uncooked. Remove from freezer, and bake at 350 degrees until golden brown.

Yield: 50 to 60 triangles

Greek Festival
Submitted by Mrs. Evan Alevizatos Chriss

Avgolemono (Chicken Egg-Lemon Soup)

Egg-Lemon sauce:

4 eggs
   Juice of 3 medium lemons,
   strained

Salt and pepper

In a blender, beat eggs, and add lemon juice, salt and pepper. Beat thoroughly.

Soup:

2 quarts chicken broth or
   bouillon
2 tablespoons butter

Salt and pepper to taste
¾ cup uncooked rice
   Egg-lemon sauce

Bring broth to a boil, add butter, salt, pepper, and rice. Simmer 15 to 20 minutes until rice is tender. Add 2 cups hot broth to egg-lemon mixture, beating constantly until well mixed. Gradually pour back into remaining broth, stirring constantly and remove from heat at once. Stir a few minutes longer, until mixture has thickened. Serve immediately. Do not simmer, boil, or reheat as soup may curdle.

Note: The egg-lemon sauce may be used alone on chicken, lamb, asparagus, artichokes, or stewed celery.

Serves 6 to 8

Greek Festival
Submitted by Mrs. Evan Alevizatos Chriss

Moussaka

2 medium eggplants (3 pounds)
2 onions, finely chopped
3 tablespoons butter
1 teaspoon salt
½ teaspoon pepper
1½ pounds ground beef

1 clove garlic, minced
1 cup canned tomato puree or tomato sauce
½ cup red wine
½ teaspoon cinnamon
Vegetable oil
¼ cup bread crumbs

½ cup Parmesan cheese, grated

Slice eggplants ¼-inch thick, sprinkle with salt, and place in colander until meat sauce is ready. Sauté onions in butter over medium heat with salt and pepper until limp. Stir in ground beef and garlic and cook for about 10 minutes until meat is browned. Add tomato, wine, and cinnamon; mix and cook for 15 minutes. Preheat oven to 350 degrees. Broil eggplant slices slightly in greased shallow pan. Turn once. Add vegetable oil when needed to prevent sticking. Arrange half of the cooked eggplant slices in 12- by 9- by 2-inch greased pan sprinkled with bread crumbs and a little grated cheese. Pour meat over eggplant and then arrange remaining cooked eggplant slices on top of meat. Sprinkle with cheese and bread crumbs. Bake for 30 to 45 minutes. Cut and serve in squares.

Note: Salad and a red wine are good accompaniments. May be made ahead and frozen. A basic Béchamel sauce may be added before final sprinkle of cheese and breadcrumbs.

Serves 6 to 8

Greek Festival

Souvlakia (Lamb on Skewers)

2 pounds lamb cut into 1½ inch
   cubes

Marinade:
2 medium garlic cloves, crushed
   or slivered
2 teaspoons salt
½ teaspoon pepper
1 teaspoon oregano

½ cup salad oil
⅓ cup lemon juice
1 cup dry red wine
1 bay leaf
1 medium sliced onion

Mix all ingredients for marinade. Add meat cubes. Mix gently, cover and
refrigerate 30 to 40 minutes or overnight. Drain and arrange meat on
skewers about 5 or 6 inches long. Place three to four pieces on each. Grill
over coals 15 minutes, turning once, or broil 3 to 4 inches from heat for 10
minutes. Turn and broil 10 more minutes, basting occasionally with marinade. Serve on bed of buttered rice.

Serves 4

Greek Festival
Submitted by Mrs. Evan Alevizatos Chriss

Mozzarella Balls

½ pound mozzarella, softened
1 tablespoon flour
1 egg

Salt
Pepper
Flour

Olive oil

Place cheese in a bowl. Be sure that it is soft enough to work. Add flour,
egg, and seasonings to taste. Mix well with your hands. Shape into 1-inch
balls and roll in flour. Heat olive oil in a deep fryer or skillet and fry balls
quickly until brown.

Yield: 2 to 3 dozen

Italian Festival

Minestrone

2 quarts water	1 cup cooked lentils (or other
½ cup peas	dried bean)
1 cup green beans	2–3 cloves garlic, chopped
2 small potatoes, diced	1 tablespoon fresh basil,
2 cups cabbage, shredded	chopped
2 stalks celery, diced	Salt to taste
1 small zucchini, diced	½ cup Parmesan cheese

3 tablespoons olive oil

Bring 2 quarts water to a boil. Add all the vegetables and cook slowly until tender. Add garlic, basil, and salt to taste. Simmer briefly and add cheese and olive oil. Heat thoroughly and serve.

Note: Vary vegetables according to availability and preference. Add elbow macaroni or other pasta to soup and cook with vegetables, or add small uncooked meatballs to simmer with vegetables.

Serves 6 to 8

Italian Festival

Kugelis (Potato Pudding)

10 large potatoes	3 large eggs, beaten
2 medium onions	3 teaspoons salt
10 slices bacon	¼ teaspoon pepper
½ cup hot milk or evaporated	Sour cream
milk	

Peel and finely grate potatoes and onion. Cut bacon into narrow strips; fry until almost crisp. Pour bacon and fat over potatoes and onions. Add hot milk. Add beaten eggs one at a time; then add salt and pepper. Pour into greased 9- by 13-inch casserole dish. Bake at 400 degrees for 15 minutes. Reduce heat to 375 degrees. Bake 45 minutes longer. Cut into squares and serve hot with sour cream.

Note: Evaporated milk gives a much richer taste than regular milk. For a crusty result, bake in a cast iron pan. May be served as an entrée or as side dish instead of potatoes or stuffing.

Serves 8 to 12

Lithuanian Festival
Submitted by Vito Banys

Vegetable Biryani

1 tablespoon oil
½ medium onion, finely chopped
½ clove garlic, minced
½ bell pepper, seeded and thinly sliced
½ tomato, chopped
2–3 cardamom pods
3 cloves
1 inch stick of cinnamon, broken into small pieces

1 cup Basmati rice, washed and drained
2 cups mixed fresh vegetables (peas, string beans, carrots), cut into bite-sized pieces
2 cups water
¼ teaspoon or more Cayenne pepper
1 tablespoon salt
Juice of ½ lemon

Heat the oil in a large pot over low heat. Add the onion and cook for two minutes, stirring constantly. Add the garlic and bell pepper and continue cooking for a few more minutes until the onions are soft. Add the tomato pieces and cook for several minutes, stirring the mixture until the tomato is well blended. Add the cardamom pods, cloves, and cinnamon, stirring to blend well. Add the rice and sauté for two minutes. Add the mixed vegetables and sauté for another minute. Add the water, Cayenne pepper and salt and gently boil the mixture for 5 minutes. Cover the pot and cook over low to medium heat for 15 minutes or until all the liquid is absorbed. Squeeze the lemon juice into the mixture just before serving.

Note: Biryani can be served with plain yogurt. You can find cardamom pods and Basmati rice at an Indian food store.

Serves 4

Indian Festival
Submitted by Mr. N. Pal. Singh Suri, Jai Hind Restaurant

Chicken Curry

5 tablespoons oil	1 teaspoon garam masala
1½ pounds onions, finely chopped	¼ teaspoon turmeric
	½ teaspoon cumin powder
¼ pound fresh ginger, peeled and chopped	½ teaspoon coriander powder
	3 pounds chicken pieces, skinned
6 cloves garlic, minced	
¾ pound tomatoes, chopped	2 cups hot water
1 teaspoon salt	4 tablespoons fresh coriander leaves
½ teaspoon ground hot peppers	

Heat the oil in a large frying pan over medium heat. Add the onions, stirring until dark brown. Add the ginger and garlic and continue stirring for about 5 minutes. Then add the tomatoes, salt, ground hot peppers, garam masala, turmeric, cumin powder, and coriander powder. Stir this mixture for about 5 minutes, then add the chicken, stirring for another 2 minutes. Cover and turn the heat down; cook for about 15 minutes, stirring occasionally. Add the hot water, cover and cook on low heat for 15 to 20 minutes, until tender. Sprinkle fresh coriander leaves on top of the curry and serve with Basmati rice or chapatis (bread).

Note: You can find garam masala, ground hot peppers, turmeric, cumin powder, coriander powder, fresh coriander leaves, Basmati rice, and chapatis at an Indian food store.

Serves 6

Indian Festival
Submitted by Mr. N. Pal. Singh Suri, Jai Hind Restaurant

Noodle Kugel Pudding

2 pounds medium egg noodles
8 large eggs
¾ cup raisins

⅓ pint vegetable oil
10 ounces granulated sugar
¼ ounce cinnamon

Boil noodles until done. Rinse thoroughly. Add all other ingredients and blend with noodles. Grease pan and fill with mixture. Bake in 350 degree oven for approximately 1¼ hours or until lightly browned. Cut and serve. If prepared in advance, cut portion sizes before reheating.

Note: Can be frozen and reheated.

Serves 6 to 8

Jewish-American Festival
Submitted by Schleider Caterers

Passover Potato Kugel

6 peeled potatoes
½ pound onions
6 eggs

⅓ cup oil
½ pound matzo meal
1 teaspoon salt

Grate potatoes and onions and combine in a large bowl with other ingredients. Pour into a greased 8- by 10-inch pan. Bake for approximately 1¼ hours in a 350 degree oven.

Note: Can be frozen or made ahead and reheated.

Serves 6 to 8

Jewish-American Festival
Submitted by Schleider Caterers

Kim Chee (Cabbage Pickles)

1 large head Chinese cabbage	1 tablespoon hot red pepper
2 tablespoons salt	flakes
4 green onions and tops	1 teaspoon grated fresh ginger
1 large clove garlic, minced	root

1 tablespoon salt

Cut cabbage in pieces 1-inch long and 1-inch wide. Sprinkle with 2 table-spoons salt, mix well, and let stand 15 minutes. Cut green onions and tops in 1½ inch lengths, then cut lengthwise in thin slices. Rinse and drain cabbage. Combine cabbage, onions, garlic, pepper, ginger, 1 tablespoon salt, and enough water to cover. Mix well. Cover and let stand at room temperature for two days. Taste mixture daily. When it tastes acidic, cover and refrigerate up to 2 weeks.

Yield: 1 quart

Korean Festival
Submitted by Hak J. Chang, Gallery Restaurant

Boolgoki (Barbecued Beef)

1 pound chuck roast cut 1½ to	1½ teaspoons sugar
2 inches thick	½ teaspoon black pepper
2 tablespoons sesame oil	1½ teaspoons crushed, toasted
¼ cup soy sauce	sesame seeds
3 cloves garlic, crushed	1 green onion and top, sliced

Cut meat across the grain in very thin slices. Place meat in a bowl with oil, soy sauce, garlic, sugar, pepper, crushed sesame seeds, and onion. Mix with hands until well blended. Cover and chill in refrigerator for at least 4 hours. Grill over charcoal fire or broil in oven. Serve hot.

Serves 3 or 4

Korean Festival
Submitted by Hak J. Chang, Gallery Restaurant

Golabki (Cabbage Rolls)

1 head cabbage	¼ teaspoon salt
½ cup rice, uncooked	Dash of pepper
1 onion, chopped fine	1 tablespoon ketchup
2 tablespoon butter or	1 cup water
margarine	2 beef bouillon cubes
¾ pound ground beef	1 8-ounce can tomato sauce
¾ pound ground pork	1 16-ounce can tomatoes
1 egg	1 tablespoon sugar

Remove core from head of cabbage. Scald the cabbage in boiling water. Remove a few leaves at a time as they wilt. Cool before using. Prepare rice according to package directions, cooking only until rice is half done.

Sauté onion in butter or margarine until it becomes transparent. Combine with meat, egg, rice, seasonings, and ketchup and mix well. Spread each leaf with meat, about an inch thick. Fold in the two opposite sides and roll, starting with one of the open ends. Fasten with white cotton thread or toothpicks.

In a large frying pan or a large pot, heat the cup of water until it boils and add the beef bouillon cubes, tomato sauce, tomatoes (squeeze the tomatoes before you put them in) along with the juice from the can, and sugar. Stir together and then add the cabbage rolls. Cook slowly until the ground meat is done, basting rolls from time to time. It usually takes about an hour to cook depending on the thickness of the meat. Serve with sour cream on the side.

Note: When reheated the next day, they are even more delicious.

Serves 6

Polish Festival
Submitted by Shirley Kalinowski

Ukrainian Borsch

1½ pounds soup meat,
　　include bone
10–12 cups cold water
1 teaspoon salt
1 medium onion,
　　chopped
2 beets, cut in strips
1 carrot, cut in strips
1 medium potato, diced
½ cup celery, diced

½ cup string beans, diced
2–3 cups cabbage, shredded
¾ cup strained tomatoes or
　　tomato juice
½ clove garlic crushed
1 tablespoon flour
3 tablespoons cold water
½ teaspoon lemon juice
Salt and pepper to taste
Chopped dill

½ cup sour cream

Combine meat with cold water and add salt. Bring slowly to a boil and skim fat. Cover and simmer for 1½ hours. Add onion and beets and cook 10 to 15 minutes or until beets are almost tender. Add carrot, potato, celery, and string beans. Continue cooking for 10 minutes. Put in cabbage and cook until tender. Stir in tomatoes or tomato juice and crushed garlic. Blend flour with 3 tablespoons of cold water, and spoon some soup liquid into it. Stir this mixture into the soup. Add lemon juice and season to taste with salt and pepper. Bring just to a boil and remove from heat. Flavor with chopped dill. When ready to serve, add a spoonful of sour cream to each bowl.

Serves 8

Ukranian Festival
Submitted by Oksana Palijczuk

Menus

Make-Ahead New Year's Day Brunch

Bloody Marys° *and* Fresh Orange Juice
Broccoli Soup°
Beaujolais wine
Ham and Cheese Strata°
Luscious Fruit Compote°
Martha's Muffins° *and* Blueberry Crunch Cake°
Coffee and Tea

Teen-Age Party

Gagi's Stuff and Nonsense° *and* South of the Border Dip°
Homemade Pizza°
Ice Cream Sundae Bar using Chocolate Sauce°,
Peanut Butter Sauce°, and other toppings
Melt-In-Your-Mouth Yummmmms°
Soft Drinks

Oriole Opening Day Lunch

Gazpacho°
Chenin Blanc wine
Crab Cakes°
Antipasto Salad°
Herb Bread Sticks°
Marbelous°

° *Hunt to Harbor* recipes

Preakness Celebration
Cocktails and Light Buffet

Black-eyed Susans°
Hot Spinach Dip°
Byrd Chardonnay
Canapé Lorenzo° *and* Pâté Mold°
Steak Tartare° *and* Italian Chicken Bits°
Maryland Beaten Biscuits° with Country Ham
Stuffed Edam Cheese° *and* Marinated Carrots°

Star-Spangled Fourth of July Picnic

Sangria°
Pickled Shrimp°
Hawaiian Short Ribs° *or* Neighborhood Chicken°
Confetti Rice Salad° *and* Curried Spinach Salad°
Four Beans Baked°
Banana-Chocolate Chip Cake° *or* Classic Apple Pie°
Watermelon

Oregon Ridge Summer Symphony Supper

Caribbean Coolers°
Terrine Maison°
California Gerwurtztraminer *or* Riesling wine
Cold Seafood Pasta Salad° *or* Beef and Avocado Salad°
French Bread°
Carrot Cake°
Fresh Fruits and Cheeses

° *Hunt to Harbor* recipes

Maryland Crab Feast

Smoked Oyster Log°
Crab Claw Soup°
Steamed Maryland Crabs
Fresh Corn
Broccoli Salad° *and* Tomato-Onion Salad°
Beer or Iced Tea
Peach Cobbler°

Football Tailgate

White Zinfandel such as Boordy Vin Gris
Hot Apple Cider
Fruit Dip with Assorted Fruits° *and* Sesame Toast°
MacBain's Tomato Chowder°
Pita Bread Sandwiches°
Toffee Bars° *and* Bavarian Apple Torte°

Children's Halloween Party

Stromboli°
Deviled Eggs
Celery and Carrot Sticks
Halloween Monster Cookies° and Vanilla Ice Cream
Orange Luscious°
Apples for Bobbing

° *Hunt to Harbor* recipes

Hunt Breakfast

Broiled Grapefruit
Pinot Noir wine or Champagne
Scotch Eggs° *or* Maryland Kidney Stew°
Zucchini and Bacon Casserole°
Fried Apples
New England Blueberry Muffins° *and* Cinnamon Buns°
Coffee and Tea
Fruit Juices

A Maryland Thanksgiving

Dry Sherry
Diamond Back Terrapin Soup°
Côte du Rhone, Chateauneuf du Pape wine
Roast Goose°
Berrywine Turkey Dressing°
Escalloped Oysters°
Sauerkraut and Fresh Broccoli
Sweet Potato Pecan Balls°
Cranberry Chutney°
Miniature Southern Biscuits°
Sherried Pumpkin Chiffon Pie° and My Mama's Pecan Pie°

Christmas Morning Breakfast

Mimosas
Orange and Grapefruit Sections
Oven French Toast° *or* Egg Baskets°
Bacon and Sausage
Julekake°
Coffee and Tea

This and That
Recipes Using Leftover or Unusual Ingredients

Anchovy Paste
Caesar-Lime Salad — 187
Oysters Rockefeller Casserole — 98
Avocado
Aunt Binny's Tomato Salad — 197
Ave Avocado — 309
Avocado Crab Dip — 16
Beef and Avocado Salad — 183
Bricklayer's Sauce with Cheese and
Avocado — 17
Curried Avocado Soup — 63
Curried Spinach Salad — 190
Guacamole — 17
Banana
Baked Curried Bananas — 158
Banana-Chocolate Chip Cake — 264
Fruit Slush — 3
Hot Fruit Mélange — 323
Pineapple-Banana Pound Cake — 263
Whole Grain Muffins — 179
Beef, Cooked
B-B-Q Beef — 130
Beef and Avocado Salad — 183
Frosted Sandwich Loaf — 75
Bourbon
Bittersweet Chocolate Bourbon Cake — 307
Classic Apple Pie — 241
General's Punch — 8
Marinated Round Roast — 125
McKee Eggnog — 10
Mint Julep — 314
Pâté Mold — 20
Real Lane Cake — 261
Whiskey Sour Punch — 7
Ye Olde Kentucky Bourbon Balls — 293
Brandy or Cognac
Chicken Diane — 105
French Onion Soup Gratinee — 66
Grilled Shrimp Kebabs — 90
Luscious Fruit Compote — 160
Mocha Balls — 277
Moselle Bowl — 8
Old Style Cocktail Sauce — 207
Pots au Chocolat — 216
Reed's Chicken Tarragon — 109
Terrine Mâison — 21
Buttermilk
Broiled Coconut Chocolate Cake — 267
Fresh Blueberry Crunch Cake — 229
Martha's Muffins — 178
Orange Glazed Muffins — 180
Rhubarb Cake — 260
Candied Fruit
Fruitcake Cookies — 282
Jamaican Style English Plum Pudding — 362

Julekake (Norwegian Christmas
Bread) — 166
Real Lane Cake — 261
Capers
Mediterranean Chicken — 108
Pickled Shrimp — 23
Steak Tartare — 22
Veal Biloxi — 335
Cardamom
Julekake (Norwegian Christmas
Bread) — 166
Tandoori Chicken — 345
Vegetable Biryani — 372
Chicken, Cooked
Australian Chicken — 329
Chicken and Crescent Almondine — 114
Chicken Puffs — 39
Chicken Soufflé Sandwiches — 79
Curried Chicken and Rice Soup — 65
Lobster and Chicken Marengo — 100
Open Face Chicken Sandwich — 77
Oriental Chicken Noodle Soup — 67
Paella — 101
Vietnamese Chicken Salad — 185
Vietnamese Spring Rolls — 40
Chicken Livers
Fillet of Beef Roll — 124
Liver Pâté — 20
Marinated Chicken Livers with Rice — 117
Sautéed Chicken Livers — 29
Terrine Mâison — 21
Chutney
Chicken Chutney Salad — 185
Chicken in Rum — 106
Chicken, Turkey, or Crab Curry — 115
Curry Chutney Cheese Ball — 15
Old Style Cocktail Sauce — 207
Clam Juice
Cheesy Clam Sauce for Spaghetti — 49
Cream of Crab Soup — 343
Linguine with Clam Sauce — 52
Coffee, brewed
Chocolate Irish Mist Cake — 266
Pots au Chocolat — 216
Coffee, powered instant
Grandma Beeman's Brownies — 289
Irish Cream — 5
Kahlua Cordial — 314
Mocha Balls — 277
Mocha Punch — 5
Corned beef, cooked
Immortal Reuben Salad — 184
Reuben Casserole — 130
Sauerkraut Balls — 31

Corn flakes
Chicken Breasts with Wine Sauce	105
Chicken Soufflé Sandwiches	79
Green Bean Casserole	144

Cottage cheese
Caraway Puffs	172
Noodle Pudding	59
Palacsinta (Hungarian Crêpes)	235
Spinach Cheese Triangles	37
Spinach Lasagne	56
Spinach Stuffed Manicotti	58

Crisped rice cereal
Humdingers a la Hall	282
Choco-Peanut Butter Balls	292

Dates
All-Natural Fudge	290
Date Swirl Cookies	281
Humdingers a la Hall	282
Sinful Chocolate Creole Cake	268

Eggs, Hard-Cooked
Delmonico Salad (1)	189
Herbed Four-Bean Salad (2)	191
Liver Pâté (2)	20
Creamy Ham and Eggs (3)	44
Steak Tartare (3)	22
Winter Potato Salad (3–4)	194
Baked Crabmeat in White Sauce (4)	83
Scotch Eggs (4)	43
Mock Terrapin Soup (6)	320
Frosted Sandwich Loaf (6)	75
Berrywine Turkey Dressing (1 pound)	351

Egg Whites
Flounder Fillets with Cheese Sauce (1)	95
Julekake (Norwegian Christmas Bread) (1)	166
Crème Marron (2)	220
Frozen Grand Marnier Soufflé (2)	218
Pavlova (2)	223
Raspberry Wonder (2)	222
Schaefer's Wafers (2)	323
Coconut Almond Macaroons (3)	273
Glazed Nuts (3)	294
Raspberry Paradise Pie (3)	249
Ritzy Fruit Pie (3)	243
Blueberry Bliss (4)	223
Chocolate Mousse Pie (4)	245
Frozen Raspberry Mousse (4)	218

Egg Yolks
Almond Truffles (1)	291
Cheese Beignets (1)	38
Dill Mustard Sauce (1)	208
Easy Hollandaise (1)	205
Raspberry Ripples (1)	284
Tandoori Chicken (1)	345
Toffee Bars (1)	283
Chocolate Crêpes (2)	234
Lemon Sponge Pie (2)	249
Paupiette of Salmon (2)	347
Lumpia Frito (3)	364
Steak Tartare (3)	22

Bavarian Cream Pie (4)	328
Fabulous Fillet of Beef, Béarnaise Sauce (4)	123
Grand Marnier Sauce (4)	236
Sugar Rolled Kolacky (4)	278
Potato Croquettes (8)	333

Feta Cheese
Spanakopita	156
Spinach Cheese Triangles	37
Tiropites Cheese Triangles	367

Fresh Ginger
Chicken Arroz Caldo	365
Chicken Curry	373
Ginger-Steamed Rockfish	96
Honey-Ginger Dressing	335
Kim Chee (Cabbage Pickles)	375
Oriental Chicken Noodle Soup	67
Pork Fried Rice	158
Sally's Szechuan String Beans	326
Stir-Fried Broccoli	145
Tandoori Chicken	345
Wok Chicken and Cherries	116

Ham, Cooked
Crab and Shrimp Gumbo	72
Creamy Ham and Eggs	44
Crab Meat with Ham en Casserole	85
Ham and Cheese Strata	47
Egg and Sausage Casserole	43
Frances' Ham Sandwich Spread	209
Hot Browns	79
Quiche Lorraine	44
Sauerkraut Balls	31

Honey
All-Natural Fudge	290
Baked Curried Bananas	158
Carrot Soufflé	146
Cilla's Three Wheat Bread	164
Creamy Bacon Salad Dressing	200
Honey-Ginger Dressing	335
Martha's Muffins	178
Oriental Salad with Honey Dressing	192
Plum Glazed Spare Ribs	137
Poppy Seed Dressing	199
Swedish Tea Ring	168
Whole Grain Muffins	179
Wholesome Apple Crisp	225
Williamsburg Pecan Bars	287
Wok Chicken and Cherries	116

Macaroons
Hot Fruit Mélange	323
Luscious Fruit Compote	160

Maple Syrup
Boordy Wine Loaf	352
General's Punch	8
Pork with Sauerkraut and Barley	358
Real Lane Cake (Frosting)	261

Mint
Honey-Ginger Dressing	335
Barbecued Shish Kebabs (Mint Sauce)	126
Humos	16

THIS AND THAT

Index

Perry Publishing
5087 Columbia Road
Columbia, Maryland 21044
410-997-2731. fax:410-730-6092.email:perry2@ix.netcom.com

Please send me _____ copies of Hunt to Harbor at $18.95 per copy plus $3.00 per copy for postage and handling. Maryland residents please add sales tax of $.95 per copy.
Enclosed is my check for $ _____ made payable to Perry Publishing.

Name _____

Address _____

City_____ State _____ Zip _____

- -

Perry Publishing
5087 Columbia Road
Columbia, Maryland 21044
410-997-2731. fax:410-730-6092.email:perry2@ix.netcom.com

Please send me _____ copies of Hunt to Harbor at $18.95 per copy plus $3.00 per copy for postage and handling. Maryland residents please add sales tax of $.95 per copy.
Enclosed is my check for $ _____ made payable to Perry Publishing.

Name _____

Address _____

City_____ State _____ Zip _____

We would appreciate having the names and addresses of book, gift, and gourmet shops in your area which may be interested in selling HUNT TO HARBOR. Thank you.

_____   _____

_____   _____

_____   _____

- - - - - - - - - - - - - - - - - - - -

We would appreciate having the names and addresses of book, gift, and gourmet shops in your area which may be interested in selling HUNT TO HARBOR. Thank you.

_____   _____

_____   _____

_____   _____

Perry Publishing
5087 Columbia Road
Columbia, Maryland 21044
410-997-2731. fax:410-730-6092.email:perry2@ix.netcom.com

Please send me _____ copies of Hunt to Harbor at $18.95 per copy plus $3.00 per copy for postage and handling. Maryland residents please add sales tax of $.95 per copy.
Enclosed is my check for $ _____ made payable to Perry Publishing.

Name _____

Address _____

City_____ State _____ Zip _____

Perry Publishing
5087 Columbia Road
Columbia, Maryland 21044
410-997-2731. fax:410-730-6092.email:perry2@ix.netcom.com

Please send me _____ copies of Hunt to Harbor at $18.95 per copy plus $3.00 per copy for postage and handling. Maryland residents please add sales tax of $.95 per copy.
Enclosed is my check for $ _____ made payable to Perry Publishing.

Name _____

Address _____

City_____ State _____ Zip _____

We would appreciate having the names and addresses of book, gift, and gourmet shops in your area which may be interested in selling **HUNT TO HARBOR**. Thank you.

_____   _____

_____   _____

_____   _____

- -

We would appreciate having the names and addresses of book, gift, and gourmet shops in your area which may be interested in selling **HUNT TO HARBOR**. Thank you.

_____   _____

_____   _____

_____   _____